Ride Utah!

Dave Magdiel

Copyright © 2007, 2013 by Dave Magdiel. All rights reserved. No part of this book may be reproduced or transmitted in any form or by any means, electronic or mechanical, including photocopying, recording, or by any information storage and retrieval system, without permission in writing from the publisher.

Abajo Media LLC
2697 S. Kenwood St.
Salt Lake City, UT 84106
www.abajomedia.com
Printed in the United States of America on acid-free paper.

Ride Utah!

Cover design by Dave Magdiel
Copyright © 2013 by Dave Magdiel

Publisher's Note: While every effort has been made to provide accurate, up-to-date information, the author and the publisher accept no responsibility for any loss, liability, risk, injury, or inconvenience by any person using this book.

ISBN-13: 978-0-615-77524-1
ISBN-10: 0615775241

Photos & maps by Dave Magdiel (unless otherwise indicated). All rights reserved.

This book is dedicated to my best friend and wife, Brenda.

ACKNOWLEDGMENTS

I'm very grateful to my friends Richard Mucha, Brent Kelly and Max Mucha. Their support and encouragement has kept this project alive and moving forward. Without their help with research, editing and promotion, this second edition of *Ride Utah!* would never have come to fruition.

Thanks go to my riding buddy, Henry Pannunzio for his willingness to embark on epic road trips when I get that wild urge to roam. Hank, the miles we've ridden looking for America have been priceless. I'm grateful for your friendship and companionship.

From Canada to Mexico, from Monterey Bay to Milwaukee, from Puget Sound to the Gulf Coast of Florida, I have met many kindred spirits on the road. Thank you, my brother and sister bikers for your kindness. I've enjoyed riding with you for a spell, as well as the cold beer and road stories you've shared. Bikers renew my faith in humanity!

No one deserves more gratitude from me than my partner in life and on the road, my wife, Brenda. Her support and encouragement have made my creative projects possible. She is always there to read, critique and edit when I need her. Without her I'm just another idiot with a bike and a pen. Thanks, Sweetie!

CONTENTS

Introduction	**vii**
Section I – Northern Utah	**1**
Bear Lake Loop	3
Golden Spike Run	19
Mirror Lake Run	31
Heber – Duchesne Loop	43
Wasatch Front Quickies	55
East Canyon / Dixie Hollow Loop	56
Provo Canyon / Alpine Loop	64
Oquirrh & Eureka Loops	72
Trappers Loop	80
Section II – Central & Eastern Utah	**87**
Mount Nebo Loop	89
San Pitch Mountains Loop	97
Fish Lake Run	107
Rock Creek & Moon Lake Runs	117
Flaming Gorge Run	129
Eccles & Huntington Canyons Run	141
Great Basin Loop	151
Section III – Southern Utah	**165**
Cedar Breaks Loop	167
Legacy Loop Highway	179
Snow Canyon Loop	189
Zion Park Run	197
Escalante Run – SR 12	209
Black Canyon to Bryce	223
Capitol Reef to Canyonlands	233
Moab Area Rides	251
Four Corners Loop	269
Section IV – Riding Through	**283**
I-15 Alternatives	285
East – West Routes	296
Appendix A – Motorcycle Dealers	**303**
Appendix B – Clubs & Organizations	**310**
Appendix C – Motorcycling on the Web	**315**
Appendix D – Travel Information Resources	**317**
Index	**321**

Contents

Articles

Utah Motorcycle Laws	18
Before You Ride	42
Utah Climate	54
Be Prepared	106
Utah Facts	116
How Cold Is It?	164
Riding Safe	208
Mileage Between Utah's National Parks	232

INTRODUCTION

There's no better place in the world to be a biker than Utah. OK, maybe there are some places that might be as good, but there are definitely none better. Within the borders of a single state *and* in relatively close proximity to one another, we can enjoy the grandeur and majesty of the Wasatch Range, the rugged splendor of the High Uintas, or the breathtaking, multi-colored panoramas of the Colorado Plateau. A good network of paved roads ties these spectacular landscapes together in such a way that even a casual glance at the map will tell you that if you ride, sooner or later, you *must* ride here.

I started riding motorcycles as a teenager, taking my dad's big road bikes out for a scoot around town or a run through the hills, sometimes even with his knowledge and approval. I was hooked, captured by the spiritual high one gets from chasing a river down a canyon along a winding two-lane highway. But after a while life's more basic demands began to intrude. Somewhere along the way I got married and started a family, and for years I became preoccupied with irritating minutia like college and career, earning a living and paying bills. I'd see a bike and think, 'Boy, that was sure fun. I'm going to have to do that again someday.'

Fast forward to 1993 — I had recently returned to the US from a stint in Europe with the Army and still had a serious case of tunnel vision as I focused on a new career. I was fully immersed in work, without a single thought for leisure or relaxation, when my dad called me one day and said he was going on a motorcycle ride.

"Why don't you come with me?" he asked.

"Where you goin'?" I shot back, thinking the answer would be something like 'down to the hardware store' or maybe 'to Grandma's house'.

"Canada", he replied.

Whoa! Was he suggesting we ride hundreds, no thousands of miles on motorcycles? The thought had never occurred to me but it sounded like an intriguing concept! Although I had some reservations, I decided 'what the hell, I'll go', and was thus introduced to the world of touring.

Returning from this first long distance motorcycle trip, I was again hooked, but on a much deeper level. You might even say that the experience was an epiphany of sorts. Anyone who has spent a week on the road with just their bike and whatever gear they can carry knows what I'm talking about. Motorcycle touring is therapeutic. It's rejuvenating. It cleans out your head. It enables you to view the world from a perspective that is not available via any other mode of transportation. It's good for the soul.

Today I would sooner piss on a sparkplug than take a vacation or leisure trip in a car. My automobile has been relegated to the role of mere transportation — a way to get from point A to point B. In the last twenty years I've ridden all over the US and Canada. I've seen some wonderful places and experienced them in ways I never would have in a car. As a biker, you know what I'm talking about. Motorcycles are so much more than just mechanical vehicles. They are the means by which we experience our world, rather than just pass through it. They are our companions, almost living, breathing entities, with unique personalities and souls of their own.

Motorcycle touring is about freedom. To many, including myself, it is an inherently unstructured activity, unbounded by the mundane strictures of normal travel. We seek our own road, reluctant to follow someone else's map.

Why this book, then? Many years ago, as a young officer in the Army, I learned the value of reconnaissance. Today, whether I'm on a planned ride or just going wherever the wind blows, that lesson still serves me well. Knowing a little about what to expect, what services are available and what to look for, make even a relatively unplanned trip more enjoyable.

Think of this book as a menu of ideas. Use it as a reference to mix and match different routes as you create your own adventure. Let it be your tour guide as you embark on one of the rides described within or perhaps just a source of suggestion as you wander with the wind.

I've organized *Ride Utah!* into three regions, offering you some of my favorite rides in Northern Utah, Central / Eastern Utah and Southern Utah respectively. These rides might be either runs (a ride with a distinct start and end point) or loops (a ride that begins and ends in generally the same place). The beginning point on a loop is, of course, arbitrary in most cases. Jump in anywhere! Pick a ride to fill a summer Sunday, or string several runs and loops together for an extended journey of discovery. A fourth section describes alternative routes to consider when traveling through or within the state.

Most of the rides I've described will take up roughly half a day, leaving the rider with the flexibility to blast through the route or stretch the ride into a full day of leisure in the saddle. Included also are a

Introduction

handful of "quickies" — short scoots ideal for blowing out the pipes after work or grabbing a fast dose of adrenaline. Each ride discussion includes a map, route description, area highlights and history, and support information such as gas, food, and lodging. I haven't tried to be comprehensive in listing gas stations or hotels, but rather have noted a few choices that are directly on or very near the route described. The eateries listed under "recommended dining" notes are establishments that I have patronized and enjoyed or were recommended to me by fellow riders. Appendices provide information on dealerships where riders may find maintenance support, club and motorcycle organization contacts, motorcycle related websites and sources of travel and tourism information.

Utah is truly a national treasure. The rich diversities of geology, terrain and climate are found nowhere else. Whether you live here or are planning a trip to Utah from elsewhere, I hope this book helps you to more fully savor this treasure. Get out there and experience the splendor of the Beehive State from the saddle. Experience *life in the moment* on two wheels. Get out there and **Ride Utah!**

Section I

Northern Utah

The first region we'll explore is comprised of a block of eleven northern counties. This region stretches from the Idaho border 160 miles south to the southern shores of Utah Lake. Dominated by the Wasatch Mountains in the east and expansive salt deserts in the west, with the Great Salt Lake right in the middle, northern Utah is home to the majority of Utah's population. "The Wasatch Front", a major urban concentration, runs from Ogden in the north nearly 100 miles south to Provo.

In spite of its large population, northern Utah also has plenty of wide open space and spectacular wilderness diversity, not to mention some of the best riding opportunities in the state. The Wasatch Range is full of canyon routes from which to escape the urban valleys. These passages into the mountains offer great day rides, as well as portals to grander adventures beyond.

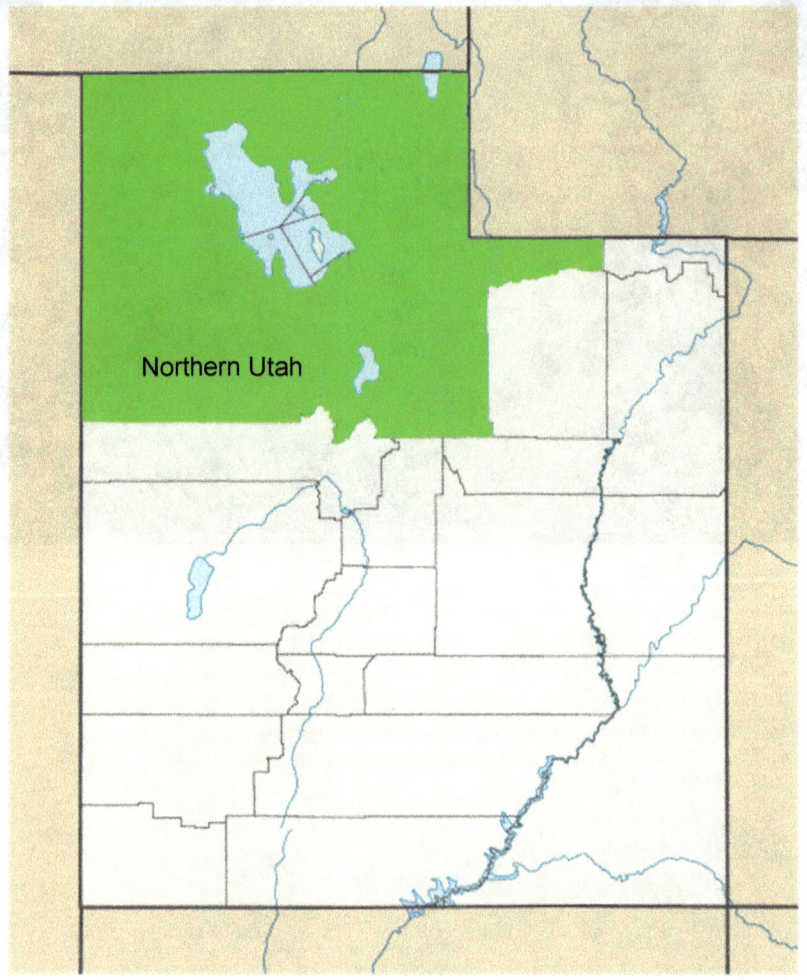

Bear Lake Loop
"Raspberry Run"

View from Bear Lake Overlook on US Hwy 89

Running through Utah's scenic "Bridgerland" country, the Bear Lake Loop is a great ride any time of the season. Vibrant wildflowers dot the landscape in the spring, while an explosion of color presents itself in the fall. In the height of summer, this is the ride to take to escape the heat of the Wasatch Front. This route offers three great canyon segments; Sardine Canyon, Logan Canyon and Ogden Canyon. If that's not enough, this ride also runs the length of SR 39 over Monte Cristo. The Bear Lake Loop is a fun day ride, but offers enough side attractions to make it a perfect overnighter as well.

Be prepared with cold weather gear on this ride. Snow can linger well into June on the Monte Cristo stretch of SR 39 and it's always cool up there even after the snow is gone. It never hurts to have rain gear on this loop. Summer showers can pop out of nowhere and hang onto the mountain ridges. Enjoy!

Ride Utah!

Bear Lake Loop
Route Map

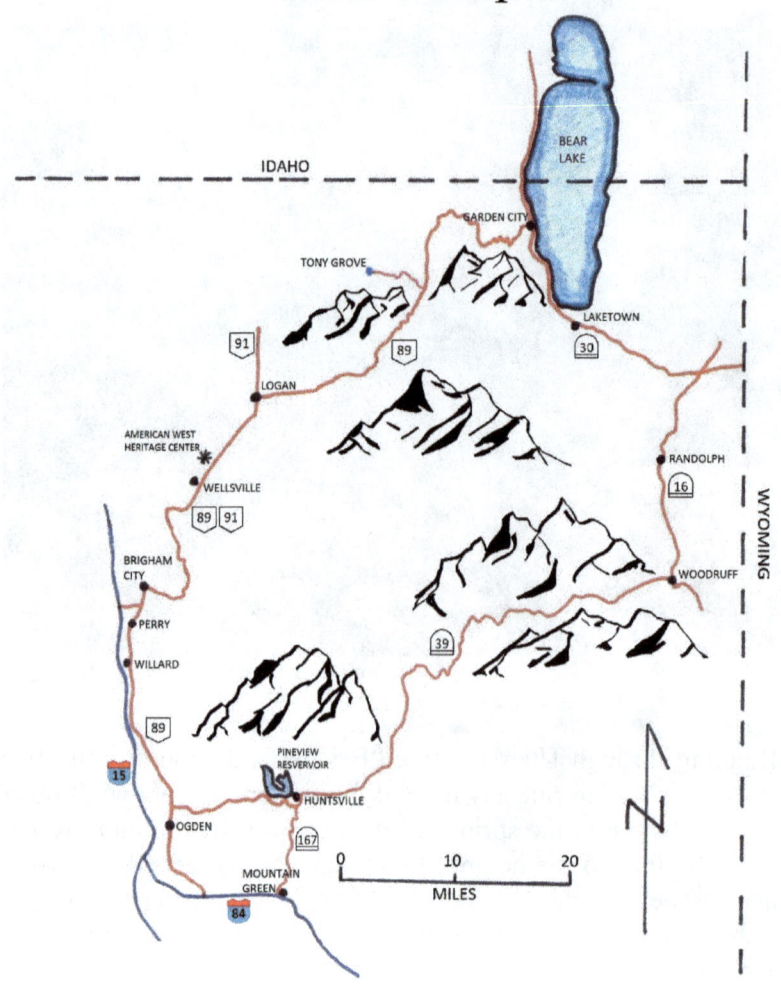

ROUTE: From Ogden, go north on US 89 or I-15 to Perry (exit 362). Take US 89/91 northeast to Logan. From Logan, take US 89 (400 North in Logan) east through Logan Canyon to Bear Lake and Garden City. From Garden City, take SR 30 south to Sage Creek Junction. At Sage Creek Junction, go south on SR 16 to Woodruff. At Woodruff, take SR 39 west to Huntsville. From Huntsville, continue on SR 39 westbound, around Pine View Reservoir and down Ogden Canyon back to US 89 in Ogden.

Section I: Northern Utah

On the road...

It's Saturday morning, your chores are done, and suddenly you have a craving for a fresh raspberry milkshake. What do you do? Grab your jacket and keys, throw your leg over the saddle and make a "Raspberry Run" to Garden City — the best place on earth for all things raspberry — on the Bear Lake loop.

This route is an easy day ride from anywhere along the Wasatch Front, but also makes a great overnighter. This is one of my favorite rides because of the great scenery, but I also love it as a way to beat the summer heat. Even on a sweltering hot day in the valley, it always seems to be several degrees cooler — just right for riding — once you start up the canyons. Besides, I love raspberries!

Taking US 89 out of Ogden is not the quickest way out of town but I find it preferable to the freeway. The highway parallels I-15 and takes you through rural communities and farm country. Known as "Utah's Fruit Way", an abundance of farmer's markets on the highway between Ogden and Brigham City make this corridor a great place to find treats of fresh fruit and produce.

A word of caution about this section of US 89: there is a notorious speed zone in the community of Willard. My experience has been that the local *gendarmerie* is quite aggressive about enforcing posted speed limits. It must be a revenue generator for them, for the highway is a wide, modern four-lane affair that wants to sucker you into a higher speed. You'd be wise to watch the speed limits here and do your best to stay under them. I-15 is a high-speed alternative if you wish to bypass the slower pace of US 89. If you choose to go northbound on the freeway, take exit 362, the Brigham City / Logan exit.

At the south edge of Brigham City, US 89 merges with US 91 and heads northeast into the mountains. This portion of the route takes you over a fabulous section of modern, high-speed four-lane highway, popularly known as Sardine Canyon. This moniker is not quite accurate. The real Sardine Canyon runs down the mountain from Sardine Summit, away from the highway. But to paraphrase ole' Bill, 'this road by any other name is still one hell of a sweet ride!' Plenty of sweeping curves and great scenic vistas make this stretch of US 89 a true joy.

Dropping down on the other side of the mountain the road levels out in a long strait stretch that takes you into Logan. Just past Wellsville, on the west side of the highway you will find the American

West Heritage Center. This is a living museum dedicated to preserving the history and heritage of the Old West from 1820 through the early twentieth century. Recognized as one of the top attractions in North America, it is well worth a stop for the history buff. Each year the center sponsors the *Festival of the American West*. This award-winning festival of living history presents visitors with a realistic, accurate, and vibrant experience of the American West. Check it out. Dates vary — for more information call 1-800-225-3378 or see www.awhc.org.

Continuing north brings you into Logan. While in Logan, check out Center Street. Designated as a National Historic District, this quaint boulevard is home to many beautiful historic mansions. At the west end of Center Street is one of Utah's finest old railroad stations, beautifully restored and now home to Café Sabor, serving fine Mexican cuisine. If you're hungry, I recommend it. If you are in the mood for a more traditional American meal, head back to Main Street. The Bluebird Restaurant, near Main and Center, has been serving customers since 1914, making it one of Utah's oldest continuously operating diners. You'll enjoy the authentic (and still functioning) marble soda fountain.

Also worth checking out is the Logan Tabernacle (1891) on Main Street and the Logan LDS Temple (1884), which dominates the town on a hillside at 200 South and 200 East. These buildings are classic examples of nineteenth century Mormon architecture, and are truly stunning in their aesthetic impact. The Tabernacle is open to the public and free tours are available daily. The basement of this historic meeting hall houses the second largest genealogy library in Utah. The staff claims "give us an hour, and we will locate the records of one of your ancestors."

As long as you're looking at old churches, St. John's Episcopal Church (1909), located at 85 E 100 N is worthy of inclusion. Built in the Gothic style, this church contains magnificent stained glass windows.

You may want to check your gas gauge here. So far, gas stations have been fairly plentiful, but the next opportunity for fuel after Logan is forty miles away. There are two gas stations on the corner of 400 North and Main, which is where US 89 splits off from Main Street (US 91) and threads up Logan Canyon.

Section I: Northern Utah

(Photo by Evi Green)　　　　　　　　　　Riders in Logan Canyon

Taking 400 North eastbound, you will climb a hill and ride past Utah State University to the mouth of Logan Canyon. One of Utah's Scenic Byways, Logan Canyon is perhaps the best stretch of road on this ride. The Utah Association of Travel Regions says Logan Canyon is rated as one of the top nine places in America to view fall colors. While they don't say who bestowed this auspicious designation, I'll buy it. This Scenic Byway is truly spectacular in the fall, but I find it to be equally colorful in the springtime when the wildflowers are blooming. Framing the colorful foliage are vertical limestone walls and rock formations laden with fossils.

About fourteen miles up the canyon you will come to Temple Fork Road. This road is unpaved, but depending on the time of year, it's not bad for a dirt road. If you're feeling adventurous and have the urge to explore, six miles up Temple Fork you will find the grave of "Old Ephraim", a grizzly bear said to be the largest ever shot. Frank Clark killed the bear in 1923 after ten years of trying. Old Ephraim's huge skull was displayed at the Smithsonian Institution for a time and can now be viewed at the Tourist Information Center, 160 North Main in Logan.

A couple of miles past Temple Fork Road (at mile marker 390) you will come to Ricks Springs, an interesting place to stop and poke

Tony Grove Lake

around. Set back in a small cave just off the highway, water flows from underground into a small, crystal clear pool and runs off into the Logan River. Thought by early pioneers to be a natural artesian spring, it is actually an underground aquifer that draws water from the Logan River through the cave and dumps back into the river on the surface.

Five or six miles beyond Ricks Springs is the cutoff to Tony Grove Lake. Look for a sign marking the cutoff. If you get to Red Banks campground, you've gone too far. Turn around and double back a half-mile or so and you'll find it. This cutoff is a worthwhile side trip. It's a seven-mile road, all paved, winding up the mountain to a beautiful glacial lake. You'll find Tony Grove is a good place to stretch your legs, take pictures, have a picnic or cool your feet.

After a short run up US 89 from the Tony Grove cutoff you will reach the top of the canyon. At the summit you will have climbed about 3,100 feet from an elevation of 4,700 feet at the mouth of the canyon to nearly 7,800 feet at the top. Just over the crest of the mountain is the Bear Lake Overlook, which offers a stunning view of the Bear Lake valley.

Wind down the hill to the lakeshore and you will reach one of the primary objectives of this ride, fresh raspberry treats! If you have

Section I: Northern Utah

pushed the limits of your gas tank getting here, fear not. There is a gas station just before you reach the bottom of the hill and another just a bit farther at the junction of US 89 and SR 30.

Now for the good stuff. Coming off Bear Lake Summit and winding down the hill to the edge of the lake, US 89 meets SR 30 at the little community of Garden City. Aside from being a picturesque town poised on the shores of a brilliant blue mountain lake, the area is famous for raspberries. Each August the town hosts Bear Lake Raspberry Days. Contact the Bridgerland Travel Region at 1-800-882-4433 for more info.

While in Garden City, you owe it to yourself to get off the bike and enjoy a raspberry shake. My favorite places to do so are the Hometown Drive-In, one block north of the junction of US 89 with SR 30, and Merlin's Drive-In right next door. The Quick 'n' Tasty Drive-In at the highway junction and La Beau's just a half-block north are also good choices.

After you have slurped your fill of milk shakes, head south out of Garden City on SR 30. This will take you around the south end of Bear Lake past Rendezvous Beach, where in 1826 the Rocky Mountain Fur Company held the first mountain-man rendezvous. The rendezvous was a regular event in this area for several years but died with the extinction of the mountain-man lifestyle triggered by the mass influx of white settlers in the 1840's. Or maybe it was just eclipsed in popularity by the Bear Lake Raspberry Days festival. You decide.

As you ride through Laketown on the south side of the lake you will come to a cute and colorful little canyon that will carry you up to the farm country beyond. Not too far into the canyon you will come upon some slow-speed ninety degree turns. Be ready for them. Take the warning signs seriously and slow down. It's not that these turns are particularly challenging on a bike, but the car and truck traffic can be. Remember that this is a main route into a major outdoor recreation area. It's the guy in a one-ton pickup towing a guided missile frigate coming at you on his way to Bear Lake, with one hand in a bag of potato chips and the other adjusting his radio as he swings wide into your lane, taking the twenty mph turn at thirty when he should be doing it at ten... well, you know how it goes. We've all seen them. It's the kind of chance meeting in a tight turn that can ruin an otherwise pleasant afternoon.

Coming up out of the little canyon will put you on a fairly straight stretch of road to Sage Creek Junction. Watch for cattle out here. Most of them are behind fences but I have occasionally encountered some on the road in this area.

At Sage Creek Junction, you'll meet SR 16. Turn south and enjoy a fairly straight run through ranch country and the little town of Randolph. In Randolph, look for the restored home of Mormon Church president Wilford Woodruff, built in 1871. Woodruff was a key figure in Utah's struggle for statehood and in that era's political conflicts between the church and the federal government.

Eighteen miles south of Sage Creek Junction you will arrive at the town of Woodruff and the junction with SR 39. Turning west on SR 39 will take you into the next treat on this ride, the run over Monte Cristo to Huntsville. This stretch of road is one of my perennial favorites. I don't know why. Of course it's very scenic but no more so than many other roads throughout the state. I guess it's because at the summit I feel like I'm on top of the whole state of Utah and can see a hundred and fifty years into the past and forever into the future.

Again, a word of warning is in order about cattle, the dumbest creature on the face of the earth and a natural enemy of the motorcycle. SR 39 near the junction at Woodruff is often lousy with the ignorant beasts! One day you may not see the slightest hint of these four legged dinner entrées, while on the same road a couple of days later you will find yourself picking your way through a herd that looks like the cattle drive scene from Red River. I have had two nearly unfortunate encounters with these obnoxious critters on this road and so now, whenever I ride here, I look for manure on the pavement. If I see it, my alert posture goes way up lest I become part of it!

A short way up the road you will be past the beef and into a stunning ride. Get ready for some grand vistas and some really fun twisty road. Notice the temperature variation from Woodruff to the summit. It's fascinating how cool it can stay at the top all year round. I've seen the remnants of great snowdrifts well into the month of June. Even in August, I rarely make it over in just my shirtsleeves. Have your jacket handy.

Coming down off the summit on the west side you will come to a paved road that cuts off SR 39 to the east. At this intersection is Red Rock Ranch, a neat little general store that affords an opportunity to stop and stretch while you enjoy a cold drink.

Not far from here the road levels off and straightens out as it runs into Huntsville. Huntsville is just a nice place plain and simple. Every time I ride through, someone in the group, if not me, comments on

(Photo by Tom Green) SR 39 near the summit of Monte Cristo

what a delightful place it would be to live. Happily, everyone who feels that way does not act upon the impulse or it would soon cease to be the picturesque little town that it is and become just another city.

On the way into Huntsville look for the sign marking the Trappist Monastery just off the highway. The monks make delicious creamed honey which they offer for sale to the public. Several times a day, they gather at the chapel for Gregorian chants. Visitors are welcome.

At the edge of Huntsville, SR 39 intersects a local road. Turning left will keep you on SR 39 and take you around the south side of Pineview Reservoir for the continuation of this ride. Go straight at the intersection to take a detour into Huntsville. Turning right would take you to Eden and the north side of Pineview.

Huntsville is home to the Shooting Star Saloon (7350 E 200 S), where you will find some of the finest greasy biker cuisine in Utah. Try the Shooting Star Burger, a mountain of beef, cheese and sautéed onions with a Polish sausage and a cold draft. The Shooting Star,established in 1879 is Utah's oldest saloon. It's a biker friendly joint that's just loaded with atmosphere. Sign a dollar bill and tack it to the ceiling when you're there. Look for your friends' offerings while you're at it.

The Shooting Star Saloon, Uth's oldest, est.1879 - Huntsville

Just around the corner, you'll find another biker favorite, the Huntsville Barbecue Company (located on 7400 E across from the park). If Texas style barbecue hits your fancy, this is the place.

If you can still walk after a Shooting Star Burger, you're doing great. Throw your leg over the bike (it's OK to use your hands to lift your leg across the saddle — nobody is watching) and get back on SR 39. The road loops south for a short distance and then turns west again. As you pass the dam you will find yourself at the mouth of Ogden Canyon, the last scenic canyon segment of this ride.

Ogden Canyon is eight miles of narrow winding road. The speed limit is low and invariably you will encounter enough car traffic to keep you under it. That's o.k. though because this stretch of road is one of the most scenic and enjoyable on the route. Sit back, relax, and enjoy the final stretch of this ride because you're not going anywhere fast.

Halfway down the canyon, on the left side of the road you will discover another good eating establishment — The Oaks. You'll find tasty burgers and sandwiches here, with cold drafts, as well as breakfast and dinner menus. If you didn't stuff yourself in Huntsville and you're hungry, The Oaks is worth a stop.

Too soon, you'll be at the lower mouth of the canyon where the mountain opens up to expose the city of Ogden, but not before passing by some stunning vertical rock formations and a rather spectacular little waterfall careening off the cliffs and crashing down the canyon wall.

Staying on SR 39 as the canyon dumps you into Ogden puts you on 12th Street. Continue straight ahead and the road intersects with US 89 (Washington Blvd.) or just a little way further west with I-15 (at exit 344), which is about where this ride started.

Next time consider a couple of interesting route variations. Instead of taking US 89/91 (Sardine Canyon) into Logan, try SR 38 north through Brigham City to SR 30 and come into Logan from the west. On the tail end, rather than riding down Ogden Canyon, turn south at Huntsville on SR 167 (Trappers Loop) and ride through Mountain Green to I-84. Take I-84 westbound (Weber Canyon) to US 89 or I-15.

Fresh raspberries and cool mountain landscapes make the Bear Lake loop a superb summertime treat. If it's not already, this ride is sure to become one of your favorites. Don't worry about your diet. Everyone knows that riding a bike is great exercise. Hell, you'll probably burn off all those ice cream calories and carbs before you finish the loop.

Bear Lake Loop – Notes

Pit Stops:

Ogden:
Chevron
1207 Washington (US 89)
(801) 399-0325

Chevron
1177 12th Street (SR 39)
(801) 393-6126

Brigham City:
Chevron
1095 S. 500 W. (US 91)
(435) 723-1052

Logan:
Chevron
398 N. Main
(801) 392-9516

Garden City:
Chevron
604 W. Logan Rd. (US 89)
(435) 946-3604

Laketown:
Sinclair
431 N. Main (SR 30)
(435) 946-3372

Huntsville:
Chevron
520 S. Hwy 39
(801) 392-9516

Chevron
369 Washington (US 89)
(801) 394-1474

Phillips 66
1192 12th Street (SR 39)
(801) 392-9966

Flying J
1080 S. 500 W. (US 91)
(435) 723-3924

Phillips 66
404 N. Main
(435) 753-2522

Sinclair
25 N. Bear Lake (SR 30)
(435) 946-8685

Randolph:
Sinclair
60 N. Main (SR 16)
(435) 793-2475

Sinclair
7435 E. 900 S. (SR 39)
(801) 745-3833

Accommodations & Camping:

CAMPGROUNDS
National Forest Campgrounds info: (877) 444-6777 or www.reserveusa.com.
   Bridger – US 89, Logan Canyon
   Guinavah-Malibu – US 89, Logan Canyon
   Lewis M. Turner – US 89, Logan Canyon
   Lodge – US 89, Logan Canyon
   Preston Valley – US 89, Logan Canyon
   Red Banks – US 89, Logan Canyon
   Spring Hollow – US 89, Logan Canyon
   Tony Grove Lake – US 89, Logan Canyon
   Wood Camp – US 89, Logan Canyon
   Sunrise – US 89, Garden City
   Monte Cristo – SR 39
   Weber Memorial Park – SR 39
   Willows – SR 39
   Meadows – SR 39
   South Fork – SR 39
   Perception Park – SR 39
   Botts – SR 39
   Hobble – SR 39
   Magpie – SR 39
   Jefferson Hunt – SR 39, Huntsville
   Anderson Cove – SR 39, Huntsville

BLM Campgrounds info: (801) 977-4300
   Birch Creek – SR 39

Utah State Park Campgrounds: info: (800) 322-3770 or www.stateparks.utah.gov
   Bear Lake Marina – US 89, Garden City
   Eastside – US 89, Garden City
   Bear Lake Rendezvous Beach – SR 30, Laketown

Commercial Campgrounds:
  Beaver Mountain – US 89, Logan Canyon
  (435) 753-0921

  Bear Lake KOA – 485 N. Bear Lake Blvd.,
  Garden City (800) 562-3442

HOTELS:
Ogden:
Best Western
1335 W. 12th Street
(801) 394-9474

Alaskan Inn
435 Ogden Canyon
(801) 621-8600

Brigham City:
Howard Johnson Inn
1167 S. Main (US 89)
(435) 723-8511

Crystal Inn
480 Westland Dr.
(435) 723-0440

Logan:
Best Western Weston Inn
250 N. Main
(435) 752-5700

Comfort Inn
2002 S. Hwy 89/91
(435) 787-2060

RECOMMENDED DINING:
Logan:
The Bluebird Restaurant
19 N. Main
(435) 752-3155

Café Sabor
600 W. Center St.
(435) 752-8088

Garden City:
Quick 'n Tasty
28 N. Bear Lake Blvd
(435) 946-2875

Hometown Drive-Inn
105 N. Bear Lake Blvd
(435) 946-2727

La Beau's Drive Inn
69 N. Bear Lake Blvd
(435) 946-8821

Merlin's Drive-In
149 N. Bear Lake Blvd.
(435) 946-8499

Section I: Northern Utah

Huntsville:
The Shooting Star Saloon
7350 E 200 S
(801) 745-2002

Huntsville Barbecue Co.
235 S 7400 E
(801) 754-2745

Ogden:
The Oaks
750 Ogden Canyon
(801) 394-2421

Gray Cliffs Lodge
508 Ogden Canyon
(801) 392-6775

Utah Motorcycle Laws

- Motorcycle operator's license (endorsement) required

- Safety helmet required for riders and passengers under age 18

- State funded rider education is available for all eligible applicants

- Successful completion of rider education course waives license skills test

- Daytime use of headlight is not required. Modulating headlights permitted

- Passenger seat and footrests are required if carrying a passenger

- Mirror required

- Annual safety inspection required

- Maximum interstate speed limits – 75 mph rural (80 mph some segments), 65 mph urban

Golden Spike Run

Golden Spike National Historic Site - Promontory, Utah

    The Golden Spike Run takes you to Box Elder County, settled by Mormon pioneers in the 1850s. To this day, the area retains its "rural America" charm and pioneer flavor.

    This ride is one for the history enthusiast, a ride to take when the sightseeing urge hits you. Enjoy Brigham City, a town that feels like the set for a 'Back to the Future' movie. Head out to Promontory and stand where the last spike in the Transcontinental Railroad was driven, bringing America's greatest engineering and economic endeavor of the nineteenth century to fruition. A couple of miles away, visit ATK/Thiokol, the cradle of our nation's rocket booster development which made possible one of the twentieth century's greatest achievements, the space program. See the geology of prehistoric Lake Bonneville or look for bald eagles in their natural habitat near the Salt Creek Waterfowl Management Area. Throw your swim trunks in the saddle bag and wrap this ride up with a soak in the soothing waters of Crystal Hot Springs. Enjoy!

Golden Spike Run Route Map

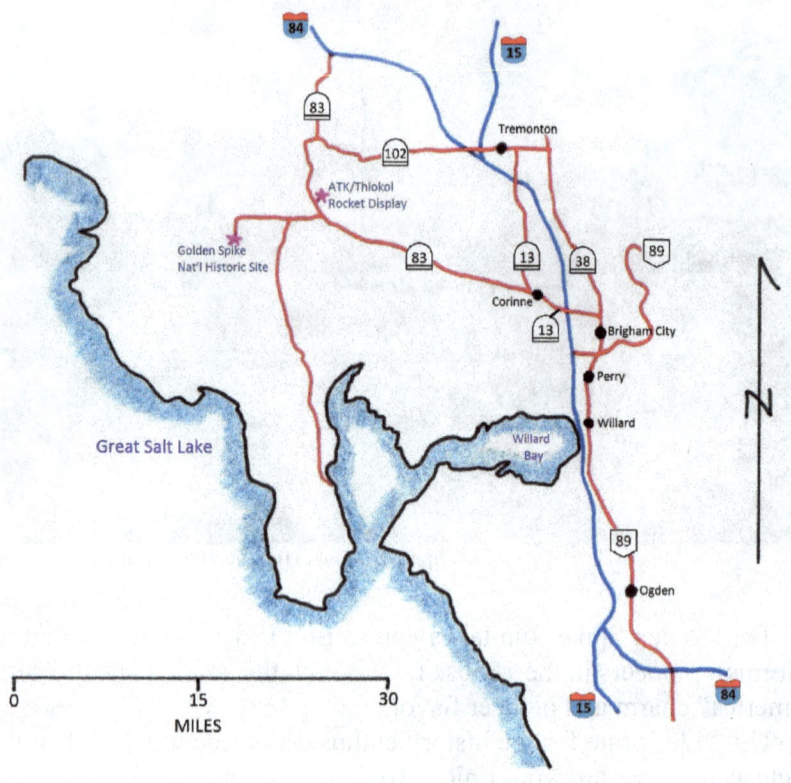

ROUTE: From the central Wasatch Front, go north on US 89 or I-15 to US 91 (exit 362 on I-15). At the intersection of US 91 & US 89, go north on Main Street (SR 38) through Brigham City to its junction with SR 13. Take SR 13 west to the junction with SR 83 at Corinne. Continue west-northwest on SR 83, 17 miles to Golden Spike Road. Take Golden Spike Road west and follow the signs to Golden Spike Nat'l Historic site. Return to SR 83 and turn north. Proceed approximately 6 miles to the junction of SR 102 (Faust Valley Road). Take SR 102 east through Tremonton to SR 38. Turn north on SR 38 to SR 30 to visit the Hampton's Ford stage stop. Go south on SR 38 to return to Brigham City.

On the road...

Historian Stephen Ambrose called it the nineteenth century equivalent of going to the moon. In a triumph of American will, such an achievement of ingenuity and courage was seen to fruition at Promontory, Utah on May 10, 1869. There, the Central Pacific and Union Pacific railroads joined two ribbons of iron rail totaling 1,776 miles, linking Omaha with Sacramento and transforming a journey that had taken six months into one of six days. How poetic it is then, that when we did land on the moon a century later, the journey began, in no small part, at ATK's rocket engine testing facility just a few short miles from where the Golden Spike was driven.

I thoroughly enjoy this ride, for what it may lack in scenic quality compared to other rides, it more than makes up for in historical appeal. This is a ride that makes you appreciate American determination, ingenuity and achievement as well as the strength reflected in Utah's pioneer heritage.

Jump in anywhere on the northern Wasatch Front and take I-15 north. If you like to "slab" it, stay on the freeway all the way up to exit 362 (the Brigham City / Logan exit) then go east to the second traffic light. This is where US 91 and US 89 merge. Turn left (north) at this intersection and you will be headed into Brigham City on SR 38 (Main Street). By *slabbin'* all the way up to Brigham City though, you miss a lot of enjoyable riding up secondary roads.

I prefer to get off the freeway at exit 324 in Farmington and take US 89 north. Between here and Ogden, the highway is a modern four lane road that offers a leisurely run skirting the suburban communities of Kaysville and Fruit Heights. Farther north, the highway intersects I-84 at the mouth of Weber Canyon before climbing the hill into South Ogden.

When you come to the second traffic light at the top of the hill, you are presented with two options to get through Ogden. Going straight through the intersection keeps you on US 89 and takes you through town on Washington Blvd. This is slow going, with a traffic light almost every block. I like to jump off US 89 by turning right (north) at the light and taking Harrison Blvd. (SR 203) through to 12th Street (SR 39), then turn left (west) to take 12th Street back to Washington Blvd./US 89. This way seems slightly quicker, with fewer traffic lights, but it's probably a wash either way.

At 2nd Street, Washington Blvd. forks, with US 89 veering left. This takes you north out of Weber County and into Box Elder County along "Utah's Fruit Way". Take advantage of the many farmers' markets and grab a snack of fresh fruit. Watch out for the speed zone in Willard, though. (See page 5.)

While you are passing (slowly) through Willard, note the many stone houses in Willard's historic district. This area boasts the greatest concentration of Welsh style stone houses in the state, a real glimpse into Utah's pioneer past.

At the south edge of Brigham City you'll come to the traffic light where US 89 and US 91 intersect. From this route, continue straight (north) through the intersection to SR 38 (Main Street) in Brigham City.

To me, Brigham City is the quintessential American small town. Main Street reminds me of movies I've seen, set in the 1950s or 60s, conforming to the stereotype image I have constructed in my mind of the world in which my parents grew up. As I ride through town, I almost expect to see Wally and "the Beav" walking down the sidewalk.

In September, the weekend after Labor Day, Brigham City hosts the annual Peach Days festival. This is the oldest continuing harvest festival in Utah, and it's just a whole lot of fun! I enjoy the antique car show and, of course, the ride-in bike show. The Dutch oven cook-off and all the homemade, hometown treats are sure to please as well. It's worth planning this ride during Peach Days weekend.

Coming into town on Main Street, you will pass the LDS Box Elder Tabernacle (1890), a rather impressive specimen of nineteenth century religious architecture. The site is said to have been chosen by Brigham Young himself and Young laid the cornerstone with territorial surveyor Jesse W. Fox in 1868. Of all the nineteenth century churches extant in the region, I find this Tabernacle to be one of the most visually appealing. Free guided tours are available in the summertime.

In the geographic center of town, Forest Street bisects Main Street. Turn left (west) and go eight blocks for a look at the historic Brigham City Depot. In keeping with the dominant railroad theme of this ride, this is a worthy detour. The depot was once a fairly significant shipping hub for the Union Pacific railroad. Today it is an education center and museum dedicated to the preservation of rail history.

There are plenty of places to get a quick lunch in Brigham City, including all of the regular fast food franchises. But for a quick burger

Box Elder Tabernacle – Brigham City

and fries, a milkshake or just an ice cream treat, I like the local flavor of the Peach City Ice Cream Drive-In at 306 N. Main. If you're hungry, give 'em a try.

At the top (north) end of Main Street, SR 38 meets SR 13. Turn left (west) and follow the signs to the Golden Spike National Historic Site. You'll be on a long straight stretch of road through farm country leading to Corinne.

Corinne was the last town to spring up on the transcontinental railroad. It is unique among the communities in the region because it was not founded and settled by Mormons. Originally populated by a cross section of outsiders from multiple religions, as well as those professing no religion at all, it has been known by such sobriquets as "City of the Ungodly" and "Gentile City".

Within two weeks of being laid out in 1869 by Union Pacific, Corinne had over 500 frame and tent buildings. The town became a substantial shipping center for the railroad and home to several major businesses, seven different churches, livery stables, blacksmith shops, hotels, gambling halls, banks, newspapers, an opera house, a cigar factory, saw mill, smelter and as many as eighty "sporting" women. The founders had designs on Corinne becoming the capitol of the State

Brigham City Depot

of Deseret. Today it is a quiet little farming community whose appearance bellies its colorful past.

SR 13 comes to a fork in Corinne as it forms a junction with SR 83. Take the left fork, which is SR 83 and following the signs to Golden Spike. Before you do though, consider a stop at Mim's Bar & Grill. It's a biker friendly saloon located right at the junction of highways 13 and 83 where you can get bite to eat and a cold draft.

Pulling out of Corinne on SR 83, you are again on a long straight stretch of highway, cutting through flat farm country. On the near horizon you can see Little Mountain forming a point at the road. As you round this point, take a deep breath. No, that smell is not your flatulent riding companions doing something vulgar (at least not all of it anyway). You're riding past Stinky Springs, a sulfurous spring just off the highway. If anyone comments about it at the next stop, look them right in the eye with a straight face, swear you didn't smell anything, and ask them to pull your finger.

As you round the point of Little Mountain, the farmland gives way to wild salt marches comprising the Salt Creek Waterfowl Management Area. Along with the many species of waterfowl and wading birds that populate the area, look for the occasional bald eagle.

Section I: Northern Utah

Historical re-enactors drive the Golden Spike

These magnificent birds of prey are truly thrilling to see in their natural habitat.

Seventeen and a half miles from the beginning of SR 83 back in Corinne, you will come to an intersection called Lampo Junction. This is where Golden Spike Road cuts off of the highway and takes you to the National Historic Site. Turn left (west) at the intersection. The road is clearly marked. Just follow the signs.

Heading west on Golden Spike Road you will see the Promontory Mountains stretching across your path and running south on the Promontory peninsula. As you get closer, notice the horizontal terraces marking the ancient shorelines left behind by the receding waters of Lake Bonneville. It's not hard to imagine the mountains before you as a chain of small islands in this prehistoric lake. For a closer look, you can take the left fork in the road at the sign marked "Promontory". This road runs south along the mountains onto the Promontory peninsula for about twenty miles before the pavement ends. There is really not much else to see out there though, so a good pair of binoculars is probably just as good as riding out on this road. Take the right fork in the road to go to the historic site.

Entering the historic site, you can clearly see the old original road cuts from both the Union Pacific and Central Pacific crews. There are several roads and trails within the site that allow visitors to explore

"119" rolls down the rails at Golden Spike Nat'l Historic Site

these various excavations; unfortunately all are unpaved. It is probably inadvisable to take a road bike on any of these dirt roads (they're rough and loose) but if you're up for a hike, there are turnouts in which to park and venture the trails on foot.

Following the paved road will take you to the visitor center, where you can view films and artifacts. Behind the center, 1.7 miles of track has been re-laid on the original roadbed. Here, fully functioning replicas of "Jupiter" and "119" (the original Central Pacific and Union Pacific engines respectively) operate all summer. After a demonstration run, both locomotives park nose to nose at the spot where the rails were joined. Platforms next to the rails allow you to climb up for a look at their control houses. Both engines can be inspected up close and hands-on. The National Park Service staff who operate the site are fabulous. They'll do everything they can to help you enjoy the experience.

Once you're satisfied that you have a new appreciation for one of America's greatest nineteenth century achievements, throw your leg back over your mount for a short run to the twentieth century. Let's go see some rockets!

ATK Rocket Display

Back at Lampo Junction turn left and go north on SR 83. Two miles up the road you will come to the ATK Rocket Display. ATK/Thiokol's solid rocket engines have propelled America into space from the earliest days of unmanned satellites to the Space Shuttle. The centerpiece of the display is an SRB motor like those used on the Space Shuttle. Pull over and take a closer look. The display is open year-round at no charge. Occasionally, the boys and girls at Thiokol used light one of these babies off in a killer fireworks display (they called it testing) that could be seen from the highway. Sadly, with the end of the shuttle program these shows are a thing of the past. However, when America develops its next generation space vehicle, ATK will surely play a key role and once again wow us with fiery exhibitions in the name of science.

Continue north on SR 83 and the road will veer around to the east. You will come to a T-intersection where SR 83 turns abruptly to the north. Go straight at this point, leaving SR 83 and continue east on Faust Valley Road (SR 102).

This road winds gently through the Blue Spring Hills and puts you on a long straight run back through farm country into Tremonton. As you pass through Bothwell, you'll ride past Eli Anderson's place

(8790 W. Hwy. 102). Eli has the largest private collection of horse drawn vehicles in the West and he'll show them to you by appointment. Check out www.wagonlandadventure.com or call (435) 730-3368 for more information.

Stay on SR 102 past the freeways, through Tremonton and back to SR 38 at Deweyville. For the real die-hard history buff, a short side trip presents itself here. If you turn left at the junction (north) and run up SR 38 to the next highway junction at SR 30, you will be able to see an historic stretch of the Bear River. Look for explorer J. C. Fremont's river crossing from the highway (indicated by a historical marker). At SR 30 turn left (west) and just a short distance past the junction you will come to a road leading to the right (look for the "Old Barn Theater" signs). This road leads you to Hampton's Ford. Built as a stagecoach stop in 1866, the building has been restored and is one of the best-preserved specimens of an Old West way station you'll find. It is now a bed and breakfast inn.

Going south on SR 38 points you back towards Brigham City. This stretch of highway is quite scenic, running down the Bear River Valley through quiet rural communities. About half-way between Deweyville and Brigham City you will come to Honeyville. Look for Crystal Hot Springs Resort on the west side of the highway. Here's your chance to relax after a day's ride and treat your bones to the soothing warmth of a mineral hot springs pool.

You've just completed a run through over one hundred years of history. Make your way back to Brigham City via SR 38 if you're done for now, or better yet, flip through these pages and find your next ride.

Golden Spike Run – Notes

Pit Stops:

Brigham City:
Chevron
1095 S. 500 W. (US 91)
(435) 723-1052

Flying J
1080 S. 500 W. (US 91)
(435) 723-3924

Tesoro
249 N. Main (SR 38)
(435) 723-0872

Schifty's
472 N. Main (SR 38)
(435) 723-1875

Corinne:
Sinclair
3870 W. 2450 N. (SR 13)
(435) 744-2603

Tremonton:
Chevron
2410 W. Main
(435) 257-7249

Tesoro
1420 W. Main
(435) 257-5107

Phillips 66
979 W. Main
(435) 257-5661

Chevron
110 E. Main
(435) 842-8475

Accommodations & Camping:

CAMPGROUNDS
Utah State Park Campgrounds
    Willard Bay State Park – 900W. 650 N., Willard
    (800) 322-3770 or www.stateparks.utah.gov

Commercial Campgrounds
    KOA Campground – US 89 south of Perry
    (435) 723-5503

Crystal Hot Springs – 8215 N. Hwy. 38, Honeyville
(435) 547-0777

HOTELS:
Brigham City:
Crystal Inn
480 Westland Dr.
(435) 723-0440

Howard Johnson
1167 S. Main
(435) 723-8511

Bushnell Motel
115 E. 700 S.
(435) 723-8575

Galaxie Motel
740 S. Main
(435) 723-3439

Tremonton:
Western Inn
2301 W. Main
(435) 257-3399

Sandman Motel
585 W. Main
(435) 257-5675

Marble Motel
116 N. Tremont
(435) 257-3524

RECOMMENDED DINING:

Brigham City:
Peach City Ice Cream Drive-In
306 N. Main
(435) 723-3923

Corinne:
Mim's Bar & Grill
4020 W 2450 N (Jct. SR13 & SR83)
(435) 744-2206

Mirror Lake Run

Mirror Lake

This run is all about wind in your hair, winding road, scenic mountain backcountry motorcycle riding. Not much in the way of historic diversions or tourist attractions here, just a whole lot of the most spectacular scenic byways ever made for two wheels.

On this ride, you'll trace the Provo River upstream through a forested canyon, wind past a series of pristine high mountain lakes and cross the Uinta Range at the edge of the High Uintas wilderness. You had better have a speedy bike because you'll need it just to catch your breath.

A jacket is mandatory equipment on this ride, and chaps, sweater and heavy gloves aren't a bad idea either. The temperature differential from start to finish is dramatic and deceiving. It's always cold on Bald Mountain Pass. I usually toss some rain gear in the bag as well. Maybe it's just my luck, but I've caught rain at least half of the many times I've taken this run. Don't let that deter you though. It's just part of the fun of riding the High Uintas. Enjoy!

Mirror Lake Run Route Map

ROUTE: From northern Wasatch Front – take I-84 eastbound to Echo Jct. Take I-80 westbound to SR 32 [exit 155]. Take SR 32 south to Kamas.

From central Wasatch Front – take I-80 eastbound to jct. with US 40. Take US 40 eastbound [south] to SR 248. Take SR 248 east to Kamas.

From southern Wasatch Front – at Orem, take SR 52 / 800 No. [I-15 exit 272] to US 189. Take US 189 northbound to US 40 at Heber City. Take US 40 westbound [north] through Heber to SR 32. Take SR 32 east to Kamas.

At Kamas, take SR 150 east and north to Evanston, WY.

On the road...

OK, we're through with field trips, for the time being. Not that there's anything wrong with field trips, mind you, but this run is a motorcycle ride, pure and simple. Time for a wind in your hair, bugs in your teeth scoot on one of Northern Utah's most beautiful scenic byways, SR 150.

For all intent and purpose, this ride begins in Kamas at the junction of SR 32 and SR 150. But getting to Kamas is a great ride in itself, so let's visit the road to Kamas briefly before we head up river.

From the north, the best way to Kamas takes you up Weber Canyon, through the Morgan Valley and then the Upper Weber Canyon to Echo Junction. This route is entirely on the I-84 freeway. Now I usually avoid freeways where secondary roads are available, and they are available here. However this stretch of freeway is really quite an enjoyable ride. Weber Canyon is a scenic ride, the Morgan Valley is quite picturesque, and traffic is rarely noticeable. On this route, you'll pass the communities of Morgan and Henefer (which have basic services) and scenic Devil's Slide.

From the central Wasatch Front, the way to go is up Parley's Canyon. This route is likewise a freeway run, this time on I-80. These two stretches of freeway (Weber Canyon and Parley's Canyon), along with the Echo Canyon segment of I-80, are some of the only worthwhile pieces of interstate highway for motorcyclists. These segments are enjoyable roads, worthy of planning into your ride. Most other portions of the interstate system are merely efficient routes, which to the biker should translate as "routes to avoid".

Parley's Canyon is not only loaded with scenic beauty, it is a thoroughly enjoyable piece of road on which to give your mount the spurs, so to speak. From the mouth of the canyon in Salt Lake City to Kimball Junction just outside Park City, the road presents a wide, well maintained, three to four lane high speed freeway. This road is one of my favorite speed runs. It presents many sweeping curves, designed and built for high speed. Traffic can occasionally be heavy, but usually moves at a good pace. Open it up and have some fun (within the limits of reason and prudence, of course). Blast up I-80 to the junction with US 40 (Silver Creek Junction). Take US 40 four miles south to SR 248, which goes east to Kamas.

Approaching from the south, jump off I-15 at exit 272 onto 800 North in Orem. This street is also known as SR 52. Take it east to US 189 at the mouth of Provo Canyon.

Provo Canyon is a fun ride by itself — a great road with plenty of mountain scenery. You'll find more on Provo Canyon in the chapter on "Wasatch Front Quickies".

Follow US 189 up the canyon to the junction with US 40 in Heber City. Go north on US 40 through Heber to SR 32, then take SR 32 into Kamas.

By the time you arrive in Kamas, you've already had a good ride. Now is a good time to check your gas. Once you roll out of town, the next opportunity for gas, food or drink is in Evanston, approximately 79 miles away. You might as well pull over and top off, stretch your legs and grab a snack or cold drink. You'll find a gas station and C-store at the junction of SR 32 and SR 248 and another a couple blocks north on SR 32 where it intersects SR150. If you're ready for a more substantial meal, try the Gateway Grill at the SR 248 / SR 32 highway junction. Here you'll find a good country menu at a good price.

From SR 248, go north on SR 32 to SR 150, the Mirror Lake Scenic Byway. This is the road that goes east off of Main Street at the Chevron station. For the next 60 miles or so you'll be on one of the best bike routes in Utah.

SR 150 follows Beaver Creek east out of Kamas, gently climbing through ranch and recreational properties before meeting the Provo River. About six miles out of Kamas you will come to a US Forest Service station where information and recreation passes are available. If you plan an extended stop between here and the Wyoming border, you'll need a recreation pass. Posted signs warn that all parked vehicles must display a pass, but if you're riding through, don't bother. My experience has been that brief stops along the way without a pass will not cause you to run afoul of the authorities. On the other hand, if you wish to camp overnight or even stop to fish or picnic, you'll probably need one. Better to stop and ask than find out the hard way. If you decide later that you need a pass, self-service stations are located at several spots along the highway.

About thirteen miles out of town you will come to the Provo River overlook, the first of several scenic points of interest on this ride. The view is much better in the spring and early summer when the river is swollen with runoff from melting snow pack. In the late summer and fall, particularly in drought years, the scene is not as dramatic.

Section I: Northern Utah

The Mirror Lake Scenic Byway - east of Kamas

Five miles or so up the road look for the Duchesne Tunnel. You'll see the signs marking it on the south side of the highway. An interesting diversion, (a really bad pun, I admit) the tunnel is part of the greater Provo River water project, designed to provide adequate and reliable water supplies to the Utah and Salt Lake valleys. It diverts water from the Duchesne River (part of the Colorado River drainage) into the Provo River (part of the Great Basin drainage) through a man-made aquifer running six miles underground at a maximum capacity of 600 cubic feet per second. Begun in 1940, work was ceased in 1942 due to manpower and material shortages during the war years. Construction resumed in 1947 and the tunnel was opened in 1952.

Not far beyond Duchesne Tunnel, the highway changes direction from generally east to generally north. You will now be in a somewhat narrower, forested canyon carved by the Provo River. Ahead on the horizon to the north you'll catch your first glimpse of Bald Mountain.

You'll be riding over the pass there in a moment, but right now, take note of the temperature. This stretch of highway is another on which the temperature differential is always dramatic and fascinating. The road starts to rise a little faster here and though you may be enjoying balmy shirt-sleeve temperatures at the moment, shortly

Duchesne Tunnel

you'll be looking at the goose bumps on your arms and debating with yourself whether to stop and put on a jacket.

Four or five miles up the road you'll come to Slate Gorge overlook. There's not a lot of room to park here but if you're inclined to stop, I promise you'll be impressed. From the highway you can look down over a steep embankment into a rock-strewn slate gorge through which the Provo River cuts a path in a bold expression of Nature's sculpture.

A couple of miles beyond, you'll find the Provo River Falls overlook. Like the Provo River overlook back down the road, this scenic attraction is much more dramatic in the spring and early summer when the river surges with heavy runoff. Unlike the other viewpoint however, this one is worth stopping to see late in the year or even in times of severe drought. You'll see the river cascade down a beautiful granite staircase into deep pools below. The setting is at once dramatic and serene. The bold rock formations sculpted by the river stand in stark juxtaposition to the soft peacefulness of the surrounding forest and create a sense of wonder and awe.

Continuing past Provo River Falls, the road starts to climb faster. The ambient air temperature will be getting nice and cool from here and the wind chill as you ride through it will be brisk and refreshing.

Provo River Falls

    Bald Mountain looms large in the picture as you near the pass. The highway so far has been fairly straight, with gentle, sweeping turns but for the next fifteen miles or so you'll be in the "twistiest" portion of this ride. As you climb to Bald Mountain Pass you'll encounter some tight turns, including three 180-degree switchbacks, with which to have some fun. You'll also run through a series of pristine glacial lakes that add to the already superlative beauty of the landscape.

    Bald Mountain overlook at the top of the pass affords a spectacular view of the valley through which you just climbed. If you look due west you can spot Wall Lake in the distance and to the south of that, some of the many smaller nameless lakes that dot the landscape. This area was sculpted by once great glaciers that carved the mountains and scooped out depressions that became the lakes you see today.

    On the north side of the summit at Bald Mountain pass, look for Hayden Peak overlook. This overlook offers a stunning view of the western end of the Uinta Range and Hayden Peak in particular. The Unita Mountains are one of only three ranges in the western hemisphere that run east-west rather than the more typical north-south orientation, and form the nation's largest east–west range. The mountains before you stretch 150 miles to the east and include Kings Peak, Utah's tallest mountain. Hayden Peak in the foreground rises 12,479 feet.

Riders on Bald Mountain Pass

Winding down from Bald Mountain Pass and the Hayden Peak overlook, you will rapidly approach Mirror Lake on the east side of the highway. Look for road signs clearly marking the turnoff into the camping and picnic area.

Mirror Lake is a pristine, crystal clear body of water with a surface as smooth as glass, the only occasional ripples coming from jumping fish. This is a lovely place to take a break, enjoy the view and maybe have a picnic. If you decide you need one, self-service recreation area passes are available. If you stop nowhere else along this ride, stop here. The serenity and beauty of this mountain jewel are most worthwhile.

Leaving the Mirror Lake area, turn right on the highway and continue north. You've still got a few enjoyable twisty turns ahead of you as you climb to Hayden Pass. Have fun with them, for the road beyond the pass reverts to its previous relatively straight, gently curving character. Beyond the pass begins a long gentle descent as you roll down the north side of the Uintas. Notice how the character of the forest changes as you come down from the higher elevations. From the pass, it's less than twenty-five miles to the Wyoming border.

Section I: Northern Utah

Crossing the border, you'll be in forested hills for a while, but soon the landscape opens up into Wyoming prairie. You'll be on a long straight home stretch into Evanston and nearly all the amenities you could possibly need. Where Highway 150 crosses I-80 at exit 5 you'll find gas, food and by venturing into town, lodging. Enjoy dinner and lager up in Evanston while you plan your next ride or turn this run into a loop by hopping on I-80 and shooting down Echo Canyon back towards Salt Lake City.

The Mirror Lake Run is northern Utah's answer to the adrenaline junkie jonesin' for some in-the-wind excitement. For the aesthete, it's a marvelous venue in which to appreciate Nature's beauty. The true renaissance rider, such as yourself — one who has demonstrated the highly refined nature of their character by, oh…say reading this book — who is equally at home in either camp, will find this ride to be a fantastic two wheeled escape. I'll see you out there.

Mirror Lake Run – Notes

Pit Stops:

Kamas:
Phillips 66
220 So. Main (Jct. SR 248 / SR 32)
(435) 783-4359

Chevron
2 No. Main (Jct. SR 32 / SR 150)
(435) 783-4375

Evanston, WY:
Chevron
106 No. 3rd St. (I-80, exit 5)
(307) 789-1813

Maverik
350 Front St. (I-80, exit 5)
(307) 789-1342

Accommodations & Camping:

CAMPGROUNDS:
National Forest Campgrounds info: (877) 444-6777 or www.reserveusa.com.
(Campgrounds listed are located on SR 150 and listed in order from Kamas to the Wyoming border.)

Ponderosa	Washington Lake
Yellow Pine	Trial Lake
Beaver Creek	Lilly Lake
Taylors Fork	Lost Creek
Shingle Creek	Moosehorn
Pine Valley	Mirror Lake
Lower Provo River	Butterfly Lake
North Fork	Sulphur
Soapstone	Beaver View
Shady Dell	Hayden Fork
West Portal	Stillwater
Cobblerest	Bear River
Upper Provo Bridge	East Fork

HOTELS:
Evanston, WY:

Best Western Dunmar Inn
1601 Harrison
(307) 789-3770

Super 8 Motel
1710 Harrison
(307) 789-2777

Days Inn
1983 Harrison Dr.
(307) 789-0783

Motel 6
261 Hwy 30
(307) 789-0791

RECOMMENDED DINING:
Kamas:

Gateway Grille
215 S. Main
(435) 783-2867

Uinta Drive Inn
235 Center St.
(435) 783-4312

Evanston, WY:
Don Pedro Mexican Restaurant
205 Bear River Dr.
(307) 789-3322

Before You Ride

Taking a few minutes before each ride to inspect your bike is a habit of all safe and responsible riders. A simple pre-ride inspection can make the difference between a full, satisfying ride and a frustrating, perhaps painful experience. Before you hit the road, give your bike the once over to check for potential problems. Such an investment in time always pays off in the long run.

Start with your tires and wheels. Remember, your life depends on the structural integrity of your wheels and the rubber on them. The contact patch between tire and road is no bigger than your fist, so this is not something to take lightly. Make sure your tires are inflated to the proper pressure (check your owner's manual) and that sufficient tread remains – no less than 3/32 of an inch. Check for cracks, cuts or signs of abnormal wear. Inspect your rims for dents or cracks. Spokes should be straight and tight.

Make sure all controls operate properly. Check the front and rear brake controls, your clutch, shifter and throttle for smooth operation. Inspect your throttle, brake, and clutch cables to insure they move freely without binding. It's better to find a frayed or broken cable in the driveway than on the highway.

Inspect your headlight, signal lights, taillight and brake light for proper operation. These critical components will help you be seen by others on the road.

Consult your owner's manual regarding oil and fluid levels, as well as battery inspection. Always check your engine oil before you ride, and other power train fluids as directed by your owner's manual. If your battery is not of the sealed maintenance-free variety, check and maintain proper water levels. Doing so will assure a trouble free ride and can double the life of your battery.

Make sure the chassis is in sound shape. Check for cracks or other signs of distress. Inspect the accessory mounts. Turn your handlebars through their full range to insure smoothness and proper damping, as well as fluid leaks. Consult your owner's manual regarding your final drive. Check for proper tension on belt and chain drive models. Inspect for cracks or leaks on shaft drive models.

Finally, inspect your kickstand for proper operation to avoid and embarrassing (and potentially dangerous) failure. Check your mirrors for proper adjustment before you start rolling. Take a look at your fuel level and decide if you need to top off before you get too far into your ride, and you should be ready to go.

Making these simple pre-ride checks a part of your routine will go far towards avoiding trouble on your ride. It only takes a few minutes and can prevent hours of frustration down the road. Don't let the assumption that everything is fine creep into your thinking and cause you to cut corners. You'll be glad you took the time and your bike will love you for it.

Heber – Duchesne Loop

Riders on US 40

So you've got a few hours to kill. You pull out a map and ask, "Where shall we ride today?" If this loop doesn't leap off the page at you, you're not spending enough time in the saddle.

Stretching about 150 miles (depending on subtle variations you choose) over some of the best motorcycle roads in northern Utah, this loop has much to recommend it as a spontaneous afternoon escape. You can run it on one tank of gas, but the ride easily stretches into three or four hours to fill up half a day in the wind. With Heber City, Duchesne and Park City on or near the loop, you can plan it around a lunch or dinner ride. Road conditions are great throughout the entire route, road character is wonderful — allowing you to explore the mysteries of g-force, torque and lean angle — and traffic is generally light. If all this is not enough, the landscape on this little jaunt is classic northern Utah: alpine forests, canyons, mountain passes, high desert, and colorful rocky draws.

Within easy reach of the greater Wasatch Front, this is a super loop to run when you want to get away by yourself for a few hours. It's also a fun getaway for the gang to do some riding and relaxing over a cold draft and a burger. If your club is planning a poker run, this is an excellent route. Whatever the reason, let's go get our knees in the breeze. Join me on the Heber-Duchesne Loop. Enjoy!

Heber – Duchesne Loop Route Map

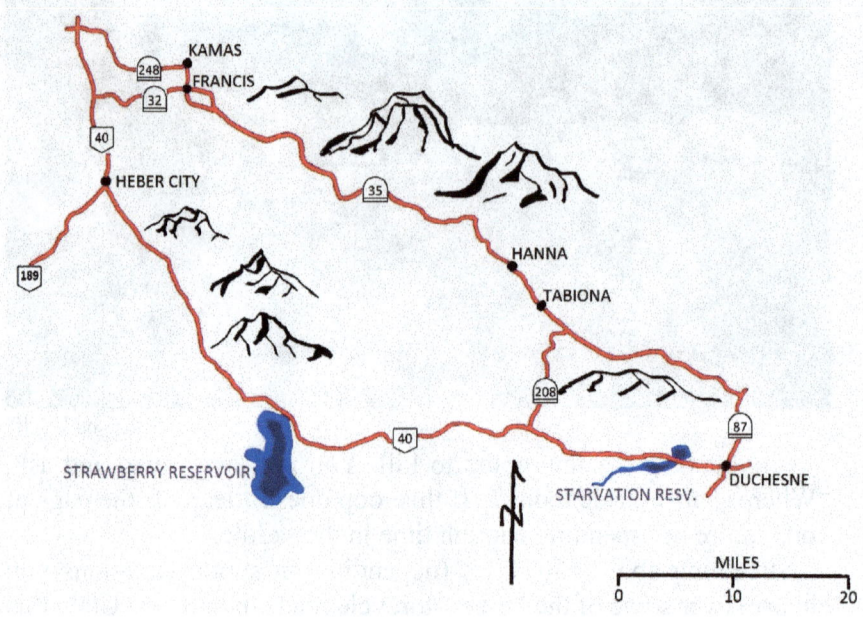

ROUTE: From Heber City, take US 40 eastbound to SR 208 or to SR 87 in Duchesne. Take SR 208 or SR 87 northbound to SR 35. Take SR 35 westbound to SR 32 in Francis. Take SR 32 westbound to US 40 near Heber City.

Section I: Northern Utah

On the road...

Living on the Wasatch Front gives northern Utah bikers access to some fantastic riding opportunities without having to plan for an extended absence from home. With multiple canyon avenues out of the valley, we can escape into the cool mountains, spend the day winding through alpine forests, and make it home to sleep in our own beds at night. This loop is one such idyllic ride. Running over some of my favorite motorcycle roads through some of my favorite mountain countryside, passing through some of my favorite mountain towns, I can't help but wonder why I don't ride this loop more often than I do.

We'll begin our ride in Heber City, Park City's less-glamorous stepsister. (Relax, denizens of Heber. I jest!) Heber City is a lovely little burg nestled in the Wasatch Mountains that hasn't yet been tainted with that cheesy resort community atmosphere or attracted the attention of out-of-state developers and speculators. Here you will find plenty of gas, food and lodging options (for those of you whose own beds are not within brief scoot range). This is the time and place to fill the gas tank and get a snack / drink. If your itinerary includes an extended stop for lunch or dinner, Heber City would also be an excellent venue for either, whether at the beginning or end of the ride.

Take US 40 (Main Street) south through town. At the bottom end of Main Street, US 40 meets US 189 at a traffic light. Veer slightly to the left through this intersection to stay on US 40 as it leaves town.

Running away from Heber, US 40 is a flat straightaway for about five miles to the mouth of Daniels Canyon. Here, the road opens up with a passing lane on the eastbound side that will give you two lanes to maneuver almost all the way to the summit. Also here, the rural valley gives way to mountain forests as you begin your ascent up the canyon. The canyon road is in good shape and mildly twisty so you'll no doubt want to open up and have some fun with it.

Daniels Canyon is a delight. The road makes a comfortable climb from about 5,600 feet elevation in Heber City to 7,980 feet at Daniels Summit. Crisp mountain air and the smells of the forest make a soothing background ambience to the stunning scenery of rock canyon walls and the vibrant green of pine and aspen groves.

The road summits at Daniels Pass, where you will find a lodge, café, general store, and gas. Since our ride has just begun, a rest stop makes little sense, but if you were to need one this is a great place.

Strawberry Reservoir

Cresting the summit, the road drops into the no-name valley in which lies Strawberry Reservoir. The forest disappears, replaced by grassland, and so do the *twisties* for the moment as US 40 makes a dash by the reservoir along the edge of the hills. Bending around the north shore of the lake, the road climbs over Windy Ridge and meets Deep Creek on the other side for a tandem run through Deep Creek Canyon.

Here begins another delightful segment of our ride. The forest reappears, gentle *twisties* are back, and the rock walls of the canyon complete the scene. The only thing wrong with this stretch of the run is that it's too short.

Coming out of the canyon, the terrain opens up into a broad, high-desert valley. The road is fairly straight here as you approach and pass through Fruitland. Except for a bend where the route crosses Red Creek and climbs a small hill, it's a straight, flat dash through the valley to the junction with SR 208.

At SR 208 we have the option to turn north and take the short loop or continue on US 40 to Duchesne for the long loop. In truth, adjectives like short and long are misleading, as going through Duchesne only adds 31 miles to the loop. This distance is hardly significant, and in fact, the practical road speed is probably faster on

Rounding Blacktail Ridge on SR 208

the long loop, so the time difference is minor. It all comes down to a matter of personal preference. Given that the road and landscape have nothing extraordinary to offer by going around the long way, and I have no need to avail myself of Duchesne's services if I gassed up and hydrated in Heber, I tend to prefer the so-called short loop. You decide for yourself.

Turning left on SR 208 takes you north on a fairly straight dash through rangeland. Watch for stock on or near the road. The desert gives way gradually to cedar forest, and on your left, a series of draws and hollows spill off of Tabby Mountain rising in the distance to the northwest. SR 208 is only ten miles long, connecting US 40 with SR 35. Near the end of this short road, it plunges into one of these draws, making a couple of tight loops back upon itself before bending around the western end of Blacktail Ridge and spilling into Hidden Valley. Here it finds a junction with SR 35, ending a brief but lovely dash.

Bypassing SR 208 and remaining on US 40 offers you more of the relatively flat and straight speed run through the desert valley that you've enjoyed since Fruitland. About 13 miles from the SR 208 junction you'll find Starvation Reservoir. The highway crosses a finger of this man-made lake over a bridge that offers an interesting view. Five miles beyond the reservoir, you'll find yourself in the heart of the Duchesne metropolitan area.

Duchesne isn't really a metropolitan area, but you knew I was being sarcastic. It is, however, a nice little rural community with all the services you're likely to require. You can find food, cold drinks, and your last chance for high-octane fuel until we climb back over the mountains to the Wasatch valleys where we began this ride.

In roughly the center of town, SR 87 runs due north out of Duchesne. Tracing the Duchesne River upstream, the road climbs a bench to the edge of the Uinta Basin and in six miles finds the junction with SR 35. Turn left (westbound) here onto SR 35.

Those who know me well know that SR 35 is one of my favorite motorcycle roads. It might be accurate to say it's on my Top Ten list in the nation, so bear with me as we discuss the next segment of our loop. I'll try to moderate the hyperbole. Only 62 miles from end to end, this relatively new highway (the middle segment was just paved in the last decade) is in great shape, is possessed of outstanding road character with marvelously tight twisties, and makes an aggressive climb and descent spanning more than 3,600 ft. in elevation through a scenic mountain forest. The only thing that could make SR 35 better would be to make it longer. I have discussed this road in detail from west to east in the *Rock Creek / Moon Lake Run* chapter, so I could refer you to those pages and have you read them backwards for this ride. That would be lazy of me though, so without being redundant, let's examine this superb highway briefly from east to west.

The first few miles of SR 35 run through dry desert terrain to a spot marked as Utahn on the map. The scenery quickly changes, however, as the road drops into a little draw formed by the Duchesne River. Now it is SR 35's turn to run the river upstream, and as it does so it finds its way back into green vegetation. The first 17 miles, to the junction with SR 208, is a gently bending, increasingly scenic ride. Coming to the highway intersection at Hidden Valley, you'll find yourself in a pastoral setting of farms and ranches surrounding Tabiona.

Tabiona sits about three miles from the SR 208 junction. With nothing more than a small café, there's not much to recommend stopping here. Less than five miles up the road lies Hanna, a much better choice for planning a rest stop.

Hanna is home to that biker favorite, The Hanna Café, a good place to stop if a nice sit-down lunch or dinner is on the agenda. Across the street you'll see the Hanna Country Store, the place to stop for a quick break and a light snack. The gas pumps out front only spit up regular

Section I: Northern Utah

Hanna Country Store

grade, none of the 91-proof sweet stuff so many of today's modern bikes have grown accustomed to. This shouldn't be a problem though, if you topped off the tank at the beginning of our ride.

Running northwest out of Hanna, excitement and anticipation should start to build because you're coming upon the best stretch of today's ride. From here to the Stockmore Guard Station the road traces a relatively straight course beside the colorful cliffs and benches, still tracking upstream along the Duchesne River. At Stockmore though, SR 35 bends west away from the river and plunges into the mouth of Wolf Creek Canyon.

This is where our road earns its place on so many "top rides" lists. Beginning a vigorous climb to the summit, the highway also gets tightly twisty here. The road surface is in great shape and supports an aggressive run over the top for those inclined to give their mounts the spurs. I liken this segment of highway to a black-diamond run on the ski slopes. For the skilled rider on a high-performance bike, a thrilling slalom speed run lies ahead. Don't take the black-diamond analogy too literally, though. Those not interested in tackling the trek over the mountain in an aggressive fashion need not shy away. Taking it easy, one may enjoy a pleasantly twisty and relaxing ride through an exceptionally scenic landscape. Roadside turnouts abound and passing

Running the *twisties* on SR 35

lanes open up near the top, allowing more sedate riders to safely pass or be passed as circumstances dictate.

A campground with a restroom and a large dirt parking area sits on the road summit at Wolf Creek Pass. I find this to be a good spot to take a break and rest the horses, so to speak (and frankly, a chance to let your adrenaline return to safe levels before shooting it up again on the descent). You'll find the temperature here at the summit is always much cooler than the valleys below and the dark forest surrounding this turnout makes it a lovely rest stop.

Cresting the hill, our highway dives into another canyon with no loss in road quality or character. Not far from the top, the road picks up the South fork of the Provo River and chases it downstream in a delightfully twisty romp that is every bit the equal of the climb up the east side of the mountain. I've never learned the proper name for this splendid canyon so I've taken to calling it South Fork Canyon. Apropos, I suppose, but until someone else does so as well, my name for this segment will lack a certain legitimacy. You can call it what you like. It's one hell of a ride!

Halfway down the hill there is an interesting roadside marker, the Goto Monument. See page 120 for the story. If you can pry yourself away from the twisties for a moment, you may find this tidbit of Utah history intriguing.

With a final series of zig-zags our downhill run rounds a bend and comes upon Nobletts Trailhead. From here, the ride settles down into a much straighter and gentler run through a broader valley, hugging the edge of the river in places as the road brings us through Woodland. Just past Woodland the highway veers suddenly to the right, much as Utah politicians often do, and climbs a bench to bring us to Francis.

Francis is a small rural community on the outskirts of Kamas. The greater downtown area consists of a small gas station at a four-way intersection, where SR 35 sadly ends. Going straight (westbound) through the intersection or turning right (northbound) both put you on SR 32. Either way will allow you to make your way back to US 40 and close this loop.

Westbound SR 32 makes a pleasant and scenic run along the south shore of Jordanelle Reservoir to join US 40 just north of Heber City. Turning left (south) on US 40 returns you to Heber City where we began our ride. If you chose to go northbound on SR 32 from Francis, two short miles of straight road have brought you to Kamas. Here you will find the junction with SR 248. Turn left (west) on SR 248 and you will enjoy another pleasant, scenic run, this one along the north shore of Jordanelle Reservoir. Follow this road all the way into Park City and you will find a veritable cornucopia of food and drink over which to celebrate a perfect ride.

Well, there you have it — a hundred and fifty miles of excitement loaded into half a day. Next time, try riding it in the opposite direction—but be sure to remember to read this chapter backwards when doing so. I know it sounds tricky but it works. Trust me.

Heber / Duchesne Loop – Notes

Pit Stops:

Heber City:
Texaco
220 N. Main St
(435) 654-0838

Mountainland Sinclair
1175 S. Main St
(435) 654-5530

Duchesne:
Bonanza Sinclair
94 E. Main St.
(435) 738-2393

Hanna:
Hanna Country Store
SR 35
(435) 848-5752

Accommodations & Camping:

CAMPGROUNDS:
National Forest Campgrounds info: (877) 444-6777 or www.reserveusa.com
SR 35:
Wolf Creek

HOTELS:
Heber City:
Swiss Alps Inn
167 S. Main St.
(435) 654-0722

Holiday Inn Express
1268 S. Main St.
(866) 307-5578

Daniels Summit Lodge
Hwy 40, Daniels Pass
(866) 599-6674

RECOMMENDED DINING:

Heber City:
Hub Café
1165 S. Main St.
(435) 654-5463

Sidetrack Café
94 S. Main St.
(435) 654-0563

Chicks Café
154 S. Main St.
(435) 654-1771

Hanna:
Hanna Café
SR 35
(435) 848-5564

Don Pedro's
1050 S. Main St.
(435) 657-0600

Granny's Drive-In
511 S. Main St.
(435) 654-3925

Daniels Summit Lodge
Hwy 40, Daniels Pass
(866) 599-6674

Utah Climate

Utah's climate has four distinct seasons. Low humidity and lots of sunshine are two characteristics of Utah weather that make it ideal for motorcycling. The table below shows average high / low temperatures in degrees Fahrenheit, with average monthly precipitation in inches, for the typical riding months of March through October. For current weather conditions and forecasts see:
        www.wrh.noaa.gov/slc/
        www.weather.com
        www.wunderground.com/US/UT

	MAR	APR	MAY	JUN	JUL	AUG	SEP	OCT
Bear Lake	45/22	57/30	67/37	75/43	85/50	85/50	74/42	60/33
	1.02	1.39	1.69	1.2	0.6	0.77	0.8	1.27
Logan	47/28	58/36	68/43	78/51	87/59	86/58	75/48	62/39
	1.89	2.02	2.05	1.22	0.64	0.81	1.22	1.69
Brigham City	51/29	61/37	73/46	82/54	93/62	91/59	80/50	66/39
	1.95	2.25	1.74	1.62	0.3	0.73	1.21	1.54
Ogden	52/30	63/37	73/45	82/52	92/60	90/58	80/48	67/38
	1.65	2.05	1.86	1.3	0.56	0.77	1.2	1.58
SLC	53/32	62/38	72/46	83/55	93/63	90/62	80/51	66/40
	1.75	2.07	1.76	0.9	0.72	0.8	1.07	1.29
Park City	43/22	55/31	63/36	75/44	82/50	80/50	71/41	60/32
	2.13	1.19	1.64	1.13	1.85	1.6	1.76	1.48
Provo	57/33	65/39	75/46	86/54	94/60	92/59	82/50	68/39
	1.95	1.9	20.8	1.2	0.86	1.14	1.58	1.91
Tooele	51/30	60/38	70/46	80/54	88/62	87/61	77/51	64/40
	2.13	2.17	2.02	1	0.79	0.86	1.16	1.52
Nephi	54/28	63/34	73/42	84/50	93/58	91/56	82/47	69/37
	1.55	1.54	1.39	0.89	0.73	0.98	0.97	1.34
Duchesne	50/23	62/31	72/38	81/45	87/52	85/51	76/42	63/31
	0.68	0.74	0.85	0.79	0.93	1.23	1.06	0.95
Vernal	51/22	62/30	73/38	83/45	90/52	87/50	78/41	65/31
	0.63	0.81	0.84	0.71	0.54	0.72	0.83	1.02
Price	53/28	63/35	73/43	84/52	90/58	88/57	80/48	65/38
	0.73	0.5	0.69	0.57	0.89	1.04	1.1	1.22
Moab	62/33	72/41	82/48	93/56	98/63	95/61	87/51	73/39
	0.81	0.81	0.73	0.42	0.79	0.86	0.85	1.02
Bluff	61/31	71/38	81/46	91/54	96/62	94/60	86/50	72/38
	0.61	0.49	0.42	0.21	0.69	0.85	0.81	0.95
Escalante	55/26	63/33	73/40	84/47	89/54	86/53	78/44	67/35
	0.84	0.57	0.6	0.47	1.2	1.82	1.16	1.05
Panguitch	51/19	60/25	70/32	79/38	85/46	82/44	76/36	65/26
	0.79	0.65	0.63	0.51	1.39	1.65	0.99	0.9
Cedar City	52/28	60/34	70/41	79/49	85/56	83/55	76/47	66/37
	1.91	1.63	0.93	0.55	1.48	1.53	0.94	1.2
St. George	68/36	77/43	86/51	96/59	102/67	100/65	93/55	80/43
	0.93	0.51	0.39	0.19	0.67	0.76	0.61	0.67

Wasatch Front Quickies

Riders on Alpine Loop

Living and working along the Wasatch Front has much to offer, not the least of which is the myriad of enjoyable short rides to choose from when you're looking for a Sunday afternoon diversion or perhaps just a quick scoot after work.

The following rides are just the ticket. Each route is convenient to hit from virtually anywhere along the Wasatch Front. They will typically run two to three hours and will give you the opportunity to get your minimum daily requirement of wind in your hair without committing to a full day in the saddle or an overnight excursion.

Some of these rides beg to be done repeatedly throughout the year as the landscape evolves from early spring awakening through verdant summer foliage to the neon explosion of fall colors. But that's what these rides are all about — keeping you in the wind as often as possible. Enjoy!

East Canyon / Dixie Hollow Loop

East Canyon is one of my favorite afternoon rides. With several subtle variations, you'll find that this is a great ride to repeat several times throughout the season. You can complete the loop in 2 to 3 hours, depending on how you want to stretch it out. It's a fun little scoot, along some winding mountain roads, past a reservoir or two and through some high country farmland.

We'll start in Salt Lake City, at the end of the Mormon Pioneer Trail. We'll be backtracking along the route of the early Mormons as we climb into the Wasatch Range.

Section I: Northern Utah

I like to take Sunnyside Ave. eastbound to the mouth of Emigration Canyon, near Hogle Zoo and This Is The Place Heritage Park. The parking lot at Hogle Zoo is a good rally point to link up with friends at the start of this ride. When you're ready to go, continue east into the canyon.

Not far from the mouth of the canyon you'll come to another good rally point and a great place to grab some lunch. Ruth's Diner is located about two miles from Hogle Zoo up Emigration Canyon Road. Ruth's has been a fixture in the canyon for what seems like forever. They serve excellent burgers, as well as other light lunch and dinner fare.

This stretch of road is one of the more enjoyable urban rides in the Salt Lake City area. Take note as you ride, however, that the canyon is populated with many homes, several of which have blind driveways that empty directly onto the road. Respect the residents as well as your own safety by taking it easy in the lower part of the canyon.

Emigration Canyon was the original point of entry into the Salt Lake Valley for the early Mormon pioneers, as well as the route of the ill-fated Donner-Reed Party. You'll see the occasional historic marker as you venture out of the city and, surveying the terrain, it's easy to imagine the building excitement these settlers must have felt as they struggled to negotiate the last difficult stretch of their journey over a primitive trail in covered wagons. Unfortunately for these hardy souls, the Harley-Davidson Motor Company was still fifty-six years in their future, with the advent of Honda and others still over a hundred years away. Too bad. A motorcycle would have cast this journey in a whole new light. Personally, I would have waited.

After cresting a hill about 7.5 miles from the mouth of the canyon, Emigration Canyon Road descends for a mile and a half to a T-intersection with SR 65 at Little Dell Reservoir. To the right lies Parley's Canyon and I-80. Instead, turn left and take SR 65 up Mountain Dell Canyon.

Just east of the intersection, near the parking turnout at Little Dell Reservoir, is a gate which closes SR 65 between mile 3 and mile 13 in the winter, as weather conditions dictate (typically October through May). Often the gate has remained locked well into May when riding season is in full swing in the valleys and lovely spring weather draws riders into the canyons.

On one such spring weekend, I rode up to Little Dell to see if the road was open. Coming to the parking turnout at the reservoir, I saw numerous bikes in the lot and riders milling about chatting. Sadly, the gate still stretched across the highway, which explained the impromptu biker gathering. My friends and I pulled into the lot and dismounted to stretch and chat with fellow riders. Soon, I heard a lone bike approaching and looked up to see a new Ultra Classic Electra Glide® coming around a slight bend in the road at about 50 mph. Both rider and passenger were looking at the crowd in the parking turnout and not at the road ahead. I could tell by the engine sound that the beautiful, brand-new bagger was not slowing down but was actually accelerating. Glancing quickly at the heavy steel gate blocking the road and back at these riders smiling and waving to the crowd as they passed, I thought 'this is going to be ugly. Wanting to jump scream and point at the gate, I was frozen, unable to manage so much as a wave. Thankfully, someone in the crowd was able to make a feeble gesture towards the looming obstacle. At what can only be described as the very last nanosecond, the rider looked up and saw the closed gate. Executing the most beautiful panic stop I have ever witnessed, this seemingly doomed rider brought his heavy touring bike to a dead stop at the gate without once locking either wheel. This was before the availability of anti-lock brakes on H-D models and with absolutely zero margin for error. From my perspective, when the bike stopped rolling, one could not have slid a sheet of paper between the bike's front tire and the steel bars of the gate. I would love the opportunity to meet this guy and shake his hand.

Sadly, I did not get the chance. Our intrepid colleague sat on his bike for a while at the gate before turning about and speeding off in the other direction, without a glance or wave to the incredulous crowd. I assume he needed a moment to pry his passenger's fingers from between his ribs and restart his heart. Upon doing so, I imagine embarrassment, and perhaps a fair amount of fecal material pooling in his boots, made it necessary for him to depart quickly. But we can all draw a couple of lessons from the incident. First, pay attention to the road! Motorcycling is an activity that is particularly unforgiving of inattentive behavior. Getting swept away in the joy of the moment could have disastrous consequences. Second, hone your riding skills every chance you get. Danger avoidance maneuvers, such as emergency stopping, can be very tricky and delicate. The rider in this story saved his own life and the life of his passenger because he was very skilled and did not panic when executing a "panic stop". Enough said. Let's get back to our ride.

SR 65 makes a twisty climb up Big Mountain

For the first three miles past the Emigration Canyon Road/SR 65 intersection, the highway is gently rolling and nearly straight, with only a few gentle curves. The foliage grows nearly to the roadside, creating a verdant tunnel of vegetation in spring and summer and a kaleidoscope of color in the fall. You'll be out of the residential area now and will surely feel the urge to open up the throttle a bit. Be aware though that the posted speed limit on this stretch of road is quite low, much slower than your bike will want to go. Keep an eye out for law enforcement. They will enforce the posted speed limit. Watch out for the odd campground entrance or recreational trail that intersects the highway and take note of the historical markers that dot the road. You can enhance your knowledge of Utah's pioneer heritage by stopping to take a look if you're so inclined.

Rather abruptly the road begins to climb traversing the side of the mountain through a series of sharp switchbacks. Before you know it you'll be cresting the highway summit at Big Mountain Pass.

Big Mountain is a good place to stop and you'll find a large gravel parking area at the highway summit where you can do so. The view of the Salt Lake Valley is spectacular. On a clear day, without pollution clouding the air, you can see across the entire breadth of the valley to Lake Point Junction at the northern tip of the Oquirrh Mountains. In spring and summer, the mountain draws below you are vibrant with

Riders survey the Salt Lake Valley from Big Mountain Pass

thick green forests of aspen and scrub oak, giving way to the urban valley beyond. In the fall, these forests explode in color, adding to the impact of the vista. On July 19, 1847, Orson Pratt and John Brown, leading an advance party of the first Mormon pioneers to reach Utah, stood here and caught the first view of their destination. The last of the three companies comprising this first migration, led by Brigham Young, arrived here on July 23, 1847. On the other side of the parking area to the east, you can see the original pioneer trail stretching back through the high valleys of the Wasatch. This trail was originally cut by the Donner-Reed Party, who took 13 days to make their way from Henefer to the Salt Lake Valley. Thanks to their efforts, the Mormons traveled the same distance the following year in just 6 days. The route became part of the California Trail and was used by the Overland Stage and Pony Express.

Continuing east, SR 65 descends quickly down a winding path to Little Dutch Hollow before curving to the north at East Canyon Creek. Not far after the road veers north, at the southern tip of East Canyon Reservoir, you'll find East Canyon Resort on the west side of the highway. The resort offers the chance to grab some food or drink should you need it but does not sell gasoline.

Past the resort, the highway runs north along the east side of East Canyon Reservoir and State Park, a popular site for summertime camping and water recreation. Near the northeast tip of the reservoir the road forks at the junction of SR 65 and SR 66. Let's explore the left fork first.

Turning left at the highway junction puts you on SR 66. The road climbs and winds along the north shore of East Canyon Reservoir before it peaks at East Canyon Dam. This stretch of road affords you a good view of the entire reservoir and a close up look at the dam. Past the dam you'll follow East Canyon Creek as it descends down East Canyon to Porterville.

At Porterville, the road forks again, offering another sub-variation to this ride. Stay right and you'll remain on SR 66 to Morgan. If I need gas or liquid refreshment right away, this is the road I'll take. Morgan is just over four miles from this point, and offers multiple places to gas up and grab a snack or a meal.

At Morgan, cross under the freeway and turn left to head northwest on Old Highway Road (700 East). This is a frontage road that parallels I-84 and will take you through Stoddard and Enterprise all the way to Mountain Green along the northeast side of Morgan Valley past high country farms and ranches.

Not quite three miles up Old Highway Road from the junction with SR 66 sits Kelly's Roadhouse, a delightful little biker canteen. Kelly's is more than just a biker friendly joint, it's pretty much a biker's only joint (a fact that is apparent when you see the "Motorcycle Parking Only" signs out front). The atmosphere here is always friendly and relaxed, the beer always cold, and the food… well, the food is fantastic. I won't ride by without stopping and in fact, if I'm anywhere in the northern Wasatch on my bike, I often find myself heading towards Kelly's. Check it out when you're riding this loop. You're likely to run into friends there and if not, there's ample opportunity to meet new ones.

Back at Porterville, if you turn left on Morgan Valley Drive, you'll travel along the southwest side of the valley through the little communities of Richville, Littleton, Milton and Peterson. The Weber River bisects this valley and the view of mountain farm country is quite picturesque from this side. This fork bypasses Morgan however, and there are no services on this side. At Peterson, a little over ten miles down the road, cross I-84 and turn left on Old Highway Road (frontage road) to Mountain Green.

Kelly's Roadhouse

Mountain Green offers another good place to stop for gas and snacks. There is a C-Store and gas station at the intersection of Old Highway Road and SR 167 that makes a convenient pit stop.

Let's jump back to the junction of SR 65 and SR 66 at East Canyon Reservoir and take a look at the other route. Continuing straight on SR 65 takes you through Dixie Hollow and Main Canyon to the town of Henefer. This road is the route of the Mormon Pioneer Historic Trail and, while relatively straight, presents a fun ride nonetheless.

SR 65 comes to a T-intersection in the town of Henefer and offers us another sub-variation to throw into the ride. Turn right and you will be able to cross over the freeway at exit 115 and catch a local road for a side trip to Croydon, Lost Creek State Park, and Devil's Slide. Turn left just over the freeway on East Henefer Road and follow it into Croydon where you will come to a T-intersection (6800 E & 1900 N). Turn right towards Croydon City Park where the road makes a quick left. Follow this road to Lost Creek Reservoir State Park. Coming back on the same road, continue straight (east) on 1900 N after passing the park and you will come to I-84 at exit 111 just past the cement plant.

Turning left in Henefer will take you to I-84 where you can jump on the westbound freeway at exit 112. From there you can get off at exit 103 in Morgan and take Old Highway Road down to Mountain Green as previously described or take the freeway to exit 96 just before

Mountain Green. If you're so inclined, just stay on I-84 all the way to the mouth of Weber Canyon and the end of this ride.

We'll tie these variations on our ride back together at Mountain Green. As indicated above, the C-store/gas station at the corner of Old Highway Road and SR 67 makes a good pit stop for fuel and refreshment. From the gas station, head west on Old Highway Road and you will merge into the westbound I-84 freeway in about two miles, at exit 92. Continue westbound on I-84 to the junction with US 89, at the mouth of Weber Canyon about five miles down the freeway.

At exit 87, get off I-84 and onto US 89. Going north on US 89 takes you Ogden and points north. Head south on US 89 to catch I-15 and the Salt Lake City metro area.

You've just completed a short loop through the Wasatch that begs to be ridden repeatedly throughout the season. I like this ride because it always seems longer than it really is. After completing the loop, I tend to have the satisfying feeling of having ridden for a long while, only to look at my watch and realize I've just been out a few hours. Try a route variation each time you ride it and it will become one of your favorite "quickies" as well.

Provo Canyon / Alpine Loop

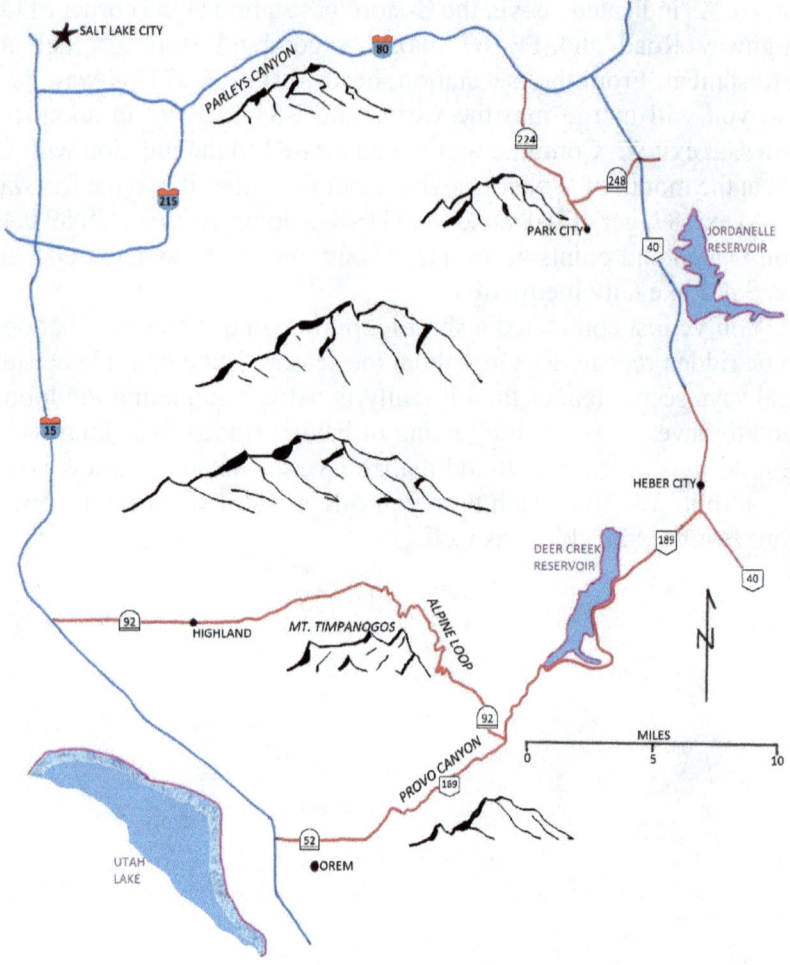

Provo Canyon and the Alpine Loop are among the most popular rides with Wasatch Front riders, and for good reason. The scenery is fantastic. The ride can be about as challenging as you care to make it, from slow and relaxing to hard and aggressive. And it offers a quick getaway from the urban rat race to the serenity of the mountains. Variations on the loop described here can run from one hour or less to about two hours, depending on traffic conditions and the route you choose. With stops, though, this ride can be stretched into a full afternoon of fun and relaxation.

Section I: Northern Utah

I'll discuss this ride from north to south, beginning in Salt Lake City and ending in Provo, but I want to emphasize before I begin that this loop should be run in both directions. Perhaps more so than other rides, this loop has a distinctively different character when ridden in opposite directions. Run it both ways to fully appreciate all that this ride has to offer.

Beginning in Salt Lake City, take I-80 eastbound out of the city and into Parley's Canyon. Parley's Canyon was the primary route into the Salt Lake Valley after 1861, used by later groups of Mormon Pioneers and California bound emigrants as well as the Overland Stage. It remains an important portal into and out of the valley today on I-80. The eastbound freeway is also one of my very favorite speed runs.

I like going up Parley's Canyon much more than going down it. Perhaps it is because I have a definite speed and power advantage over four-wheeled traffic on the uphill side. This is not necessarily true on the downhill (westbound) run, where gravity allows the cage drivers with whom you share the road to explore the limits of their squirrelly behavior. Either way, the road is a beauty, with a respectably steep grade, three to four broad lanes in which to maneuver and sweeping high-speed curves. From the mouth of the canyon to the top of Parley's Summit, this road begs to be ridden fast and hard. Of course, I would never encourage one to exceed the posted speed limit or break any other traffic laws, but it doesn't surprise me to see those laws stretched a bit here by my friends on two wheels. Know your own limits and always ride within them.

Just past Parley's Summit at exit 145 you will come to Kimball Junction where I-80 meets SR 224. Right off the exit you will find a gas station and a myriad of fast food establishments, should a pit stop be required. For a fun diversion, take SR 224 into Park City for a break.

Park City is a town loaded with history and ambience. Once a simple mining town, it has become the centerpiece of Utah's winter sports industry as well as a mecca for the nouveau riche and California transplants. Whether deserved or not, Park City has at times held a reputation for being less than a biker-friendly community. It remains, nonetheless, a favorite among bikers. Ah, the tragedies of unrequited love....

Head for historic Main Street where you will find a plethora of eateries and drinking establishments. Two of my favorites are Main Street Pizza & Noodle, in the middle of Main Street, where you can

Main Street – Park City

get built-to-order home style pizza and Wasatch Brew Pub at the top of Main Street, where you will find excellent pub fare and some of Utah's best craft beer to wash it down. Another biker favorite is the No Name Saloon, located about mid-Main Street.

When you're done in Park City, backtrack on SR 224 (Park Ave.) to Kearns Blvd. This is SR 248. Go east on SR 248 to US 40. Go south on US 40 at the junction.

If you're not inclined to visit Park City, stay on I-80 past Kimball Junction. About 2 miles east of Kimball Junction at exit 146 you will come to the interchange with US 40 called Silver Creek Junction. Take the exit and head south on US 40. (According to the UDOT, you will be going eastbound on US 40, which is probably true in a big picture sense, but for this segment of the ride, you will be traveling south.)

About fourteen miles from Silver Creek Junction, US 40 rolls into Heber City. Here you will also find everything you'll need for a successful pit stop. There are gas stations all along Main Street, offering multiple flavors of high-octane refreshment for your mount. For food, I recommend Granny's Drive-In or the Sidetrack Cafe for a classic lunch of charbroiled burgers and fries. The Hub Café on the south end of Main Street at the junction of US 40 and US 189 offers a traditional diner fare for breakfast, lunch and dinner. Don Pedro's Mexican Restaurant, nearby, serves above average Mexican cuisine. For a cold one, stop at The Other End Saloon on the west side of US 40 at the north edge of town. This biker friendly establishment offers light pub fare and ice cold beer in a comfortable setting.

For a dose of nostalgia, swing out to see the historic railroad while in Heber. You can see working examples of historic engines and rolling stock and even hop a ride on the "Heber Creeper" if you wish. The rail yard lies on the west side of town. Just follow the signs off Main Street.

At the south end of Heber City, US 40 meets US 189. Turn right and head southwest on US 189. After about three miles of flat straightaway, you'll come upon Deer Creek Reservoir. The road winds along the shore of the lake, then below the dam, dumping you into the top of Provo Canyon.

Provo Canyon is a scenic ride along the Provo River through forested mountains and granite cliffs. The road is modern and well maintained and has recently been upgraded to four lanes from top to bottom. On the way down Provo Canyon, look for Vivian Park, roughly two miles from the junction of SR 92 and just before mile marker 13. Here you will find a Heber Valley Railroad stop where, if your timing is right, you can catch the Heber Creeper or watch as the majestic steam engine puffs and bellows on its way through the mountains. Also look for Bridal Veil Falls just over two miles past Vivian Park. There is an overlook on the south side of the highway just above mile marker 11. The falls cascade dramatically off a high cliff and crash down the canyon walls. They even come complete with an Indian legend, which you can read about at the rest area. High on the cliff above the falls you may see the ruins of an old building that was perched precariously on the canyon wall, along with a derelict tram that once provided access. I'm told this was a resort/restaurant in its day but the building burned down in the summer of 2008.

Continue west down US 189 and you will find Orem at the mouth of the canyon. The road forks here at a traffic light. Go straight (the left fork) and you will stay on US 189 through Orem to Provo. Turn right and you will be on SR 52, also known as 800 North in Orem. Take this road west to find I-15, which will take you to points north and south along the Wasatch Front.

The "Heber Creeper"

Let's backtrack now and explore a significant variation of this ride – the Alpine Loop. About four miles down the canyon from Deer Creek Dam you will find SR 92 forming a T-intersection with US 189 on the right (northwest) side of the highway just before mile marker 15 and the tunnel. If you feel like stretching this ride out through some beautiful country with spectacular vistas, turn right (north) here.

The Alpine Loop is an amazing road that skirts the edge of the Mount Timpanogos Wilderness Area. I call it amazing for the almost overwhelming mountain beauty of the landscapes you will experience and the breathtaking views you will see. This of course, makes it a very popular stretch of road with sightseers and so from late spring to early fall you can expect a lot of traffic, especially on weekends and holidays. On top of this, the road gets very narrow (not much wider than a single lane) as it crosses over the mountain so plan on a slow ride. Your best chance to avoid traffic and have the road somewhat to yourself is on an early weekday: Monday through Wednesday.

About two miles up SR 92 from US 189 you will come to Sundance, the ski resort built by Robert Redford. The resort is open year round and offers a variety of food and drink. On summer weekends you can often catch musicians or local bands playing on the

Riding the Alpine Loop in early autumn

grass at the foot of the ski hill. Sundance makes for an enjoyable rest stop and a good place to grab a snack or a meal.

Roughly five miles up the road (about 3 miles from Sundance) you will come to a National Park Service fee station. The Park Service administers the land you will be riding through, including Timpanogos Cave National Monument on the other side of the mountain. If you plan to stop anywhere within the recreation area you are required to pay a usage fee. However, if you intend to just ride through, you will be allowed to pass without charge.

Just after the entrance station the road gets narrow and will remain so until you get near the bottom on the other side of the mountain. You are on the backside of the Wasatch here and will be climbing through cool mountain forests of aspen and pine. As you climb with the highway you will catch several impressive views of Mount Timpanogos, towering in imposing fashion over the mountain valleys below. You'll be able to see the scars of glaciers that carved and shaped this side of the mountain, some of which hold permanent snow pack throughout the year.

After twisting up narrow switchbacks for four or five miles through thick forest, you will reach Alpine Summit where you crest the

Riders in Provo Canyon

mountain and begin a similar winding trek down the front side of the Wasatch Range. At the road summit you will find restrooms at a hiking trailhead if you need to stop.

Winding down the front side, the road opens up a bit, offering more expanded views of the canyons and valleys below. The vistas from this stretch of the road defy description and can be particularly overpowering in the early morning or in the fall as the foliage explodes in color.

A couple of roads cut off the highway on this side, each of which comes to a dead end. The main route is clearly marked, however. Just follow the SR 92 markers and you will be on the right path.

Way too soon you will find yourself at the bottom of the hill on the front side. Here the road widens back to two lanes and straightens out as you follow American Fork Creek down American Fork Canyon. Just about two miles down from where the road enters American Fork Canyon you will come to Timpanogos Cave National Monument. This fascinating natural wonder is well worth taking the time to explore. To see the cave requires a short (less than a mile) but steep hike up the side of the mountain, and remember, if you wish to stop here you need to purchase a recreation pass.

Continuing west down the canyon on SR 92 takes you to the town of Highland, where SR 92 becomes 11000 N. You will find a Chevron station at the intersection of SR 92 and SR 74 (11000 N and 5300 W) in case your trek over the mountains has left you low on fuel. About five miles west on this road you will find I-15 and the end of this ride.

Don't think it strange if you feel like turning around at this point and doing it again. This loop is one that should be run in both directions to be fully appreciated. Explore it in different variations and this ride will surely become one of your perennial favorites.

Oquirrh & Eureka Loops

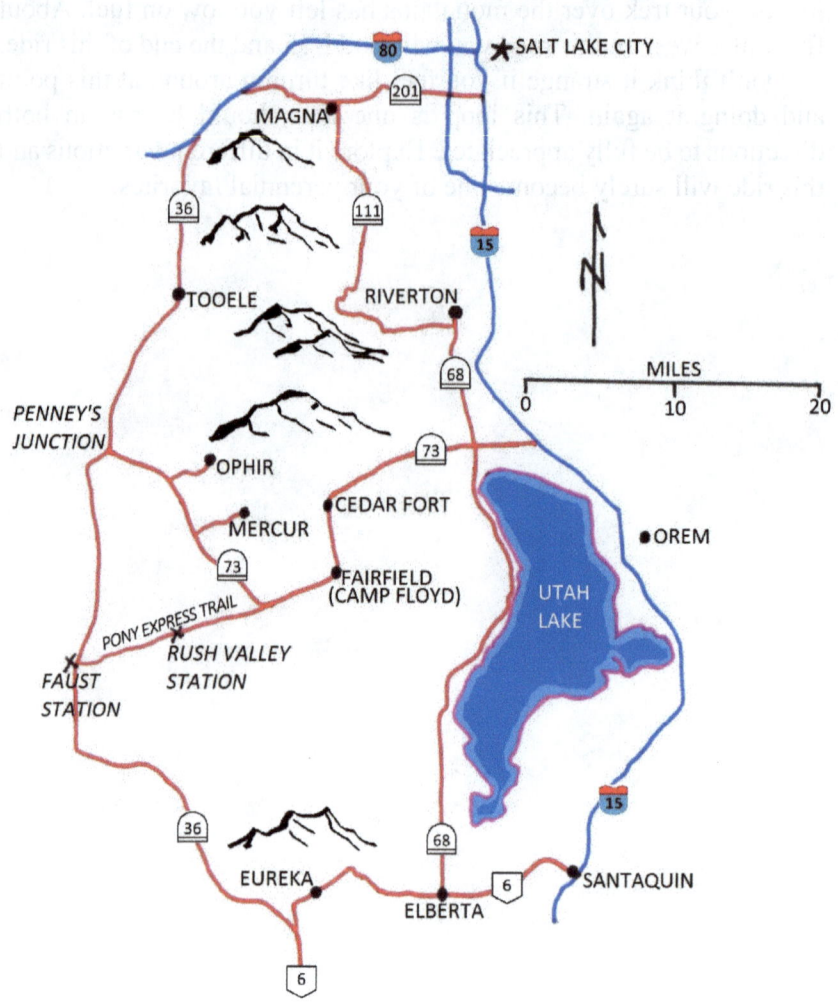

The Oquirrh and Eureka loops are west desert valley rides that are great for the early and late season. These loops sit on top of each other, forming a figure eight of sorts, which offers riders the chance to take a quick scoot when snow or cold temperatures effectively put the higher elevation rides out of reach. For years, Salt Lake Motorcycle Club has run their annual Polar Bear Ride in early March on subtle variations of the Oquirrh loop. This ride traditionally marks the "unofficial" start of motorcycle season in Northern Utah. I have ridden these routes in December and January, so if the roads are dry and you've got a bad winter itch to ride, give them a try.

As described here, these loops offer short (Oquirrh) and long (Eureka) variations. Both will take you through mining country and a century and a half of Utah's mining history. Depending on how you run them, you can be back in the garage in two to three hours, or stretch them into half a day.

We'll start in Salt Lake City but, as with any loop, the beauty is that you can jump in anywhere and, of course, run them in either direction. Take SR 201 westbound out of the city. This highway runs past Magna and the Kennecott smelter operation before merging with I-80 at milepost 102. Get on I-80 westbound for three short miles and jump off at exit 99 in Lake Point. This will put you on SR 36 southbound.

Lake Point presents one of many opportunities on these loops to gas up and grab some food or snacks. If you run the full Eureka Loop, you'll probably burn through the better part of a full tank of gas, but no worries, there are enough fuel stops on the route that you needn't give gas much thought.

Take SR 36 southbound through the city of Tooele, past Tooele Army Depot, and through the town of Stockton. As you leave Stockton, you'll be riding into the north end of Rush Valley and will see tiny Rush Lake to the west of the highway. Continue south for four miles out of Stockton until you get to Penney's Junction, where SR 73 intersects SR 36.

Just north of the junction, on the west side of SR 36 you will find one of my favorite stops for food and liquid refreshment. Penney's is a quaint little tavern that has the look and feel of being out in the middle of nowhere. It's a biker-friendly joint where you can grab a burger and a cold draft (or a hot cup of coffee).

Now we come to the point where these loops diverge. We'll look at the Oquirrh Loop first. At Penney's Junction take a turn to the east on SR 73. As you ride eastbound on 73 look off to the south of the highway. You'll see the Deseret Chemical Weapons disposal facility and the remnants of what was once one of the largest chemical weapons storage sites in the world. If you happen to see a lot of dead birds and other critters lying about, hold your breath and ride fast. (Just kidding – this site wrapped up its mission in recent years with an

Polar Bear Riders take a break at Penney's

impeccable safety record and performed an invaluable service to the nation.)

About five miles east of Penney's Junction, you'll come to the Ophir cutoff on the north side of SR 73. Remember, you're in mining country and Ophir is a quaint little mining town right out of Utah's colorful past. Founded in 1870, it was once the typical old west mining town, with saloons, gambling halls, brothels, stores, etc. At its peak, Ophir's population hit about six thousand but the boom was over by 1880. Since then it has evolved into the near ghost-town it is today. If you're not in a hurry turn up the cutoff and take a peek. In addition to being an interesting diversion, you can find a cold drink and a snack there.

Another few miles east and you will see the cutoff for Mercur, once the site of a thriving mining town and a gold mine that operated on and off for over a hundred years. The mine's last operators, Barrick Gold Corp., had an interesting little museum that showcased the mine's operation and the history of Mercur with artifacts from the town recovered in archeological excavations. Barrick shut down the mine in 1999 however, and moved everything out, including the museum. Today, there is nothing to see but dirt, so exploring this

Camp Floyd – once the largest Army garrison in the US

cutoff isn't worth the trouble, but with gold prices at all-time highs in recent years, rumor has it that mining operations will soon resume in Mercur. Maybe by the time you read this there will be something worth seeing at the end of this desolate cutoff.

After rounding the bottom end of the Oquirrh range, the highway drops down into Utah County where you'll come upon the tiny community of Fairfield. This is the site of Camp Floyd, where the US Army settled during their occupation of Utah in the so-called "Utah Rebellion" just prior to the Civil War. At the time, ca. 1858, it was the largest military installation in the United States with a garrison of about 7000 troops. All that remains today are the old Stagecoach Inn and the commissary along with some stone markers and monuments. Nearby is the military cemetery. The site is administered by the state park service.

Just up the highway about 5 miles is the small town of Cedar Fort, where you'll find a gas station and convenience store right on the highway. Here the road bends to the east and takes you about 14 miles to the junction with SR 68, also known by some as "Four Corners Junction" and more recently as Saratoga Crossroads.

At this point, let's go back and examine the Eureka loop. We'll rejoin the Oquirrh loop again here at the crossroads.

Back at Penney's Junction if you continue south on SR 36 you'll begin a 40 mile run through Rush Valley. Some riders I know claim this is an area almost totally void of scenic appeal. I couldn't disagree more. I think there is plenty of beauty to be found in this desert valley, and being on a bike certainly helps. You can also glimpse some interesting history as you ride this lonely stretch of highway.

Just south of the SR 199 turnoff, look for a state historic site marker indicating the location of William Ajax's underground store. Ajax built his 8000 square foot mercantile, which extended two stories underground, by himself with just a shovel and a wheelbarrow. The store operated from 1870 until 1914 serving travelers, local ranchers and miners. Today there's not much to see beyond the marker and a faint depression in the ground, but it's a fascinating story nonetheless.

Further south, the old Pony Express Trail crosses the highway at Faust Road. Just west of the highway here you will find a marker indicating the site of Faust Station. Pony Express stations were located every five to twenty-five miles along the trail, and roughly five miles to the east on Faust Road is another marker at the site of Rush Valley Station. Faust is named for Doc Faust, the station manager at the Rush Valley Station in 1860.

Continuing south, SR 36 bends to the east at Vernon and climbs towards the East Tintic Mountains. Here you will come to Tintic Junction, where SR 36 ends and meets US 6. Turn left at the junction and take US 6 eastbound into Eureka.

Eureka is a town that has definitely seen better days. Riding in from the west, you'll see the derelict remains of multiple mining operations and it's not hard to imagine a time when this little town thrived. Today, this sleepy little community offers a well-placed rest stop, with places to gas up and grab some refreshment.

Riding out of Eureka to the east, you will drop down through a small rock canyon. The road through here takes three low speed right-angle turns. I've never thought this was a particularly challenging or dangerous stretch of road when I've ridden it, but when talking to local residents, I have been surprised to learn of a number of fatalities here, so be careful.

After winding briefly through the hills, US 6 straightens out and runs east down to Elberta. Here we come to the junction with SR 68,

Section I: Northern Utah

where we will head north again, but before we do, let's consider a short side trip.

Continuing east on US 6 past Elberta will take you to the town of Santaquin. Now there's nothing in particular to recommend this short ride, except for the good food in town. In fact, if you're going to stop to eat on this ride, I recommend planning to eat in Santaquin. My favorite for lunch is the One Man Band Diner on Main Street. This is a real biker-friendly joint that is a favorite among local riders. Another good family style restaurant is the Family Tree, also on Main Street. You can't go wrong at either place for good food and a relaxing rest stop.

Back in Elberta, take SR 68 northbound. If you're one of those cynical souls who thought Rush Valley was a scenic wasteland, you ain't seen nothin' yet! (This time I'm inclined to agree with you.) The first 14 miles of this highway are straight, flat, and boring! But it gets better real soon. Besides, if you're doing this loop in the off-season, you're probably not riding for the scenery, but just to be in the wind. Remember, the worst day on a motorcycle is much better than the best day doing whatever comes in second place.

At the base of the Lake Mountains, the highway bends to the east and runs along the shore of Utah Lake. Suddenly, this road takes on a whole new character. It becomes mildly twisty and (even more fun) you'll find a number of rises and dips that give it a roller coaster effect. This is a thoroughly fun stretch of highway and it's a pity that it only lasts about 15 miles as it skirts the Lake Mountains. You'll be hard pressed to resist opening up the throttle here.

Near the north tip of Utah Lake the road straightens out again and runs through the community of Saratoga Springs. Soon you will be upon the Four Corners junction where we left off our discussion of the Oquirrh loop.

At the Four Corners, you'll find gas, cold drinks and snacks in case you need to stop. From the Oquirrh loop, turn north here onto SR 68. On the Eureka loop, continue straight (northbound). After passing Camp Williams you'll drop down into the suburban communities of Bluffdale and Riverton.

In Riverton, you'll come to the intersection with SR 154, the Bangerter Highway. If you're headed back into Salt Lake City you can call it quits at this point and either continue north on SR 68 (Redwood Road), turn right (east) to jump onto I-15, or turn left (west) and take Bangerter north through the west side of the valley. I like to

(Photo by Carl Benson) Riding SR 73 through the Oquirrhs

bend west and ride the full loop up the front side of the Oquirrh Mountains.

If you're with me, turn left (west) onto Bangerter Hwy and follow as it bends back to the north. At 12600 So., turn left (west) again and take this road through the town of Herriman, where it ultimately becomes Butterfield Canyon Road. Stay on this road all the way to the mouth of Butterfield Canyon, where it makes a sharp right turn to the north. Go northbound here past the Kennecott mine and you'll end up on SR 111 for a run up the front side of the Oquirrh range.

Here you'll be right in the lap of one of the largest open pit mines in the world. Seeing the magnitude of the mine from the base makes one wonder just how much copper they've pulled out of the mountain to make it worthwhile to dig such a big hole!

A short way up SR 111 you'll intersect Bingham Highway (SR 48). Taking a detour west on this road brings you into the little mining community of Copperton, a town you'll have a hard time finding on most maps.

Continuing north on SR 111 you'll run the east side of the northern Oquirrh range into the town of Magna, where again you'll find plenty of opportunities for gas, food, and drink. Here the highway comes to an end at a T-intersection with SR 201.

Section I: Northern Utah

You've now done a full loop, either a short lap around the Oquirrhs or a slightly longer loop through Eureka. Granted these loops are not in any danger of being added to the list of National Scenic Byways, but when weather makes riding the Wasatch unpleasant or impossible and you're jonesin' for some high octane entertainment, these loops are downright beautiful! Don't rule out these rides in the summertime, though. Enjoy them throughout the year. You might even try running them as a figure 8 route. They'll see you through the early season, when you're going stir crazy with spring fever and it's still too cold to ride the higher elevations and they'll see you through the late season (and even the winter) when you just can't bring yourself to put your scoot away for the cold months. In the summertime, they offer a quick getaway, close enough to the urban valleys to be the perfect after-work ride.

Trappers Loop

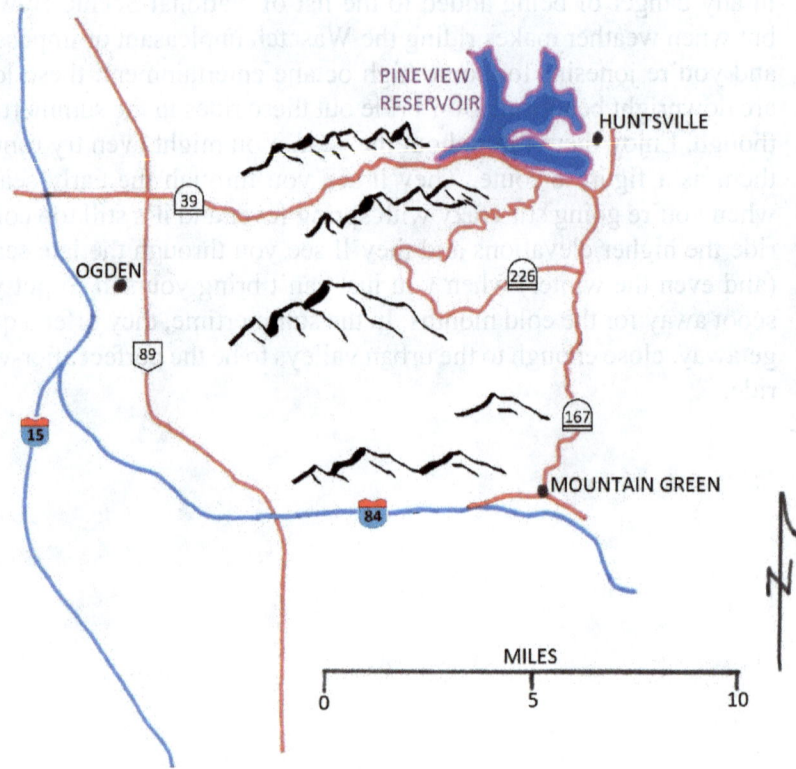

Trappers Loop is the shortest of our Wasatch Front "Quickies", making it the ideal dinner ride or perfect quick getaway when time is limited. For instance, one could, in theory, slip out of church, excusing oneself to, oh…let's say go to the restroom. Then, having one's scooter strategically pre-positioned, one could hop on, hit Trappers Loop, and be back in the pew just as the sermon ends. With proper care to remove the bugs from one's face and comb one's hair, one might even fool one's spouse. But I'm just thinking out loud here. I would, of course, never advocate such childish behavior.

I'll discuss this ride as if coming from the Salt Lake City area to the south. If you're coming from the north, simply turn the book upside-down here and read the route in reverse.

Riders take a pit-stop in Mountain Green

Come north on I-15 or US 89 (I prefer US 89) until you hit the junction with I-84. Take I-84 eastbound and you're in Weber Canyon.

This is a fun stretch of freeway. The road snakes through the narrow part of the canyon, providing some fun curves as it tracks the Weber River upstream. Just five miles from the mouth of the canyon, take exit 92. This is the Mountain Green exit.

Go left under the freeway and the road turns sharply to the east and parallels I-84. About two miles up the road you'll come to a junction with SR 167 near the community of Mountain Green.

There's a C-store at this intersection where you can grab a cold drink and a snack, as well as gas up. Turn left (north) onto SR 167. Here the road climbs rapidly and soon presents you with some broad, high speed *twisties*.

SR 167 is a road made for motorcycles. The entire route is four lanes of well-maintained asphalt that climbs and twists, then drops and twists some more. It just begs to be ridden hard. The scenery on both sides of the mountain defies description and the view from the summit is breathtaking. Running less than ten miles from end to end, it's over way too quickly and you'll likely want to turn around and run it again. Be careful though. Unless your clergyman is particularly long winded,

Riders blowing out the pipes on SR 167 – Trappers Loop

you may want to get back to church before your spouse comes looking for you in the restroom.

Near the north side of the summit, you'll find a cutoff to Snow Basin ski resort that offers a side loop to stretch out the ride. This is SR 226, which winds to the east from SR 167 to Snow Basin, then zigzags through the mountains back to the northwest, joining SR 39 about a mile and a half west of where SR 167 does. This too is a great stretch of scenic road, but not as wide and well maintained as SR 167. It is a worthwhile detour if you want to stretch the ride out.

SR 67 ends at SR 39 on the south shore of Pineview Reservoir near Huntsville. Here, you might consider detouring into town for lunch or dinner at the Shooting Star Saloon or the Huntsville Barbecue Company. Otherwise, turn left (west) on SR 39 and follow the south shore of Pineview to the mouth of Ogden Canyon.

Ogden Canyon is a wonderfully scenic stretch of road, one of the Wasatch Front's great urban rides. The road is narrow, as is the canyon, hugging the Ogden River as it winds its way downstream. About halfway down the canyon, consider making lunch or dinner at The Oaks or Gray Cliffs Lodge part of your itinerary.

Section I: Northern Utah

Enjoying a break at the highway summit on SR 167 – Trappers Loop

Coming out of the mouth of Ogden Canyon completes this fun little loop. Continue westbound on SR 39 and you will intersect both US 89 and I-15, from where you can high-tail it back to wherever you are supposed to be. Try to wipe that smile off your face though, lest you betray yourself. No one grins like that after two hours in church!

Wasatch Front Quickies – Notes

Pit Stops:

Morgan:
7-11
404 E 300 N
(801) 829-3010

Mountain Green:
Sinclair / C-store
5150 Old Highway Rd.
(801) 876-3471

Kimball Junction:
Chevron
6500 N Hwy 224
(435) 649-9934

Heber City:
Texaco
220 N. Main St
(435) 654-0838

Highland:
Chevron
5260 W. 1100 N.
(801) 756-4196

Lake Point:
Top Stop C-Store (Chevron)
8793 No. Hwy 36
(801) 250-5298

Tooele:
Top Stop C-Store (Chevron)
322 E. 2400 No.
(435) 882-0703

Holiday Oil (Sinclair)
608 N. Main St.
(435) 843-1095

Eureka:
Carpenter's Sinclair
202 W. Main St.
(435) 433-6311

Santaquin:
Conoco
300 E. Main St.
(801) 754-3470

Speedy Turtle (Chevron)
390 E. Main
(801) 754-5577

Cedar Fort:
Country Store (Conoco)
149 S. 200 E. (SR73)
(801) 768-8840

Saratoga Springs:
Top Stop (Chevron)
36 W. 1400 N. (Jct. SR73 / SR68)
(801) 766-5252

RECOMMENDED DINING:

Salt Lake City:
Ruth's Diner
4160 Emigration Canyon Rd.
(801) 582-5807

East Coast Subs
3490 So. State
(801) 685-8325

East Canyon:
East Canyon Resort
SR 65
(801) 355-3460

Morgan:
Kelly's Roadhouse
1550 W. Old Highway Rd.
(801) 829-3320

Park City:
Main Street Pizza
530 Main St.
(435) 645-8878

Wasatch Brew Pub
250 Main St.
(435) 649-0900

No Name Saloon
447 Main St.
(435) 649-6667

Red Banjo Pizza
322 Main St.
(435) 649-9901

Heber City:
Hub Café
1165 S. Main St.
(435) 654-5463

Sidetrack Café
94 S. Main St.
(435) 654-0563

Granny's Drive-In
511 S. Main St.
(435) 654-3925

Chick's Café
154 S. Main St.
(435) 654-1771

Don Pedro's
1050 S. Main St.
(435) 657-0600

Claim Jumper
1267 S. Main St.
(435) 654-4661

Tooele:
Bonneville Brewing Co.
1641 N. Main St.
(435) 248-0652

Anthony's Main Street Grill
29 N. Main St.
(435) 241-5128

Stockton:
Penney's
7766 Hwy 36
(435) 882-3277

Santaquin:
One Man Band
175 E. Main
(801) 754-3668

The Family Tree Restaurant
77 W. Main
(801) 754-3499

Section II
Central & Eastern Utah

Our next section is carved out of the middle of the state, taking in nine central and eastern counties. This large region reaches from Nevada in the west to Colorado in the east and Wyoming in the north, capturing a vast array of geography. The intersection of I-15 and I-70 in this region, along with a myriad of secondary highways makes this area the crossroads of the state and offers ease of access to its many riding opportunities. Here you'll find such treasures as Flaming Gorge and Dinosaur National Monument, the beauty of the Ashley, Manti-La Sal, and Fish Lake National Forests and the stark splendor of Castle Country: the Book Cliffs and the San Rafael Swell. You'll experience the magnificence of Skyline Drive cresting the Wasatch Plateau and sample the flavor of Utah's Mormon pioneer heritage as you wander through the middle of the state.

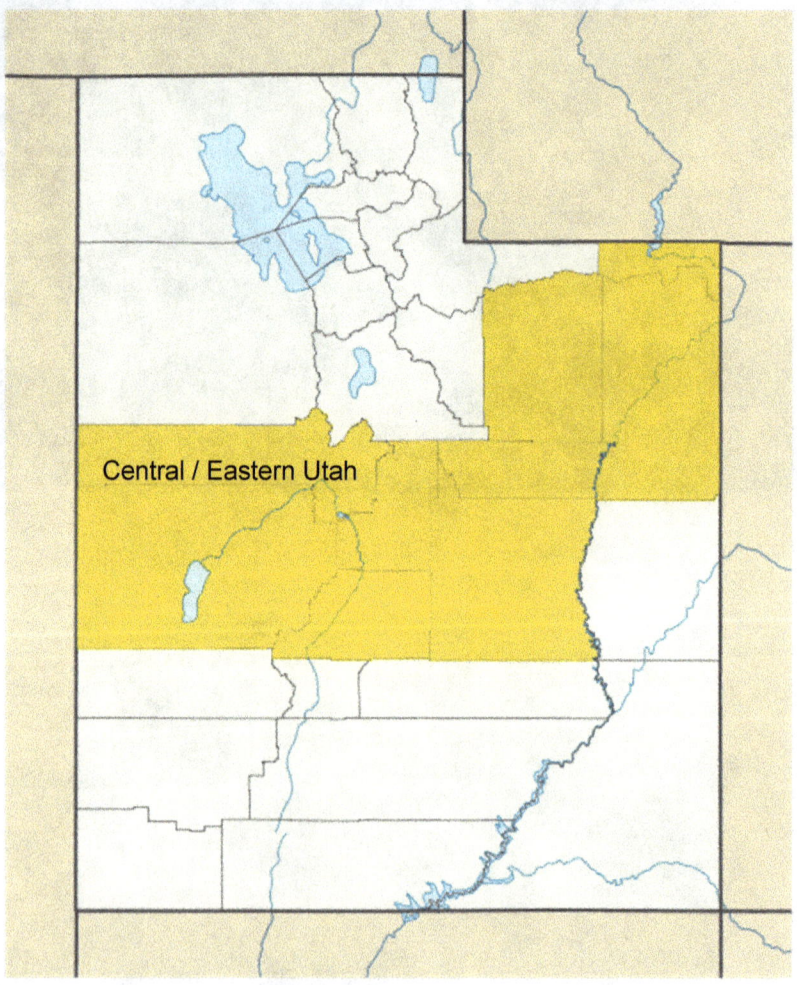

Mount Nebo Loop

Mt. Nebo – tallest peak in the Wasatch Range, elevation 11928 ft.

The Nebo Loop is a perennial favorite among Utah riders. The route follows one of Utah's great scenic byways and has been rated by various sources among the top ten rides in the west. It has been called a photographer's dream, with multiple scenic overlooks and abundant wildlife.

The geography and elevation of this ride make it an excellent escape from the summer heat. Hitting the loop in early spring may not be possible due to lingering snow pack but, barring an early snowfall, this route can be ridden late into the season. Like most rides through the Wasatch and Uinta mountains, the fall colors on Mt. Nebo are breathtaking.

Proximity to I-15 puts the Nebo Loop within easy reach of most urban centers in north-central Utah. Riders can easily fill a day with this ride and still be home by evening. On the other hand, if you are planning an extended tour, consider slipping this loop into your route as an excellent detour from I-15. Enjoy!

Mount Nebo Loop Route Map

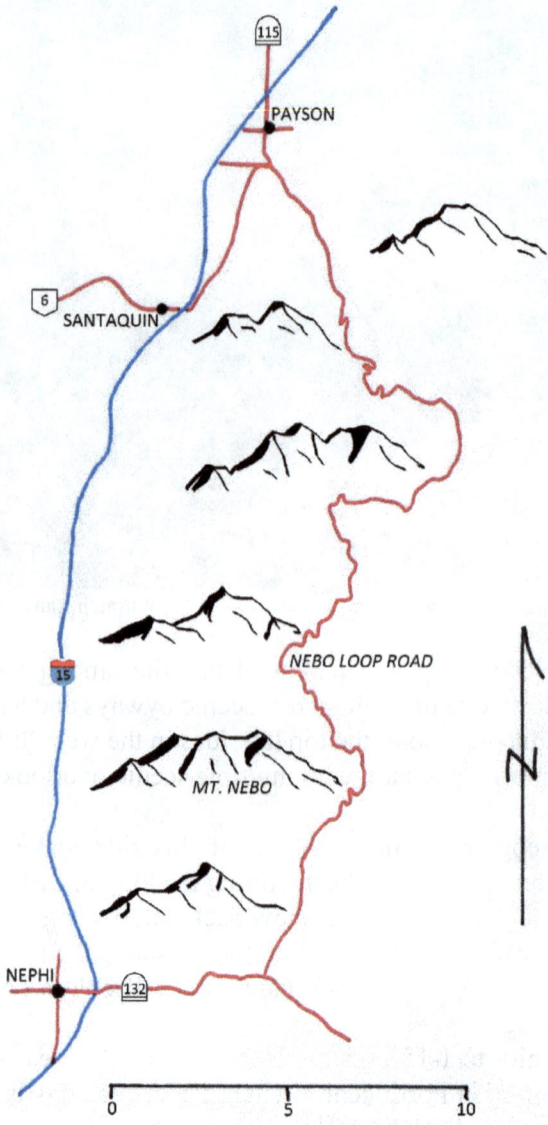

ROUTE: From I-15, take exit 225 in Nephi. Go eastbound on SR 132 approximately five miles to Nebo Loop Rd. Turn left (north) on Nebo Loop Rd. Stay on Nebo Loop Rd to 800 So. in Payson. Turn left (west) on 800 So. and continue west to I-15, exit 248.

Section II: Central & Eastern Utah

On the road...

When they surveyed and cut the Nebo Loop Road, surely they had motorcycles in mind. Riding this route you can't help but draw the conclusion that this is a road built by bikers for bikers. It almost seems incongruous to encounter a car on this ride.

I like riding the Nebo Loop from south to north, but like any loop, you should run it from both directions to fully exploit all that it offers. Furthermore, if you're traveling the I-15 corridor and time is not a factor, consider this loop as a relaxing diversion from the monotonous slabs of the freeway. This 38 mile National Scenic Byway will take about 1 hour to run.

From the south, take exit 225 off of I-15 in Nephi. This puts you on SR 132 in close proximity to the center of town. Consider availing yourself of the conveniences offered at this exit, especially gas and liquid refreshment, before you head up the mountain. It will be a while before you or your bike will have the opportunity to quench your thirsts.

Ride eastbound on SR 132 and you will begin to climb into the foothills. Roughly five miles up the road, you will come to Nebo Loop Road on the left. Turn north on Nebo Loop Road and you'll then ascend into the Uinta National Forest along the edge of the Mt. Nebo Wilderness.

As you turn onto Nebo Loop Road, take note of the terrain around you. You are about to see some interesting variations of geography and geology. Watch the rapid transition from the semi-arid Juab Valley and tan sandstone cliffs on SR 132 to the lush forest greenery as you trace Salt Creek up the mountain. Soon, amongst the thick green foliage you will see brilliant red sandstone cliffs that look as if they belong in the deserts of southern Utah's color country. Not far into the Nebo Loop Road you will pass the cutoff to Bear Canyon, where nineteenth century pioneers built a saw mill at the site of today's campground and picnic area.

The road begins to climb almost immediately, subtly at first, but soon quite steeply, traversing the mountain in a series of sharp switchbacks. You'll climb over 4000 feet on this ride and, though I have not validated it with actual measurement, my perception is that the climb is steeper from the south end of the loop (one of the reasons I like riding south to north). As you traverse this first series of

Devil's Kitchen

switchbacks you will be exposed to views that are so breathtaking that you may find it difficult to keep your eyes on the road.

At the crest of a ridge you'll soon come to the Salt Creek overlook. This turnoff provides a stunning view of the valley through which you just passed, as well as the mountain ranges rising to the east. From here you can also see the red sandstone cliffs I referred to poking out from the verdant alpine forest, dramatically juxtaposed with the granite Wasatch peaks in the background

Just a short way beyond Salt Creek overlook, you will come to Devil's Kitchen. I highly recommend stopping here to see this interesting geological formation. Eons before the Wasatch peaks appeared, this area was under water. Sediment deposits collected and formed the rocky red sandstone, called conglomerate. The conglomerate's red color comes from oxidized iron in the soil. These cliffs are literally rusted! Subsequent wind and water erosion has created the Devil's Kitchen, a formation likened to a miniature Bryce Canyon. Seeing it, you will surely agree. This odd rock formation looks strangely out of place cradled against the Wasatch.

Another short run up the road brings you to Mt. Nebo overlook. Along with Devil's Kitchen, this overlook is one of the "must see"

The backside of Mt. Nebo from Bald Mountain Overlook.

stops on this ride. If you stop nowhere else on the loop, take the time to see these two vistas. Mt. Nebo overlook offers the best view of the backside of Nebo. As you'll learn at the turnout, Mt. Nebo is a rather amazing geologic formation, with the youngest rocks at the top and the older rocks below. Now, I'm not sure I understand how this mountain got turned upside-down, but I know I like looking at it. The view from this overlook is spectacular.

The elevation at the Mt. Nebo overlook is roughly 9,165 feet, making it the highest stop on the loop. The road doesn't summit for another mile or so to the north however, climbing a few hundred more feet.

Farther along the road lies the Bald Mountain overlook, with another great view. Here you'll find a quiet mountain meadow in the foreground immediately below your viewpoint, as Bald Mountain rises just beyond. Snow will often remain in the folds of the mountains well into July.

Just ahead lies the Santaquin Canyon overlook. This turnout offers a rather interesting view of Utah Valley. From here you can see the eastern shore of Utah Lake and the urban area from Provo to American Fork. Look closely and you can glimpse the "Y" on the mountain over

Riders enjoy a break on the Nebo Loop Road

Brigham Young University. Sadly, this vista is nearly always obscured by air pollution. Were it not for the byproducts of modern urban living hanging low over the valley, this would be a stunning view.

Here the road veers to the east for a short run. I've been fascinated to find snow and ice in the sheltered folds of the mountain alongside the road, and even on the road itself, in late spring and early summer. A short way from Santaquin Canyon overlook you will find Utah Lake overlook. This viewpoint offers nearly the same vista of Utah Valley from a slightly different angle. While Provo is not so visible from here, you will be able to see most of Utah Lake, and air conditions permitting, you can view the top end of the valley where I-15 enters Salt Lake Valley at Point-of-the-Mountain. Unfortunately, like the Santaquin overlook, this vista is often limited by pollution.

Another short distance traveled brings you to the last overlook, called Beaver Dam Creek. The name puzzles me, for here I have found no beaver, no dam and no creek, but it's a colorful name nonetheless. This overlook offers a powerful vista of the mountains to the east.

From here the road begins to descend from the 8,000 ft. level, gently at first, to the Payson Lakes where you will find an excellent campground and picnic area. Consider packing a lunch and stopping here for a picnic.

Shortly after Payson Lakes, the road begins to descend more rapidly and becomes pleasantly twisty as it follows the Peteetneet Creek down Payson Canyon. You'll even find a few good 180° switchbacks on this stretch. Shortly, the road straightens out and levels off before the canyon opens rather abruptly, depositing you in Payson.

You can make your way west through Payson on SR 178 (800 So.) and you will find I-15 at exit 248, or north on SR 115 (Main Street) to hit the freeway at exit 250. Near the freeway onramps you will find plenty of gas and food, as well as lodging.

You've just completed a ride that will undoubtedly remain on your top-ten list for as long as you can throw a leg over the saddle. Run this loop often, for each season brings a unique character to the ride. No tour of Utah is complete without riding this jewel of a scenic byway.

Mount Nebo Loop – Notes

Pit Stops:

Nephi:
Walker's (Phillips 66)
830 E 100 N (SR 132 at I-15)
(435) 623-4041

Chevron
835 E 100 N (SR 132 at I-15)
(435) 623-2611

Payson:
Gas-N-Dash (Chevron)
710 N. Main (SR 115 at I-15)
(801) 465-4365

Flying J
840 N. Main (SR115 at I-15)
(801) 465-9281

Accommodations & Camping:

CAMPGROUNDS:
National Forest Campgrounds info: (877) 444-6777 or www.reserveusa.com.
Ponderosa
Blackhawk

Payson Lakes
Maple Bench

Commercial Campgrounds
Nephi KOA - Salt Creek Canyon, Nephi (SR 132 & Nebo Loop Road) (435) 623-0811

HOTELS:
Nephi:
Economy Lodge
885 E 100 N (SR 132 at I-15)
(435) 623-9000

Payson:
Comfort Inn
830 N. Main (SR 115 at I-15)
(801) 465-4861

RECOMMENDED DINING:
Nephi:
One Man Band Diner
1142 E. Hwy 132 (SR 132 at I-15)
(435) 623-7185

San Pitch Mountains Loop

San Pitch Mountains

The San Pitch Mountains sit in Central Utah just off the southern tip of the Wasatch Range and form the western wall of the Sanpete Valley which was settled by early Mormon pioneers. This loop, while perhaps not the most scenic or challenging of rides, is rich in local culture and history. Much like the Oquirrh and Eureka loops, this route presents good opportunities for early and late season riding when higher elevations are put out of reach by the weather.

This ninety-seven mile loop will take you through the heartland of Mormon-Pioneer Utah. You'll ride through communities whose names reflect their Mormon heritage, such as Nephi, Moroni, Ephraim and Manti, and roll through country where fundamentalist sects still practice polygamy. Two state parks on this route afford the opportunity for packing a picnic lunch and the history buff will find the area rich with places to investigate and explore. You can ride the entire loop in two hours or less, but don't be surprised if you get sidetracked. Enjoy!

San Pitch Mountains Loop Route Map

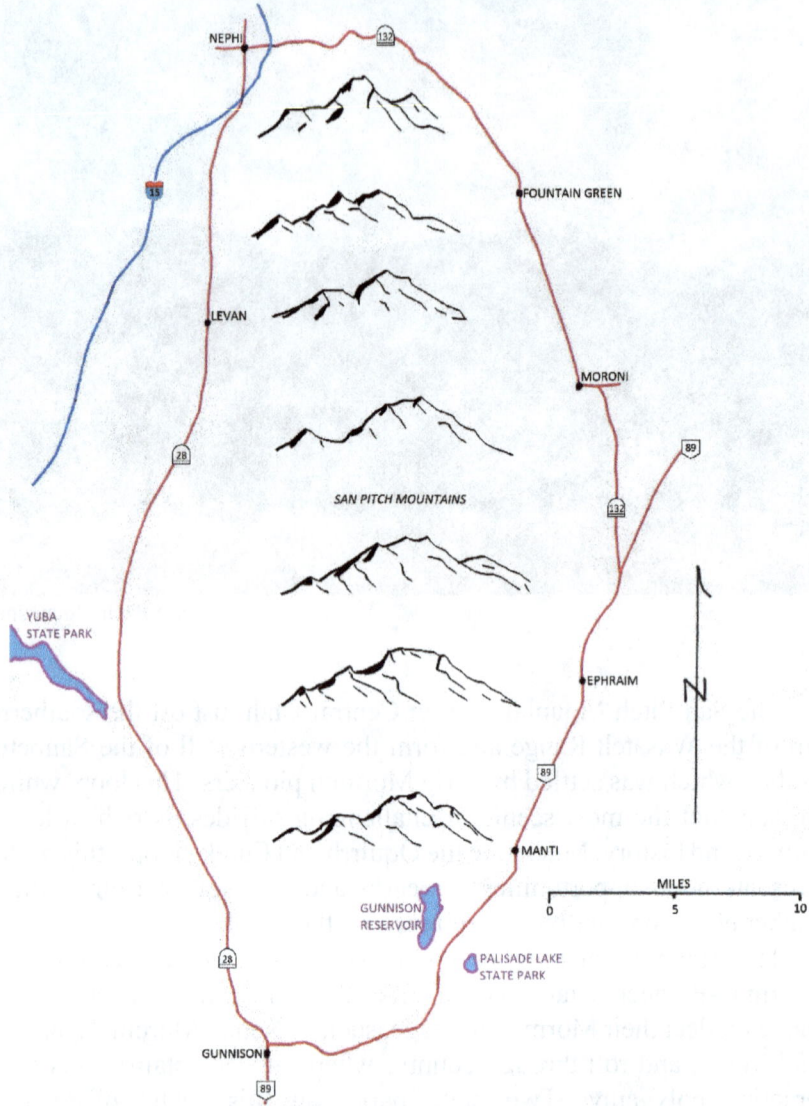

ROUTE: From Nephi take SR132 eastbound through Fountain Green and Moroni. At the junction with US89, take US89 southbound through Ephraim and Manti to the junction with SR28 in Gunnison. In Gunnison, take SR28 northbound through Levan and back to Nephi.

On the road...

Is early autumn or lingering springtime snowfall keeping you from taking a scoot on your favorite mountain run? Do you feel like sampling the flavor of Utah's pioneer heritage from the saddle of your bike? Have you got a couple of hours to kill and feel like doing it in the wind? If the answer to any of these questions is yes, then this loop may be just the ticket.

The San Pitch Mountains sit like an island at the southern edge of the Wasatch Range, encircled by SR 132, US 89 and SR 28. This loop is conveniently accessed from I-15 in Nephi, placing it within easy reach of northern and central Utah riders looking for a quick diversion.

In Nephi, head east on SR 132 and you'll begin a gentle climb into Salt Creek Canyon. Here the grey sandstone of the canyon gradually gives way to the thick foliage of the mountains on either side. Rising boldly to your right is Salt Creek Peak, with red cliff faces of iron conglomerate jutting out from the green forest. At 9,997 feet, this is the tallest peak in the San Pitch range.

Just as you come around Salt Creek Peak, about six and a half miles into the ride, look for a monument marking the spot of the Salt Creek Canyon Massacre. To call this incident a massacre may be to add a bit of hyperbole to an otherwise unremarkable skirmish between white settlers and natives in the nineteenth century unless, of course, you were one of the white settlers. Spin doctoring aside, on June 4, 1858, at this site, four Mormon pioneer settlers traveling unarmed to the Sanpete Valley were attacked and killed ("massacred") by Indians, proving again the old adage that it is always better to have a gun and not need it than to need a gun and not have it.

As the road bends to the southeast, the canyon opens to the Sanpete Valley near the town of Fountain Green. Originally settled in 1859 as a camp for Mormon colonists emigrating to Sanpete Valley, this pleasant little community seems to say "Welcome to Rural America". You'll find gas and food here, as in each of the towns along the loop.

A short ride down the highway brings you to the town of Moroni, a community much like Fountain Green. By now you will likely begin to notice the abundance of older dwellings and Victorian style architecture scattered among the newer homes. On the southeast edge of Moroni, the road forks at the junction of SR 132 with SR 116. Turn left (south) to continue on this loop.

Monument marks the site of the Salt Creek Canyon Massacre

About eight miles south of Moroni, SR 132 joins US 89. This section of US 89 is aptly referred to as "Heritage Highway". Even more descriptive perhaps, this area and the communities that dot the Sanpete Valley are known as "Little Denmark", reflecting the valley's heavy settlement by Scandinavian immigrants during the nineteenth century.

Just south of the highway junction, you'll roll into the town of Ephraim. Settled in 1854, this city has been described as Sanpete County's most "cosmopolitan" community, perhaps due to the fact that it was the first town in Sanpete to cross the US Census Bureau's population threshold of 2,500 in the 1970s to become the county's only "urban" location. Riding into town, you'll immediately feel the community's sense of its own history and heritage, seeming to flow in perfect confluence with a subtle desire to grow in the modern world. When you see the Wal-Mart Supercenter just down the street from what appears to be a (still occupied) nineteenth century log cabin, you'll know what I'm talking about.

Ephraim was the most important fort in the Sanpete Valley during the Black Hawk War, a protracted (and violent) disagreement between the Mormons and a confederation of local Indian tribes over cattle.

After hostilities ceased, the town remained an important cultural and business center. In the late 1800s, the population was 90% Scandinavian, and roughly half of all residents carried one of eight surnames. This interesting demographic quirk was undoubtedly compounded by the fact that at least 25% of Ephraim's Mormon families practiced plural marriage.

Today, Ephraim has succeeded in preserving the flavor of a classic Mormon village. Note the many examples of stone and brick Victorian style homes as you ride through town. Also worthy of inspection is a beautifully restored Mormon co-operative mercantile at the center of Main Street. To celebrate their Nordic pioneer heritage, the town hosts an annual Scandinavian Festival each May, on Memorial Day weekend. To learn more, see www.scandinavianheritagefestival.com or call (435) 283-4631.

A short, straight shot down the Heritage Highway brings you into the town of Manti. In the early rivalry for dominance in Sanpete County, Manti seems to have won out, securing the county seat as well as the site of Utah's third Mormon temple. As you roll into town from the north, you'll immediately see the temple dominating the landscape from a hill overlooking the highway.

The Manti Temple is a stunning and beautiful example of early Mormon architecture and old world craftsmanship. The temple was built between 1877 and 1888 with donated labor and local materials at a cost of $1 million. That equates to approximately... a whole lot more... in today's dollars.

Settled in 1849, Manti is the oldest community in Sanpete Valley and was the fourth settlement in Utah. Today, the town, like its Sanpete neighbors, retains the feel of a classic Mormon village. Each year in late June, Manti hosts the "Mormon Miracle Pageant", a live theatrical production of national renown. More info on the pageant can be found at mormonmiracle.org or by calling 1-866-961-9040.

Also, like the neighboring Sanpete communities, it is interesting to note that Manti has a significant fundamentalist population. The town has been featured prominently in a nationally broadcast television documentary highlighting a local fundamentalist sect that continues the fairly open practice of plural marriage here in the pastoral setting of Sanpete Valley, over one hundred years after it was abandoned by the mainstream church in order to secure statehood. Polygamy is a fascinating yet very divisive facet of Utah's history and culture, a difficult subject to broach without eliciting strong emotions on both

Manti LDS Temple

sides. But hell, I have more than one motorcycle, so who am I to comment on someone else's lifestyle?

Leaving Manti to the south, the Heritage Highway bends west as it encloses the southern end of the San Pitch Mountains. Just before the community of Sterling, you'll come to the road to Palisade State Park, a place to consider for a rest stop or picnic.

Bending around the bottom of the San Pitch and dropping gently through a minor canyon, US 89 joins SR 28 in Gunnison. Our route will take us to the right (north) at the highway junction on SR 28, but since Gunnison sits at the bottom of our loop, just over the halfway point, you might consider a detour to the left (south) into town for food, drink, and/or gas.

SR 28 runs north/south through farm country between Gunnison and Nephi. Because it runs generally parallel to I-15, it makes a great alternative to the freeway corridor. Traffic is usually sparse, and this, combined with the road's generally straight character and long distance visibility make it a high-speed route. As an added bonus, ambient temperatures along this rural highway are usually significantly lower than on the frying pan surface of the superslab, something to consider in the height of summer.

On this ride though, SR 28 is simply the last leg of our loop, running along the front side of the San Pitch Mountains back to our starting point in Nephi. Climbing and bending around the foothills north of Gunnison, the road quickly drops into the Juab Valley for the run north to Nephi. Roughly fifteen miles out of Gunnison, you'll come upon Yuba State Park, another likely place for a picnic or rest stop. Another fifteen miles, and you'll roll through the little farming community of Levan. Stay to the right at the intersection in Levan to stay on SR 28 and continue into Nephi.

A quick ten mile run from Levan brings you into Nephi and the end of this loop. You've just completed a lap around the San Pitch and a run through country representing a rich and unique facet of Utah's pioneer heritage.

San Pitch Mountains Loop – Notes

Pit Stops:

Nephi:
Walker's (Phillips 66)
830 E 100 N (SR 132)
(435) 623-4041

Chevron
835 E 100 N (SR 132)
(435) 623-2611

Fast Gas (Tesoro)
1188 E Hwy 132
(435) 623-4259

Fountain Green:
Beck Sinclair
83 So. State
(435) 445-3454

Moroni:
Silver Eagle (Conoco)
416 E. Main
(435) 436-8631

Ephraim:
Thompson Serv. (Sinclair)
109 N. Main
(435) 283-6997

Maverik
89 N. Main
(435) 283-6057

Manti:
Top Stop
300 N. Main
(435) 835-1212

Gunnison:
Gic Conoco
111 N. Main
(435) 528-7544

Accommodations & Camping

CAMPGROUNDS:
Palisade State Park
2200 Palisade Rd.
Sterling, UT 84642
(435) 835-7275
www.stateparks.utah.gov

Yuba State Park
12225 So. Yuba Dam Rd.
Levan, UT 84639
(435) 758-2611
www.stateparks.utah.gov

HOTELS:

Nephi:
Economy Lodge
885 E 100 N (SR 132)
(435) 623-9000

Manti:
Manti Country Village Motel
145 N. Main
(435) 835-9300

Ephraim:
Ephraim Homestead B&B
135 W. 100 N
(435) 283-6367

Legacy Inn Bed & Breakfast
337 N. 100 E.
(435) 835-8352

RECOMMENDED DINING:

Nephi
One Man Band Diner
1142 E. Hwy 132
(435) 623-7185

Ephraim:
Fat Jack's Pizza
81 So. Main
(435) 283-4222

The Satisfied Ewe Cafe
350 N. Main
(435) 283-6364

Manti:
Don's Gallery Cafe
305 E. Union St.
(435) 835-3663

Be Prepared

Basic ride preparation is essential for a safe and enjoyable ride. A little bit of forethought and the right gear can make the difference between fun and frustration.

BEFORE YOU GO: Whether you're taking a short day ride or heading out for a week on the road, it's important to do a basic pre-ride inspection of your bike (see page 42). Be familiar with your owner's manual and follow the manufacturer's advice If you're leaving on an extended journey, you may consider having your mechanic go over the bike. I like to take my bike in for service before I go on a long road trip, even if a scheduled maintenance is not quite due. Finally, if you are going to be gone overnight or longer, consider letting someone know where you are going, including your intended routes and a basic itinerary.

CLOTHING: I know some guys who say they wear full leathers every time they ride. I assume these guys only ride March through April and again in October and November, or they are exaggerating. Having said that, it's still a good idea to tailor your wardrobe (pun intended) to cover the unexpected. Even on day rides, I usually throw a sweatshirt and light jacket in my saddlebags. Remember, temperatures drop as you climb into the mountains. Plan your attire so that you can dress in layers, starting with a T-shirt and adding on or peeling off as conditions dictate. On longer trips, I take my leathers, even if I don't anticipate wearing them. More than once I've been glad I did when encountering sudden weather changes or having to ride after dark. Speaking of weather, it's an old biker article of faith that if you don't have your raingear, you're sure to hit rain. Remember that gloves are both a comfort item and basic safety equipment. It's a good idea to have a lightweight pair as well as a cold weather set.

BASIC EQUIPMENT: Consider taking along some basic items that come in handy out on the road. I have a small "kit" bag that I keep by the door and throw on the bike virtually every time I ride. Items I take along include earplugs, extra glasses (including nighttime eye protection), extra gloves (lightweight or cold weather), a flashlight and Leatherman tool, a small first aid kit with band aids, aspirin, etc., and sunscreen. When on an extended ride, my basic "kit" expands to include tools, spare fuses and electrical tape. Sometimes I'll carry a role of duct tape and I've heard some reflective tape can come in handy if your headlamp fails. I always take a strong cable lock and rotor lock, as well as a bike cover to make my bike a less obvious or at least, more difficult target for thieves. Spare keys have come in handy more than once, and I recommend always traveling with a set. You can pack them deep in your bags or secure them with duct tape under your saddle or inside your headlamp nacelle. A cell phone can be worth its weight in gold on any ride. Start with common sense items and build your ride kit according to both your planning and experience. You'll eventually be glad you did.

Fish Lake Run

Fish Lake

This little run of approximately 90 miles traces a lazy "W" on the map without really going anywhere – there's nothing but more road on either end of this run. But as they say: "it's not the destination, it's the journey."

Fish Lake is nestled between the Mytoge Mountains and Fish Lake Hightop Plateau at an elevation of about 8,800 feet. This six-mile-by-one-mile natural lake is the centerpiece of a relaxing scenic ride through the mountains of the Fish Lake National Forest. Twisty roads, mountain canyons, aspen forests, rivers, streams and lakes combine to give a cool refreshing quality to this summertime escape. Enjoy!

Fish Lake Run
Route Map

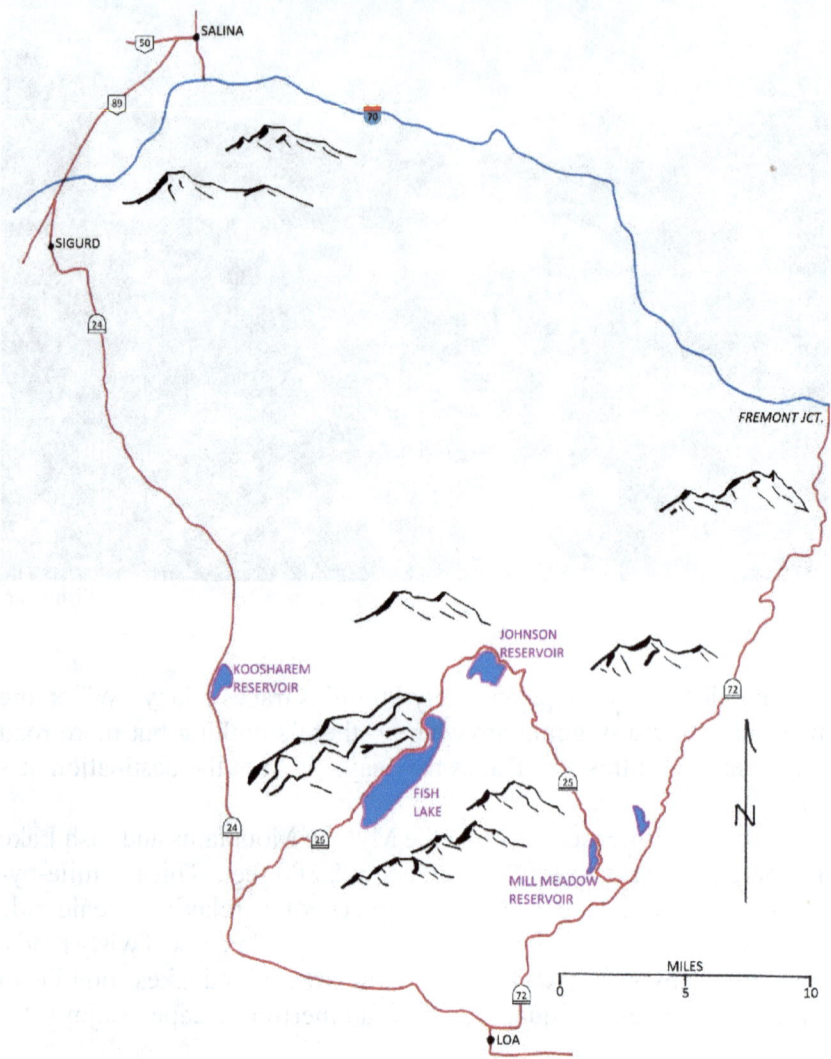

ROUTE: Take I-70 exits 86 or 91 to Fremont Junction. Go south at junction on SR72. Approx. 25 miles from Fremont Junction turn right (northwest) on Fremont River Road (SR25). Follow SR25 through mountains, past Johnson Valley Reservoir and Fish Lake to junction with SR24. At SR24 turn right (north) to Sevier Valley and junction with I-70 at exit 48.

On the road...

Here's a motorcycle run that lies almost smack dead center in the middle of the state, is near the cities of Salina, Richfield and Loa, and is conveniently located just off of I-70. In spite of all this, this run has an out-of-the-way quality about it. It doesn't really take you anywhere and doesn't quite fall into place within any larger route. But, who cares? You certainly won't after completing this ride. This is a stretch of road that you go out of your way to ride; the kind of route that defines why we tour on motorcycles.

We'll start on I-70 where SR72 and SR10 meet the freeway near a spot on the map called Fremont Junction. You can get off of I-70 at either exit 86 or 91. Find the frontage road that parallels the freeway on the south side. From exit 86 go east, from exit 91 go west on this frontage road until you come to SR72. Here, you will turn south.

SR72 is a pleasant surprise right from the start. The road climbs through Post Hollow as you move south from Fremont Junction and the ride is immediately scenic. You'll be treated to a section of "roller-coaster" road where the highway offers a series of gentle rises and dips, mixed with an ample serving of twisty curves. Just try to hold back on this fun piece of pavement, I dare you! The road begs for you to give your mount the spurs. It is well maintained and doesn't see a lot of traffic. It does, however run through open range, so be careful.

Bending through a fold in the terrain near Last Chance Creek, the road crosses into Fish Lake National Forest. Cedar and juniper trees dot the surrounding landscape, giving way to sporadic clearings and meadows.

Soon the highway rounds a hill and comes into Paradise Valley. To the east side of the road you will see the outline of Paradise Valley Lake, an intermittent lake that will most likely be dry during riding season. Too bad, for it would surely add to the picturesque mountain valley setting before you. The road makes a short run down the length of the valley and quickly begins to climb, twisting gently as it traverses another mountain.

A short, aggressive climb brings you to Hogan Pass where you may wish to take in the view at Desert View overlook. Look for the turnout on the east side of the road at the highway summit. The name sounds incongruous with the terrain through which you have been riding, but one look explains it. From here you can see the bold colorful desert mesas to the southeast and on a clear day, glimpse the rugged

Desert View Overlook – SR 72

landscape of Capitol Reef, which lies only about eight miles away. This panoramic view is worth a short stop.

After cresting at the overlook, the road begins a descent, twisty in places, along a ridge called Fox Bench. To the west, you will see Forsyth Reservoir tucked in a valley below. A couple of miles and a few amusing curves past the reservoir you will find Fremont River Road to your right. This is SR25. Look for the sign to Fish Lake. You can't miss it. (I did the first time I made this ride, but luckily for me my bike saw it and turned around.)

Turn right (northwest) on SR25. This road gently twists down into a river valley in which sits Mill Meadow Reservoir, formed by a dam on the Fremont River. At the north end of the reservoir you will begin to climb up a lovely little draw, tracing the Fremont River upstream. The ride is quite relaxing: a slow, gently twisting roll through a cool mountain forest. The river flows peacefully through the canyon bottom below, revealing the occasional meadow clearing. The road is slightly narrow through here and the posted speed limit is low, neither of which will really hold you back. There are plenty of turnouts to allow you to get around the rare vehicle traffic you may encounter or

SR 25 overlooking the Fremont River

to pull off the road yourself to enjoy the surroundings. You'll likely settle into the natural rhythm of this peaceful mountain setting as you roll up the hill.

At the top of the draw, near a road summit, you'll find a large overlook turnout offering a splendid view of the road and river valley you've just traveled. This is a great place to take a break.

Just past this overlook, the road descends down to Johnson Valley Reservoir, treating you to a grand view of the lake as you drop down near the water's edge and trace its northern shoreline. Rounding the top end of the reservoir brings you to the northern apex of SR25 and the middle of this "W" shaped route. Here the ride bends south, rounding a small hill at Frying Pan Flat and rolling down to Fish Lake.

Fish Lake has become a minor recreational resort location. As you ride along its northwest shore you'll pass a marina, cabins and summer homes, campgrounds and picnic areas, an amphitheater and resort lodges. Somewhere in all this you'll find gas, food and a place to stay. It's a great vacation spot and the development, such as it is, has not spoiled its natural wilderness appeal.

After a slow coast down the lakeshore to the bottom end of Fish Lake, you'll climb out of the valley to the southwest. Cresting a hill,

Riders on SR 25

you'll enjoy a gently twisty romp down to the highway junction with SR24. The road is in great shape, one of the benefits of development, I suppose. Property investment attracts highway maintenance dollars.

At SR24 turn right (north). Coming down out of the hills into a high desert prairie, this highway offers a speed run past the Praetor Slopes (to the right) and Koosharem Reservoir, then through the Plateau Valley before bending slightly west and climbing into Kings Meadow Canyon.

Kings Meadow Canyon is a fun stretch of road, a gently curvy, up and down (mostly down) gambol through the hills. The character of the highway is such that you can open the throttle a bit and have some fun blowing out the pipes.

Near the top end of the canyon you'll pass the Rainbow Hills. These interesting hills are striped in layers of pastel pinks and grays, making a fascinating and scenic landscape.

Bending sharply west and then north in a broad S-curve the road crosses the Sevier River and drops into Sevier Valley. Rolling up the valley through the rural communities of Sigurd and Vermillion, it brings you to junctions with US89 and I-70. Both of these highways, running roughly parallel, will take you northeast into Salina or on to your next ride.

This short ride is a fun, scenic mountain run. It needn't take more than half a day and easily provides your minimum recommended daily allowance of wind in your hair and bugs in your teeth. Basing in Salina and capping the route with I-70, it is easily made into a loop. When you find yourself in central Utah, ride the "lazy W". It's worth going out of your way.

Fish Lake Run – Notes

Pit Stops:

Salina:
Maverik
195 W. Main (US 50)
(435) 529-7990

Salina Chevron
1355 S. State (US 89)
(435) 529-3232

Don's Sinclair
215 W. Main (US 50)
(435) 529-3531

Sigurd:
Dave's Country Trading Post
20 S. State (SR 24)
(435) 896-9471

Accommodations & Camping:

CAMPGROUNDS:
National Forest Campgrounds info: (877) 444-6777 or www.reserveusa.com.
    Piute – SR 25, Johnson Valley Reservoir
    Tasha Equestrian – SR 25, Johnson Valley Reservoir
    Frying Pan – SR 25
    Bowery (& group site) – SR 25, Fish Lake
    Mackinaw – SR 25, Fish Lake
    Doctor Creek (& group site) – SR 25, Fish Lake

Commercial Campgrounds
    Lakeside Resort – SR 25, Fish Lake, (435) 638-1000

HOTELS:
Fish Lake:
Bowery Haven Resort
SR 25, Fish Lake
(435) 638-1040

Fish Lake Lodge
SR 25, Fish Lake
(435) 638-1000

Lakeside Resort
SR 25, Fish Lake
(435) 638-1000

RECOMMENDED DINING:
Salina:
Mom's Café
10 E. Main (corner US 50 & US 89)
(435) 529-3921

Fish Lake:
Bowery Haven Resort
SR 25, Fish Lake
(435) 638-1040

Fish Lake Lodge
SR 25, Fish Lake
(435) 638-1000

Utah Facts

The name Utah comes from a Ute word which means, according to various sources, "home on the mountain top" or "people of the mountains".

State Capitol – Salt Lake City, population 189,314 (2012, US Census Bureau)
Greater Salt Lake Metro area, population 1,161,715 (2012, US Census Bureau)

Statehood Day – January 4, 1896 (45th state)

GEOGRAPHY:

Land area – 82,144 square miles (rank: 12th).
Total area – 84,899 square miles (rank: 13th).

Highest point – Kings Peak (Uinta Mountains), 13,528 feet.
Lowest point – Beaver Dam Wash (Washington County), 2,350 feet.

The average elevation of the tallest peaks in each of Utah's counties is 11,222 feet., taller than the same average elevation of any other state in the US.

POPULATION:

State population – 2,855,287 (2012, US Census Bureau)
Median age – 29.1 years, youngest in US
Birth rate – 18.2/1000, highest in US
Death rate – 5.2/1000, 2nd lowest in US
Average household – 3.1, largest in US

80% of Utah's population lives along the Wasatch Front. 62.2% of Utah's population are members of the LDS (Mormon) church.

ATTRACTIONS:

Utah is home to 5 National Parks, 7 National Monuments, 1 National Historic Site, 6 National Forests, 2 National Recreation Areas and 45 State Parks.

Utah's National Parks see a combined visitation of over 6.5 million annually. In addition to being the oldest park, Zion is also the most popular with an annual visitation of almost 3 million.

MOTORCYCLES:

Motorcycles registered (2012) – 90.095
Motorcycle operators licensed (2013) – 169,813 total*

*Utah has a tiered motorcycle endorsement system:
Unrestricted endorsements – 157,329
<650cc – 7,017
<250cc – 4,262
<90cc – 1,205

Rock Creek & Moon Lake Runs

Mountain Sheep Pass near Rock Creek Ranch

    The Rock Creek and Moon Lake areas offer two fun overnight escapes from the urban grind. These runs add camping to a menu of great riding to make the perfect overnight or weekend getaway. You'll run one of the best motorcycle roads in Utah through spectacular High Uinta landscapes on this ride back to nature. Whether your idea of camping is a hotel room or pitching a tent in the forest under a blanket of stars, you'll find the opportunity to get primitive or have the amenities that allow you to avoid doing so. Weather conditions make this area accessible from late spring through early fall so if camping is on your outdoor recreation agenda, why not do it with your bike? Throw a sleeping bag on the rack and your leg over the saddle and take this short trek to a place where you can't see the air you breathe, rush hour traffic is but a fading image in the rear view mirror and the workplace feels like it's a million miles away. Enjoy!

Rock Creek & Moon Lake Runs Route Map

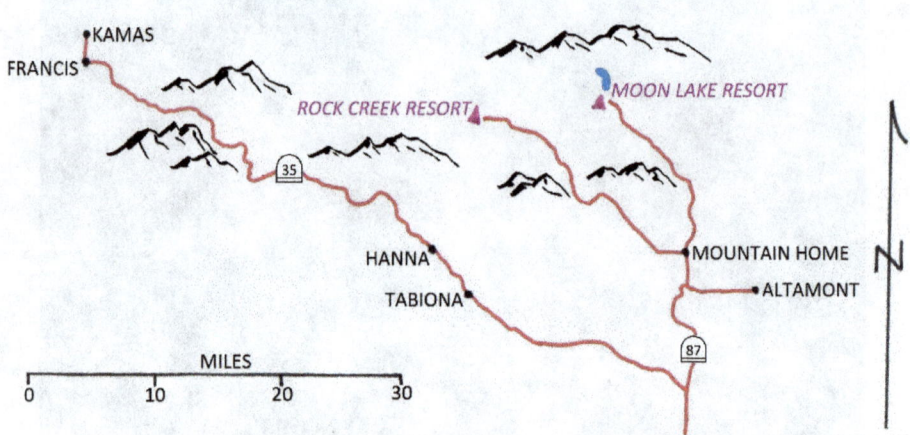

ROUTE: From Kamas, take SR32 south to the junction with SR35 at Francis. Go eastbound on SR35 over Wolf Creek Summit and continue through Hanna and Tabiona to the junction with SR87. Go north on SR87 to Route 1566. Take Route 1566 north to Mountain Home. <u>ROCK CREEK</u>: From Mountain Home go west on 6750 N. Continue on road to Rock Creek Ranch near Upper Stillwater Reservoir. <u>MOON LAKE:</u> Continue north on Route 1566 to Moon Lake.

Section II: Central & Eastern Utah

On the road...

If you love to ride and love to camp out, have I got deal for you! But wait, if you love to ride and you believe, as I do, that any night not spent in your own bed (even in a hotel room) qualifies as camping, don't count yourself out. Toss an overnight bag on the bike and join your more primitive companions on this backwoods adventure. You'll get credit for camping out without foregoing life's basic refinements such as clean bedding, indoor plumbing, and electricity.

I love this ride because it runs what I (and many others) consider to be one of the best motorcycle roads in Utah — state highway 35. You're sure to agree after running the *twisties* through high country forests and mountain valleys on this wilderness outing.

We'll begin our ride in Kamas, where you should gas up. Kamas is your only opportunity to procure high-octane fuel on this trip, so if your mount gets finicky on anything but the sweet stuff, you're wise to top off the tank or have some octane booster in your saddlebags (or both).

A short stretch due south out of Kamas on SR 32 brings you to Francis and the junction with SR 35. Turn left (east) at the four-way intersection. This is the start point of SR 35, which rolls gently through the communities of Francis and Woodland before beginning a rambunctious climb into the mountains. Here the road drifts along the South Fork of the Provo River through a pastoral landscape of ranches, farms, summer homes and recreational property. The setting is quite peaceful and quite scenic.

After a run of roughly eleven miles through this pastoral mountain ranch country, the highway bends at Nobletts Creek trailhead and the real fun starts. Quickly, the highway becomes pleasantly twisty and climbs aggressively to Wolf Creek Summit. Give your steed the spurs and get ready to enjoy a romp over the mountain that was tailor made for motorcycles.

In addition to the pleasing contour and character of the highway, you will also find it well maintained. SR 35 was unpaved in the middle until several years ago, so most of the road surface from Nobletts to Hanna is relatively new and in great shape.

Climbing up to Wolf Creek Summit you'll be treated to cool aspen groves on the left and a thick pine forest on the right. Parking turnouts abound on both the front and back sides of the summit, so at some

Riding SR 35 near Nobletts Trailhead

point consider a time-out from the thrill of the road to take advantage of the opportunity to soak in the scenery or take some pictures.

About sixteen miles from Francis you'll find a turnout with a rather interesting bit of Utah historical trivia. Look for the highway sign indicating a "memorial marker" ahead and take the corresponding turnoff. There you will find a monument to Masashi Goto, a young aviation pioneer who crashed and was killed 3000 feet southeast of this site on July 4, 1929. Goto, with his friend and partner Takeo Watanabe designed and built a small biplane to pursue a dream of flying around the world. The duo intended to hop across America, Europe and Asia by plane and cross the oceans by boat. Unable to finance a tandem venture, they decided Goto should embark solo.

Departing from Los Angeles on or about July 2, 1929, Goto flew up the coast to Oakland, carrying a folded American flag and letters to his family in Japan tucked in his flight suit. On July 3 he made the hop to Reno, Nevada, and then flew on to Salt Lake City Municipal Airport on July 4, where he was met by members of the local Japanese community who had gathered to greet him and cheer him on. Taking off out of Salt Lake City, Goto pointed his craft east towards New York, his destination on the American leg of his odyssey. Experts at the time speculated that the intrepid Goto ran into a thunderstorm as he flew over the Uinta National Forest near Woodland and attempted, with disastrous results, to fly under it, bringing a heartbreaking finale to a grand adventure.

Not far beyond the Goto monument lies Wolf Creek Summit. Cresting the hill you'll be at 9,476 feet above the sea. It's not uncommon to see temperature differentials of ten degrees or more between the summit and Francis or Hanna, both of which lie at about the 6,500 feet level on either side of the mountain. This can be quite refreshing on a hot summer day, but it also means that early or late season rainfall in the valleys can manifest itself as snow at the summit.

On top, right next to Wolf Creek Campground, you'll find a rest area with restrooms. There's plenty of wide open flat space to turn out, park and take a break.

While near the top, you'll no doubt notice how the aspen groves have thinned out. It's not hard to imagine that the timberline lies not far above this elevation. The growing season strikes me as relatively short in this area for these hardy trees. I've seen the aspens mostly bare, just beginning to sprout new leaves as I've ridden SR35 in early June. By the end of September, the leaves are in full color and beginning to drop.

As you start down the east side of the pass, note how the landscape differs on either side of the highway. The left (north) side of the road is wide open grassy fields broken by sporadic patches of aspen while the right (south) side is covered by thick green pine forests. This is the first indication of a fascinating pattern of disparate geography that continues and intensifies as the road descends to the valley below.

At this point however, you're probably not focused on botanical mysteries so much as the fantastic ride you're enjoying. The highway is as steep and twisty descending the east side of the summit as it was climbing up the front side – not too much or too little, but just right! Your brain will undoubtedly be pumping out all manner of happy hormones as you dive through the curves and the grin plastered across your face will surely be derived in part from eager anticipation of the return trip. Here the road chases Wolf Creek down the canyon to its union with the Duchesne River in the valley below.

About seven miles from the summit, the dichotomy of the terrain on either side of the canyon becomes more dramatic. The north side of the highway becomes a high chaparral landscape of desert grasses and sagebrush while the south side retains a thick evergreen forest.

Hanna Cafe

I've always been fascinated by what appears to be two strikingly different ecosystems separated only by a fold of the mountains and the road running through it.

Near Stockmore Guard Station, the road's descent becomes gentler as the canyon opens into a scenic mountain valley. Ranches and cabins begin to appear at the foot of red rock cliffs and the edge of the forest. About 18 miles from the summit and nearly 3,000 feet lower, you'll roll into the little town of Hanna.

Hanna is a good place to stop and take a break. While there, stop in at the Hanna Café for a wonderful menu of home-style cuisine. The burgers and fries there remind me of those my mom would make when I was a boy, as opposed to the assembly line product found in the big city chains. Across the street from the café you will find the Hanna Country Store, where you can get a quick snack, a cold drink, and gas (regular grade only).

From Hanna, SR 35 follows a relatively straight course along the Duchesne River through the town of Tabiona and the narrow valley beyond. Less than twenty miles past Tabiona, the highway ends at the junction with SR 87.

Turn north at the T-intersection onto SR 87. This road runs due north across a semi-desert plain before bending abruptly to the east at a fold in the hills called Big Hollow. Just past the hollow, you will see highway signs clearly marking the turn to Rock Creek and Mountain Home. Turn left (north) where the sign indicates onto a road marked as Route 1566.

About three miles north on Rt. 1566 you will come to Mountain Home and the Rock Creek Store. This is where the paths to Rock Creek Ranch and Moon Lake Resort diverge, and again, both are clearly marked by highway signs.

The Rock Creek Store is a gas station and convenience store where you can take a break and fuel up. They have pumps labeled as regular (85 octane) and mid-grade (88 octane) gasoline but interestingly, each time I have been there over a span of two years, the mid-grade pump has been marked as out of order. Coincidence or evil conspiracy? You decide. As suggested earlier, you probably ought to just swing by your favorite motorcycle dealership or auto parts store and grab a bottle of octane booster before embarking on this run.

Rock Creek Ranch

To go to Rock Creek Ranch, turn left (west) at the Rock Creek Store (6750 N.). This road runs due west, straight and flat, for about three miles before becoming pleasantly twisty and revealing some scenic vistas on par with those you left behind on SR 35. Once again, the forest becomes thicker around you and you'll enjoy picturesque little lakes and bold mountain views.

Just over 22 miles from Mountain Home you'll come to Rock Creek Ranch on the right side of the road. It is clearly marked by a road sign and lies directly across from the Rock Creek Ranger Station. The ranch offers rustic cabins (with no electricity or plumbing) as well as modern cabins which are equivalent to a quality motel room. Nearby campgrounds let you pitch a tent and sleep on the ground if you wish. Horseback rides, hiking and fishing are available to enjoy at your leisure. The lodge has a small convenience store for basic necessities and also serves meals to order from a fine menu.

While at Rock Creek, take a walk through the surrounding woods on one of the paths that crisscross the area. Upper Stillwater Dam is a short hike from the resort and the banks of the creek make a nice place to enjoy this woodland paradise. You'll also surely enjoy relaxing with

Rock Creek Lodge

friends at the lodge, on the steps of your cabin, or your campsite as evening falls on the forest and the crisp mountain moonlight dances off the chrome of your bikes in the clearing – a perfect end to a perfect day!

Moon Lake Resort

To go to Moon Lake, continue straight north on Rt. 1566 at the Rock Creek Store in Mountain Home. The road makes an L-shaped jog, right and then left, just past Mountain Home, but then continues generally north into the mountains.

The road to Moon Lake is narrow and rough – not as well maintained as the road to Rock Creek Ranch. There are no lane markings but it is paved and passable. You'll cross some semi desert terrain of low hills and sagebrush through open range. Watch for livestock on the road.

About ten miles from Mountain Home you'll come to the boundary of the Ashley National Forest and the road begins to look more like the road to Rock Creek, with green forests and mountain vistas.

The resort lies on the shores of Moon Lake about 15 miles from Mountain Home. They offer cabins which split the difference between

Moon Lake

Rock Creek Ranch's rustic and modern units. All cabins have electricity and indoor plumbing, but do not include bedding or kitchen gear. Each has an outdoor fire pit and adjacent parking. The lodge has a general store with basic necessities. As at Rock Creek, nearby campgrounds afford the opportunity for more primitive quarters.

At Moon Lake Resort you can enjoy hiking and fishing or just relax on the beach. Horseshoes, volleyball and basketball facilities are available to resort guests. Boat and fishing gear rentals are also available. Moon Lake is a peaceful escape to the serenity of the Uinta wilderness — again, the perfect destination at the end of a perfect ride.

When it's time for a quick retreat from life's routine, either variation of this run will fill the bill. SR 35 is a joy in itself and will surely become one of your favorite stretches of road if it isn't already. Besides making this run as much fun as it is, SR 35 is an excellent alternative east-west corridor to US 40. Riding season in the Uintas is short compared with other areas of Utah, but the rewards are spectacular.

Riders on Route 1566 to Moon Lake

Rock Creek & Moon Lake Run – Notes

Pit Stops:

Kamas:
Phillips 66 / C-store
220 So. Main (SR 248 &SR 32)
(435) 783-4359

Chevron / C-store
2 N. Main (SR 32 & SR 150)
(435) 783-4375

Hanna:
Hanna Country Store
SR35
(435) 848-5752

Mountain Home:
Rock Creek Store
67501 N 21000 W (Rt.1566)
(435) 454-3853

Accommodations & Camping:

CAMPGROUNDS:
National Forest Campgrounds info: (877) 444-6777 or www.reserveusa.com.

Rock Creek area:
Miners Gulch
Yellow Pine
South Fork
Upper Stillwater

Moon Lake area:
Moon Lake

HOTELS:
Rock Creek:
Rock Creek Ranch
120 S. 100 E.
Mtn. Home, UT 84051
(435) 454-3332

Moon Lake:
Moon Lake Resort
PO Box 51070
Mtn. Home, UT 84051
(435) 454-3142
www.moonlakeresort.com

RECOMMENDED DINING:
Kamas:
Gateway Grill
215 S. Main
(435) 783-2867

Summit Inn Pizza & Ice Cream
80 S. Main
(435) 783-4453

Ride Utah!

Hanna:
Hanna Café & Bar
SR 35
(435) 848-5564

Rock Creek:
Rock Creek Ranch
(435) 454-3332

Flaming Gorge Run

Flaming Gorge Reservoir

It was in the spring of 1869 that John Wesley Powell, on his first expedition to explore the Green and Colorado Rivers, observed that the red rock cliffs seemed to be aflame as the sun danced off the canyon walls, thus giving Flaming Gorge its name. Today, those flame red walls hold the azure waters of Flaming Gorge Reservoir, a jewel of manmade and natural beauty straddling the Wyoming border on the north slope of the Uinta range.

This short ride runs up US 191, the Flaming Gorge National Scenic Byway. Like so many of Utah's great roads, this highway is a journey through the ages. Wandering the eons between Vernal and Flaming Gorge, you'll ride through Jurassic and Triassic Utah when dinosaurs ruled the area. You can visit pre-Columbian Utah, where prehistoric humans left their art carved into stone. You'll roll through Utah of the Old West, where Butch Cassidy et al. rode the Outlaw Trail. And of course, you'll see modern Utah, embodied in the ambitious infrastructure projects of the late 20th century such as Flaming Gorge Dam and the Colorado River Storage Project. Enjoy!

Flaming Gorge Run Route Map

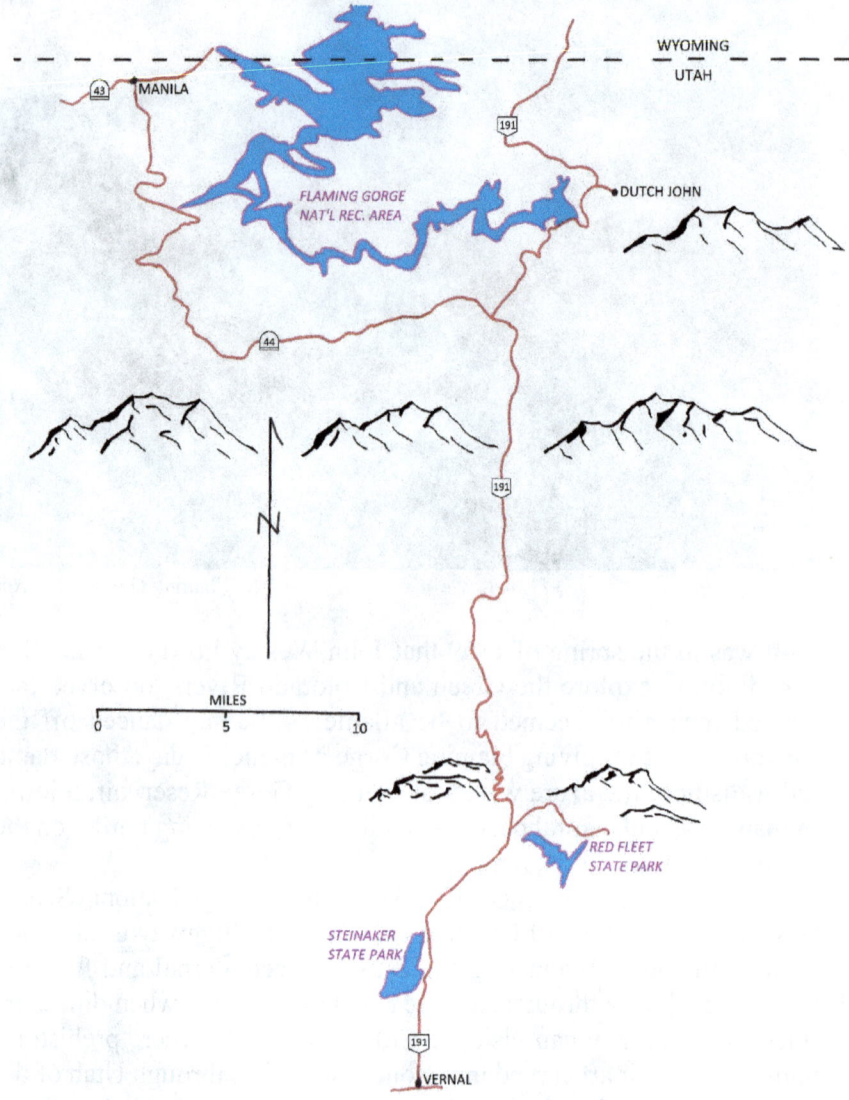

ROUTE: From Vernal, take US 191 (Vernal Ave.) northbound. At junction with SR 44, remain on US 191 north to go to Flaming Gorge Dam and Dutch John, or go west on SR 44 to Red Canyon, Sheep Creek Bay and Manila.

On the road...

One of the things I love about riding in Utah is the wonderful diversity. Each region of the state seems to have its own unique flavor. Subtle and not so subtle variations in topography, geology, climate, history and culture make Utah a patchwork quilt of wonder and beauty, sewn together with threads of similarity. While the similarities are fascinating, it's the variety that defines the experience.

In my opinion, Flaming Gorge is such a ride. It defines for me the northeast corner of Utah. The cool mountain splendor of the Ashley National Forest, the austere desert of the Uinta Basin, the distant echoes of dinosaurs roaming the hills, stone galleries of petroglyph art, the modern marvel of Flaming Gorge Dam and the timeless energy of the Green River sculpting the landscape as it flows south to join forces with the mighty Colorado – these form the unique blend that gives this region its special character.

The city of Vernal makes a good base from which to launch a day of riding and exploration and it is here that we'll begin this run. Take US 191 north out of town. (This is Vernal Ave. which intersects Main St. / US 40 near the center of town.) The highway runs flat and straight for a few miles north as it leaves the city, then begins to climb as it bends into the hills near Steinaker Reservoir & State Park.

Here the road quickly becomes pleasantly twisty and the ride gets quite scenic. Gentle turns through dramatic rock formations make this a good motorcycle road. A buff colored sandstone base underlies red rock layers of petrified dunes. Amazing swirls frozen in stone add to the spectacle.

Along the route, highway signs mark geological points of interest which add to the enjoyment of the ride. You'll note that the landscape here was formed in the Jurassic and Triassic periods. A highway sign will also alert you to the fact that you are riding in dinosaur country. While I have never seen any on the road, tracks abound in the area so stay alert lest you round a corner and encounter one of the giant lizards in your path.

Speaking of lizard tracks, about thirteen miles north and 200 million years back from Vernal you'll come to a cutoff for Red Fleet State Park, where a picturesque reservoir lies nestled among the red rock formations. There you will also find a short (2.5 mile round trip) trail that leads to dinosaur track sites. Red Fleet is a worthy detour on

DINOSAUR HUNTING LICENSE
SPECIAL PERMIT
*No. 181 - U022

ISSUED TO:

NAME _____
ADDRESS _____
CITY _____ STATE _____ ZIP ____

ISSUED BY AUTHORITY
U. S. REPTILE CONTROL COMMISSION
Restricted to Northeastern Utah Only

This license entitles holder to hunt for, pursue, and remove from that area known as Dinosaur Control Area of Northeastern Utah the following types of reptilian wild game:

- A. TYRANNOSAURUS REX - 1 Only (adult male)
- B. DIPLODOCUS GIGANTICUS - 1 Only (either sex) and not less than 5000 lbs. live weight.
- C. STEGOSAURUS - 2 Only (males) any size
- D. PTERODACTYL - 4 Only (without young)

The holder of this license agrees to remove all such game, legally bagged by him under the proper restriction, properly preserved and in sanitary condition within 5 days of time of reptile's death, and further agrees to have said game inspected by the Utah Game Warden before removal.

Signed *Al O'Saurus*

ISSUED BY AL O'SAURUS
Deputy Lizard Warden, Vernal, Utah

ALTERATIONS ERASURES OR OBLITERATIONS VOID THIS CERTIFICATE

*SPEAK the number: "I eight one, you ought to, too."
Dinosaur Hunting License copyright 1963
Dinosaurland Travel Board, Inc.

Find a Dinosaur Hunting License and info at the Dinosaurland Travel Board – www.dinoland.com
[Dinosaur Hunting License © Dinosaurland Travel Board – used with permission]

this ride, but before you go, be sure to pick up your Dinosaur Hunting License in Vernal. Imagine the pain of lost opportunity should you find a herd of *Diplodocus giganticus* or a trophy *Stegosaurus* in the park and be forced to watch them wander away because you lack the proper permit to bag one. I'm told they taste like chicken but even better, their mounted heads make killer trophies for your den and will surely impress your friends and neighbors. Dinosaur hunting licenses, and more important, a wealth of information to enhance your trip can be found at the Dinosaurland Travel Board at 55 E. Main St. in Vernal or on the web at www.dinoland.com .

Back on US 191, your journey through pre-history continues. This area contains an abundance of fossils. Crocodile teeth have been found here and the rocky draws even contain a petrified forest. What an amazing story this land has to tell, one of dynamic evolution and dramatic change. As you ride, let your imagination paint a picture of the landscape in hundreds of millions of years gone by. Lush prehistoric forests line an ancient ocean shoreline or perhaps the edge of a great inland sea. Dinosaurs roam the forests and beaches while pterodactyls soar overhead. If you've ever been crapped on by a seagull (and sooner or later riding in Utah you will be), just imagine the mess one of those great flying lizards would make of your bike in an aerial attack!

Shortly, the road climbs through a series of ten switchbacks as it ascends through mining country. Traversing the hill back and forth through these hairpins affords a grand view of the countryside behind you. To the west lies a large phosphate strip mining operation. Heavy trucks are common on this stretch of highway.

Past the mine and the switchbacks, the scenery changes as the road rolls into a mountain forest. Aspen and pine groves dot the landscape and the ride takes on a high country character. Here again you'll agree that you're riding the perfect motorcycle road. The well-maintained ribbon of asphalt gently twists and turns, up and down, through a scenic forest setting to make its way over the Uintas. Crossing the Daggett County line, the road summits at 8,428 feet.

Up on top, the highway crosses open range. There are often cattle on the roadside and deer are plentiful to the point of nuisance. Be careful.

Roughly thirty-six miles from Vernal lies the highway junction with SR 44. US 191 actually turns off to the right from the main road, while continuing straight puts you on SR 44. Highway signs clearly mark the junction. We'll explore both forks on this ride, so pick either one.

Turning right with US 191 takes you to Flaming Gorge Dam and the community of Dutch John. From the junction, the road runs relatively flat and level before beginning a steep and winding descent to the dam. Several campgrounds, as well as Flaming Gorge Lodge, are in this area. You can find gas and a C-store at the lodge.

Just past the highway junction, off of US 191, you can find an interesting piece of Utah pioneer history. Swett Ranch National Historic Site is an early twentieth century ranch preserved by the US Forest Service. Oscar Swett built the ranch on a homestead claim in 1909 and expanded his acreage over the next 58 years. He was reportedly something of a traditionalist (or perhaps eccentric is the right word), and given the ranch's remote location, operated his equipment solely with horse and human power. When construction of the dam began in 1958, bringing the modern world with it, Oscar's life

Cart Creek Bridge

must have sped out of control. He sold the ranch in 1968 and the Forest Service acquired it in 1972. Today it remains largely intact, just as the Swetts left it, preserved as an historic example of an early 1900s homestead. Swett Ranch is located about 1 mile off of US 191 on Forest Road 158. FR 158 is unpaved and its condition varies with the seasons. You may be able to ride into the ranch if you wish to see it, but even if you feel the road is too rough to ride, consider pulling over and walking in. It's a short, easy hike.

Back on US 191, after twisting down a steep grade you'll come to Cart Creek Bridge, an attractive example of highway architecture spanning a finger of Flaming Gorge Reservoir. The bridge was built in 1962 and presents a grand vista of the lake in crossing.

Shortly after the bridge you will come to the dam and visitor center. This is a good spot to take a break, enjoy the view and learn a bit more about the modern engineering marvel before you. The visitor center is open from 10:00 a.m. to 4:00 p.m. daily. Free tours of the dam begin every 20 minutes and offer a fascinating look at the power generators deep within the bowels of the structure, as well as stops overlooking the river gorge at the top of the dam and a platform on the river outlet at its base. Be aware, however that in today's post 9/11 world, security

Flaming Gorge Dam

is high at this facility where several years ago it was non-existent. You must pass through a metal detector and security checkpoint to access the dam tour. Cameras and recording devices are unfortunately prohibited. Even pocketknives are a no-no, so plan on emptying your pockets before lining up for a tour. You can also expect to see tours suspended entirely when the threat condition is elevated. Don't let any of this discourage you from venturing into the facility. The inconvenience, while irritating, is minor and touring the dam is well worth it.

Construction of Flaming Gorge Dam began in 1958 and was completed in 1964. Built mainly for water control, it captures the waters of the Green River in a reservoir 490 feet deep, extending up to 91 miles to the north with over 300 miles of shoreline. At capacity it will hold 3,788,900 acre-feet and has a surface area of 42,020 acres, neither of which means much to me but it must be a whole lot of water! The reservoir took 12 years (1962 – 1974) to fill.

Power generation began in 1964 and the dam's power plant cranks out about 500,000 megawatt-hours per year, another statistic which is meaningless to me but I am told that this will power about 150,000 homes. The dam rises 502 ft. above the river bed and contains 987,000 cubic yards of concrete (finally a number I understand). It is said that the concrete deep within its structure will not be fully cured until about the year 2067.

With this bit of dam trivia, and what you'll learn on your dam tour, you'll be so dam smart that you can impress all your dam friends before you continue this dam ride. Now aren't you glad you bought this damn book?

Leaving the visitor center, US 191 crosses the top of the dam and bends around the mountain towards the community of Dutch John. If the ride across the dam looks strangely familiar to you, you must have seen the 1999 movie *Chill Factor*, staring Cuba Gooding Jr. and Skeet Ulrich, filmed on location at Flaming Gorge Dam and in Moab.

Rounding the mountain on the way to Dutch John you'll see evidence of a recent forest fire which swept through the surrounding hills. Though the scars from the burn are still fresh, the healing is well underway and the fascinating process of forest regeneration has taken hold.

Dutch John is a little community built in 1958 to house personnel, offices and equipment used in the construction and operation of the dam. For years, the community was administered by the Bureau of Reclamation but in 1998 Congress passed legislation that provided for the transfer of responsibility to local government. You'll find a gas station, C-store and café there, and not much else.

North of Dutch John, the highway winds through the hills and crosses Antelope Flat to the Wyoming border. Continuing on US 191 would take you across the southern Wyoming desert to I-80 between Green River and Rock Springs.

Instead, let's go back to the highway junction and explore the scenic mountain environs of SR 44. Past the junction, SR 44 is a somewhat straighter ride to the west, a pleasant roll through the forest on a well-maintained highway. About five miles down the road you will come to a cutoff to Red Canyon Overlook on the right (north). This road leads to another visitor center and a beautiful view of Red Canyon

Again, the highway crosses open range and I have often encountered cattle along the roadside here. This stretch of road will beckon you to open up the throttle. By all means enjoy the ride. Just be aware of livestock and ride prudently.

A little more than eleven miles from the junction, the highway bends to the north and winds through some stunning red rock gorge country. Watch for the signs marking the Sheep Creek Geological Loop coming up on the left (west) side of the road. This cutoff loops around Sheep Creek Hill and back into SR 44. It's a scenic, interesting detour of roughly 12 miles you should consider taking either on the way out or the way back.

Rising and falling, SR 44 hugs the shape of the landscape giving you a wonderfully curving ride through each fold in the mountain. Broad sweeping switchbacks overlook a marvelous view of Sheep Creek Bay. You'll no doubt be unable to avoid a huge grin as you give it the spurs through here, so just give up and pick the bugs out of your teeth later.

After crossing Sheep Creek and rounding one last hill, the road settles into a gentle run north, down into the Lucerne Valley. At the end of the highway where it forms a T-intersection with SR 43 sits the town of Manila. Gas, food and lodging are all available in this quiet little burg on the Wyoming border.

This is where I turn around and head back to Vernal, but there are other options. Going west on SR 43 will take you into Wyoming and northwest to I-80 at Lyman. To the east, you will likewise enter Wyoming and find yourself on WY 530 running north along the Flaming Gorge NRA to I-80 at Green River.

Before you call it a day back in Vernal, consider a fun side trip. Take 500 N westbound to 3500 W and turn north. This road will take you up into Dry Fork Canyon. Here you can find a couple of different petroglyph sites. These examples of ancient Fremont Indian rock art are two of the most accessible you can find in Utah, and certainly some of the finest specimens. The pavement ends roughly ten miles into the canyon, so this is a short but fascinating ride.

So, there you have it. You've just spent the better part of a day on a ride that took hundreds of millions of years to create. Thankfully, time was kind enough to leave traces of each passing age, providing us with fascinating clues to the region's origin and history.

Flaming Gorge Run – Notes

Pit Stops:

Vernal:
Chevron
722 W. Main (US 40)
(435) 789-9999

7-11
100 N. Vernal Ave. US191)
(435) 789-2182

Flaming Gorge:
Flaming Gorge Lodge (Conoco)
1100 Flaming Gorge Meadows
(435) 889-3733

Dutch John:
Flaming Gorge Store East
US 191 & South Blvd
(435) 885-3191

Manila:
Chevron (w/ C-store)
SR 43
(435) 784-3363

Accommodations & Camping:

CAMPGROUNDS:
National Forest Campgrounds info call (877) 444-6777 or Flaming Gorge Ranger District (435) 784-3445 or www.reserveusa.com.
Dutch John area:
Red Springs – US 191
Lodgepole – US 191
Firefighters Mem. – US191
Deer Run – US 191
Cedar Springs – US 191
Arch Dam – US 191
Dutch John Draw – US 191
Dripping Springs – FR 075

Greendale East – US 191
Greendale West – US 191
Mustang Ridge – US 191
Antelope Flat – FR 145
Skull Creek – SR 44
Greens Lake – SR 44
Canyon Rim – SR 44
Red Canyon – SR 44

Manila area:
Mann's – SR 44
Willows – SR 44
Carmel – FR 218 (Sheep Creek Geo. Loop)

Lucerne Point – FR 146
Lucerne Valley – FR 146

Utah State Park Campgrounds info (800) 322-3770 or
www.stateparks.utah.gov
Steinaker State Park – Vernal
Red Fleet State Park – Vernal

Commercial Campgrounds
Dinosaurland KOA
930 N. Vernal Ave., Vernal (435) 789-2148

Flaming Gorge KOA
Hwy 43 & 3rd West, Manila (435) 784-3184

Lucerne Valley Marina & Campground
#1 Lucerne Blvd., Hwy 43, Manila (435) 784-3484

HOTELS:
Vernal:
Best Western Antlers
423 W. Main
(435) 789-1202

Best Western Dinosaur Inn
251 E. Main
(435) 789-2660

America's Best Value Inn
260 W. Main
(435) 789-1011

Weston Plaza Hotel
1684 W. Hwy 40
(435) 789-9550

Dutch John:
Flaming Gorge Lodge
1100 Flaming Gorge Meadows
(435) 889-3773

Trout Creek Log Cabin Motel
US 191 & Little Hole Rd.
(435) 885-3355

Red Canyon Lodge
790 Red Canyon Rd.
(435) 889-3759

Manila:
Flaming Gorge Motel
18 E. Hwy 43
(435) 784-3377

Vacation Inn
250 Hwy 43
(435) 784-3259

RECOMMENDED DINING:
Vernal:
Gateway Saloon
737 E. Main
(435) 789-9842

La Cabana Restaurant
56 W. Main
(435) 789-3151

Casa Rios
2650 W. US 40
(435) 789-0103

Eccles & Huntington Canyons Run "The Energy Loop"

View of the Sanpete Valley from Skyline Drive

At the risk of sounding cliché to the point of being sappy, this is a ride for the riding enthusiast. You'll easily outrun your troubles twisting through a series of superb mountain canyons. Blasting through cool dark forests, you'll forget where you just came from or where you're going. Riding Skyline Drive along the edge of the Wasatch Plateau, you'll feel like you're crossing the top of the world. Cliché? Maybe, but this run is where you go to get in touch with your inner biker.

Cobbled together from three state byways running through Eccles, Fairview, and Huntington Canyons, this run has been designated a National Scenic Byway by the Federal Highway Administration. The route is known as "The Energy Loop" (though not accurately defined as a loop) because it runs through the heart of Utah's energy producing region. But while coal mines, natural gas pipelines and coal-fired energy generation projects are found here, you'll be struck by how well they blend into the environment, maintaining the area's scenic, almost pristine beauty.

This is a riding adventure, a run where the ride itself is the attraction — a wonderful two-wheeled escape. Enjoy!

Eccles & Huntington Canyons Run Route Map

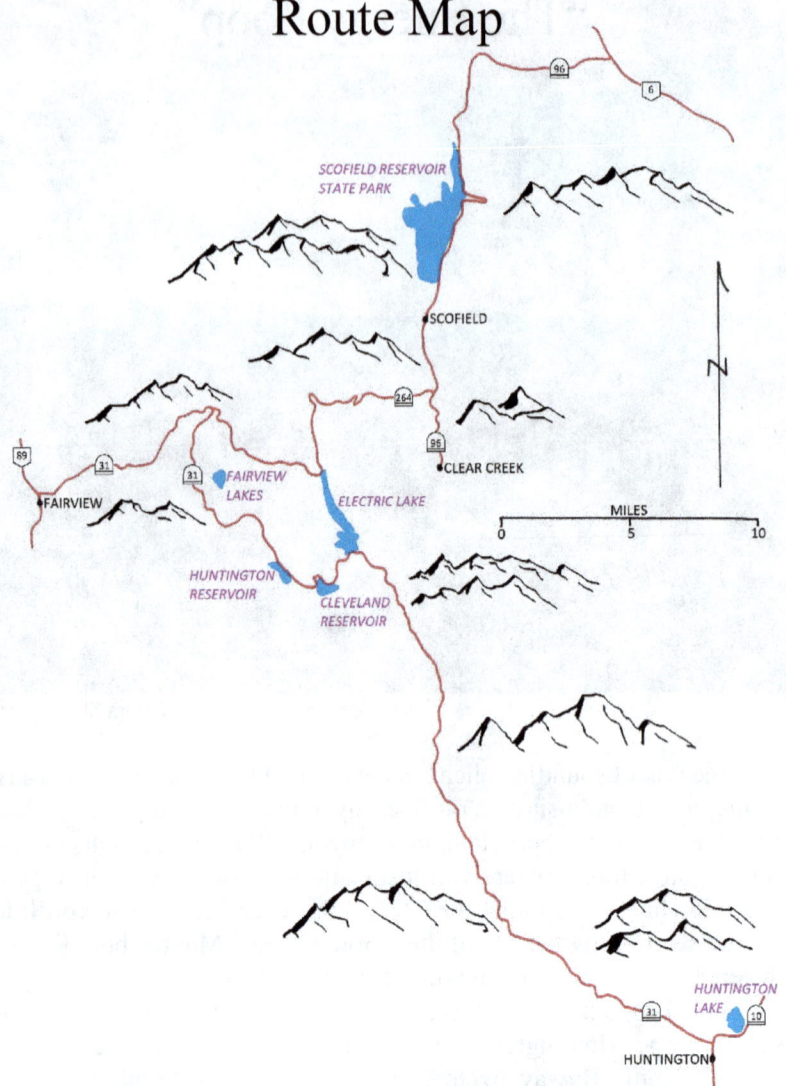

ROUTE: From US 6, find the junction with SR 96 at Colton, ca. 5 miles southeast of Soldier Summit. Turn west on SR 96 and bend south through Scofield to the junction with SR 264. Turn west on SR 264 to the junction with SR 31. Take SR 31 west through Fairview Canyon to Fairview. Return to the junction with SR 264 and take SR 31 south over Skyline Drive and through Huntington Canyon to Huntington at the junction with SR 10.

On the road...

There are some roads in Utah that are quintessential motorcycle paths. They are those rare ribbons of pavement which possess that classic, almost archetypal quality, seemingly laid out and built with nothing more in mind than the modern posterity of Gottlieb Daimler's gasoline powered bicycle. This is such a ride.

A romp through the high country, this run will send you winding through mountain canyons and across the rocky spine of the state while you traverse elevations ranging from 5,000 to 10,000 feet. Make room on your "top ten list" for this one.

Roughly five miles southeast of Soldier Summit on US 6, SR 96 cuts off the highway on the west side near a spot on the map labeled Colton. It is here that we'll begin our ride.

SR 96 is an immediate change of pace from US 6. Most notably, you will encounter far less traffic. The road runs due west for a few miles and then bends nearly due south. For the first 10 to 11 miles you'll coast through rolling hills and high meadows punctuated with groves of aspen. In the fall these meadows can explode in vivid colors.

At about this point, you'll come upon the north tip of Scofield Reservoir and State Park. A cluster of cabins and recreational properties surround the north end of the lake. Scofield Reservoir is a popular boating, camping and fishing destination. The park is home to a marina and two campgrounds.

Just over 16 miles into the ride and a mile or so past the south end of the lake, you'll roll into the town of Scofield. On the north edge of town, to the east of the highway, lies the historic cemetery, final resting place of many of the pioneer miners who carved a living out of these hills.

Scofield is an interesting little town, a colorful tile in the mosaic of Utah's history. Founded in 1879, it was one of the state's first coal towns. At its peak, the population topped 2,000 but today it teeters on the brink of ghost town status with about two hundred permanent residents. Once a contender for Emery County Seat, Scofield's population dwindled as the mines closed down.

One of the worst mining disasters in history occurred here in 1900. Winter Quarters Canyon, which runs to the west from the southern edge of Scofield, was home to multiple coal mines and a small mining camp. On May 1, 1900, coal dust exploded in one of the Winter Quarters mines, trapping hundreds of miners. The death toll ultimately

Skyline Mines

tallied one hundred ninety-nine miners, a catastrophe which devastated the communities of Winter Quarters and Scofield. At the time (and for years to follow) it was the worst mining disaster in US history. The mine reopened by the end of May with little, if any, improvement in safety or working conditions. Fed up, the miners walked out on strike in 1901 forcing the mines to address critical issues of work safety.

A couple of miles south of Scofield, the road forks. This is the junction of SR 96 and SR264. SR 96 continues for about 4 miles to the little town of Clear Creek, a small mining camp. To the right, SR 264 climbs west into Eccles Canyon. Take the right fork onto SR 264.

At the road junction sits the Skyline Mines operation. This is coal mining country and has been for over 100 years but the countryside before you belies the typical impression of a mining operation. The Skyline facility blends in quite well with its surroundings and appears to be a strikingly clean operation. Skyline Mines has done an excellent job of reclaiming the land.

SR 264 is a great road! You'll hit the *twisties* just past the Skyline Mines facility and climb through some really fun tight curves. The

(©1999, Scenic Byways Committee)　　　Burnout Canyon

winding road up this peaceful, forested mountain canyon makes it easy to lose yourself in the moment. What a great alternative to Prozac!

The highway summits near the Sanpete County line, then drops down an eight percent grade, presenting a grand view of a lovely mountain valley. Huntington Creek runs down its center, paralleled closely by the road. Broad open meadows surround the creek and you'll likely see eagles and other raptors soaring overhead. This picturesque valley is known as Burnout Canyon. A natural gas pipeline runs through here but you'd never know it. This is without a doubt the most cunningly successful environmental reclamation I have seen.

Running south through Burnout Canyon, the highway begins a gradual climb and runs some pleasant curves. Here you'll come upon the north tip of Electric Lake. This lake is an artificial reservoir built to provide power for Huntington Power Plant. At the bottom of the lake lie the remains of Connellsville, a mining ghost town.

At Electric Lake, SR 264 bends west around the mountain and climbs up to a junction with SR 31 on the ridge of the Wasatch Plateau. You'll find a rest area at the highway junction.

To the right, SR 31 makes a short run down Fairview Canyon to the town of Fairview. This canyon segment is only about eight miles long and is stunningly beautiful. The road runs some very tight aggressive turns through its steep descent into town. I highly recommend this short detour, if for no other reason than the road itself, but Fairview makes for a good rest stop as well. You'll find gas and food in this historic little Mormon pioneer community. It's a good place to grab some lunch and kick back for a bit.

After visiting Fairview and climbing back out of the canyon to the highway junction, go south (right at the intersection) on SR 31 towards Huntington. You are now on top of the Wasatch Plateau on a segment of trail known as Skyline Drive.

The Wasatch Plateau is a significant terrain feature that runs north – south nearly the entire length of the state. It divides Utah into distinct geographic regions by separating the Colorado Plateau and the Great Basin. Skyline Drive follows the crest of this plateau for much of its length but unfortunately, most of the trail is unpaved. The elevation here is high, near 10,000 feet, and you'll be running the timberline across Utah's backbone. The views from the top are spectacular. On a clear day you can see landmarks 50 miles away.

One such grand view is from Sanpete Valley Overlook where you can gaze across the breadth of the Sanpete Valley and see the town of Mt. Pleasant with the Cedar Hills and the San Pitch Mountains beyond.

In my opinion, Skyline Drive and the ensuing upper Huntington Canyon segment of this ride are the best stretches of road in the state for viewing the fall colors. This is a bold statement, I know, given the many magnificent alpine rides in northern and central Utah. Anywhere aspen, scrub oak and other deciduous vegetation takes hold in abundance, as it does throughout the mountains of Utah, the potential for spectacular autumn colors is high and many Utah rides are

Huntington Canyon

breathtakingly beautiful in the fall, as noted in other chapters. I have found Skyline Drive and Huntington Canyon however, to be beyond superlative. The autumn color can be so bold and so vibrant as to nearly overwhelm the senses. Take this ride in late September or early October and see if you don't agree.

Just past the Sanpete Valley Overlook, the road separates from Skyline Drive and drops down off the plateau. As you twist down the mountain you'll overlook Fairview Lake, Huntington Reservoir and Cleveland Reservoir, then wind around a hill to the south end of Electric Lake. Here the highway rejoins Huntington Creek for its dash down Huntington Canyon.

Huntington Canyon is a fantastic stretch of road! The scenery is breathtaking and the highway hugs the creek, making it a pleasingly twisty frolic through the woods. This road begs to be ridden hard. The descent off of the Wasatch Plateau is fairly rapid yet it doesn't feel unusually steep. There are plenty of turnouts and scenic overlooks along the way at which to stop and take in the surroundings.

Midway down the canyon you can find the Stuart Guard Station National Historic Site. This Forest Service facility was built in 1934 by the CCC. It is still operational, hosting a visitors' center and mini-museum.

The only drawback to the Huntington Canyon stretch is that it is over too soon. Shortly after Stuart Guard Station you'll come to the boundary of the Manti-La Sal National Forest where the canyon opens up and deposits you in Castle Valley. Farms and ranches appear along the highway and the road takes you past the large Huntington Power Plant. The road here is bordered by sculpted cliffs and fortress-like escarpments from which Castle Valley gets its name.

Rolling into the valley you have completed a descent from about 10,000 feet to roughly 5,800 feet. Here you come to the end of SR 31 in Huntington at the junction with SR 10 and so too, unfortunately, the end of this ride.

SR 10 runs the length of Castle Valley. To the north you will find Price and US 6. Going south takes you through Castle Dale and ultimately to I-70 at Fremont Junction, where you can hop on SR 72 and do the Fish Lake Run (see page 107).

The Energy Loop is a great ride. Once you've discovered this gem it will always be at the top of your list when the call of the wind beckons you to mount up.

Eccles & Huntington Canyons Run – Notes

Pit Stops:

Fairview:
Walker's Chevron
334 N. State
(435) 427-9304

Texaco
36 W. Canyon Rd.
(435) 427-3694

Huntington:
BK's Stop n' Shop
506 N. Main (SR 10)
(435) 687-9393

Hart's Food & Gas
135 S. Main (SR 10)
(435) 687-9336

Maverik
197 N. Main
(435) 687-9467

Accommodations & Camping:

CAMPGROUNDS:

National Forest Campgrounds: info (877) 444-6777 or www.reserveusa.com.
  Flat Canyon – SR 264   Forks of the Huntington – SR 31
  Old Folks Flat – SR 31   Bear Creek – SR 31

Utah State Park Campgrounds info: (800) 322-3770 or
www.stateparks.utah.gov
Scofield State Park - Scofield

HOTELS:

Scofield:
Scofield B & B
270 N. Rail Rd.
(435) 448-9435

Fairview:
Skyline Motel
236 N. State
(435) 427-3312

Price:
Best Western
590 E. Main
(435) 637-5660
800-937-8376

Holiday Inn
838 Westwood Blvd.
(435) 637-8880

RECOMMENDED DINING:
Fairview:
Home Plate Café
215 N. State
(435) 427-9300

Timber Creek Bakery & Deli
36 Canyon Road
(435) 427-3988

La Mariposa
44 S. State
(435) 427-9212

Great Basin Loop

Wheeler Peak – Great Basin Nat'l Park

Utah straddles two of North America's great geographic features — the Colorado Plateau and the Great Basin. While the Colorado Plateau seems to get the most attention from riders (for good reason), the Great Basin should not be overlooked. A casual glance at the map might lead one to dismiss the thought of riding the vast western deserts. This would be a mistake, for while on paper the roads look long and straight and the terrain featureless, from the saddle an entirely different picture presents itself. The Great Basin is full of scenic wonder, a fascinating bio-diversity and a stark beauty found only in North America's high deserts.

This ride is laid out in three legs of nearly-equal distance, forming an almost equilateral triangle. Gas and amenities are available at each corner of the triangle for convenient comfort stops, and points of interest — most notably Great Basin National Park — offer the opportunity to explore the area's history and landscape in detail. Each leg takes just over an hour to run, so with rest stops and sightseeing detours, the ride will easily fill half a day or more.

Situated within reach of the Wasatch Front and Utah's Dixie, this loop is an easy daylong escape for riders based in most of the major population centers of the state. So treat yourself to a day in the saddle and experience an essential sample of the wonders of the Great Basin. Enjoy!

Great Basin Loop
Route Map

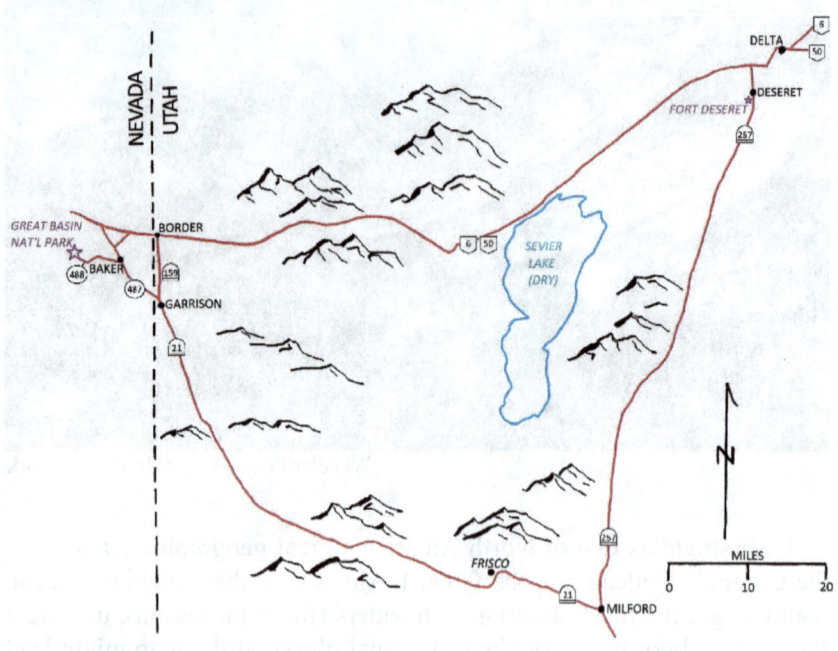

ROUTE: From Delta, take US 6/50 westbound to NV 487 (just past the Nevada border). Take NV 487 southeast to Great Basin National Park (Baker, NV). Continue southeast on NV 487 from Baker, NV. Road becomes SR 21 at Utah border. Take SR 21 southeast to Milford. At Milford, take SR 257 northbound to Delta.

On the road...

It's said that every drop of water that falls on the North American continent ends up in one of three places: the Atlantic, the Pacific, or the Great Basin. This vast region of high desert valleys and narrow mountain ranges is characterized by its lack of drainage. Rivers and streams are few, with no outlet to the sea. Water collects in shallow mud flats, salt lakes, and marshes, and then evaporates. Stretching from the Sierra Nevada in the west to the Wasatch Range in the east, the Great Basin is not a single basin but many, divided by roughly parallel north-south mountain ranges. Dry, brush-covered valleys nestled between forested mountains present a beautiful and fascinating landscape to explore from the saddle.

This is a ride that is probably best enjoyed early or late in the season. Temperatures in Utah's west desert can be brutal in the height of summer. Not to say that you shouldn't attempt this route in July or August, but be forewarned and take the appropriate precautions. April through mid-June and September through early November are likely to be easier on both you and your bike (especially if your mount is air-cooled). Take note also that regardless of the time of year, water is a must on this run. The air in this region is remarkably dry. You can almost feel it drawing the moisture from your body, even standing still. Riding with any exposed skin in this climate makes dehydration a concern. Throw a couple bottles of di-hydrogen monoxide in the saddlebags just in case and replenish your supply at each stop.

I'll begin my discussion of this ride in Delta and go counter-clockwise on the map. As with any loop, you can of course jump in anywhere and go in either direction. For riders coming from the Wasatch Front, Delta is the logical start point. Those who start their day in St. George or Cedar City can begin the loop in Milford, and, like their northern counterparts, be back in their own driveway by sundown after a full day of riding.

Start this ride with a full tank of gas. With a six-gallon tank you will easily make two legs of the loop before prudence dictates topping off. You could probably do the same on a five-gallon tank, depending on your riding style, but may want to consider topping off at each corner. Several years back, I was riding this route with some out-of-state friends and neglected my own advice. Having too much fun to pay attention to the gas gauge, five of the six bikes in our group ran dry (we were all on five-gallon tanks). Making the situation more

Sevier Lake

uncomfortable, it was I who did not run out. My new friends were less than pleased with me that day, but I think they forgave me. What can I say? I thought we'd make it. I know better now.

In addition to plenty of fuel stops, Delta offers many choices for a meal before you launch into the loop. When fueled and fed, head westbound out of town on US 6/50.

This stretch of road has a bit of historic and cultural caché worthy of note. US 6 was once the longest ribbon of highway in the United States. Tagging along for a ride on the same roadbed, US 50 is a continuation of the famous "loneliest road in America" that bisects Nevada.

The highway runs due west until Hinckley, then bends southwest for a laser-straight run to the House Range, some 40 miles ahead on the horizon. About 30 miles or so southwest of Delta you will spot Sevier Lake on your right. This is an intermittent lake, so I am told, though I've never seen it wet. Illustrative of the environmental mechanics of the Great Basin, Sevier Lake is a giant evaporation basin into which the Sevier River and seasonal runoff flow to be recycled back to the atmosphere. If you're riding by in the summertime, rather than a lake you will see a large, snow-white salt flat.

Just past the poorly-marked Sevier Lake Viewpoint (where the highway passes closest to the lakeshore) the road rises and pokes

Riding through Tule Valley

through the House Range at Skull Rock Pass. Dropping down from the pass, the highway bends northwest into the scenic Tule Valley. Here you'll enjoy a short run up and across the valley with the House Range on your right and the Barn Hills on your left as you approach the Confusion Range. A glance to your left as you enter the valley will reveal another intermittent lake.

After crossing the Tule Valley, our road climbs into Kings Canyon to take us through the Confusion Range. The short ride through Kings Canyon is quite scenic and the road becomes mildly twisty, with posted speeds dropping to 35 mph. The highway summits at a posted elevation of 6,280 ft. about 22 ½ miles east of the Nevada border and begins a straight and steep (eight percent) downgrade. At the bottom of the hill the road bends almost due west as it runs to the border.

The Border Inn on the Nevada border is one of two opportunities on the second corner of our triangle for food, fuel, and most important, water. The other pit-stop opportunity lies in Baker, NV just under a dozen road miles ahead.

From the state line, continue another six miles west on US 6/50 to the junction of NV 487. Look for the signs pointing you to Great Basin National Park.

A few miles before the NV 487 junction you will come to a cutoff on your left marked "Baker Archeological Site." This is a paved road

Riding into Kings Canyon

that runs between US 6/50 and NV 487 and basically cuts the tip off of this corner of the triangle. Its main purpose is (you guessed it) access to the Baker Archeological Site, a Fremont Indian village dating ca. 1200 – 1295. This site was excavated by Brigham Young University in cooperation with the BLM from 1991 to 1994. Several building foundations were revealed and many artifacts salvaged. The excavation was backfilled upon completion of the study, so the foundations of the original village can no longer be seen. All that remains today are a self-guided trail to some replica foundation walls (built in 2002) and a whole lot of flat, open desert. Personally, I find the cutoff to be solidly in the "not worth it" category, even as a shortcut, but if you're passionate about pre-Columbian history knock yourself out.

Turn left (southeast) from US 6/50 onto NV 487 and you will come to the Great Basin National Park Visitor Center in about four miles. There is no gate or entrance fee to this national park. The visitor center is of the same high quality one can expect at any national park and offers a wealth of information about the Great Basin's ecology and history. It's worth a stop.

Leaving the visitor center, turn right (southeast) and continue on NV 487 to the town of Baker, NV. Here is our second opportunity on this corner of the route for gas and refreshment. In the center of town,

Great Basis Nat'l Park

NV 488 intersects the highway on the right. Turn right (west) to enter the park.

Great Basin National Park was created by Congress in 1986. The park protects the South Snake Range, a wonderful example of the many desert mountain islands throughout the Great Basin. The paved trail into the park is definitely worth riding and will take you up to 10,000 ft. above sea level on the Wheeler Peak Scenic Drive. Breathtaking vistas abound on this short route, and you will have the opportunity to view the fascinating ecology of Wheeler Peak's wildlife and varied forests, including groves of ancient bristlecone pines. Near the bottom of Wheeler Peak Scenic Drive is the Lehman Caves Visitor Center. Here you will find more information on the park and can purchase a ticket for a scheduled tour of Lehman Caves. There is also a snack bar and gift shop at this site.

Leaving the park, take NV 488 back to Baker, NV and turn right (south) on NV 487. Remember as you roll through Baker that you've got about 85 miles of hot desert highway between your current location and the next gas and water. Enough said.

About seven miles from Baker the highway crosses the state border at Garrison, UT and becomes SR 21. There are no services available in the small community of Garrison.

SR 21 is a well-maintained highway running south-southeast from the Nevada border to Milford. This is a delightful stretch of road to ride and an excellent opportunity to not only view but experience the typical topography of the Great Basin. The next 75 miles will take you over multiple north-south mountain ranges, separating broad flat valleys of desert grass and sage.

The first such segment runs south down the Snake Valley from Garrison. You'll see the Burbank Hills on your left (to the east) and a few miles south of Garrison, you'll see Pruess Lake on the right (west) side of the highway. Making a straight run down the valley, the road rises over a low gap at the bottom of the Burbank Hills and drops into Antelope Valley.

Antelope Valley is a lovely, broad basin nestled between the Mountain Home Range and the Burbank Hills on the west and the Halfway Hills and Tunnel Spring Mountains on the east. A straight run of roughly eight miles takes you across this scenic valley as you enjoy unfettered vistas on both sides of the highway. On the east side of the valley, the road climbs into the Halfway Hills with some mild twists and takes you up to 6,300 ft. at Halfway Summit before spitting you out into the next basin.

Pine Valley is an even broader basin than the last, sitting between the Wah Wah Mountains ahead in the distance, the Halfway Hills through which you just passed, and The Needles over your right shoulder to the southwest. This time a dash of about 15 miles carries you across an equally scenic valley as you race towards the mountains blocking your path. By now, your keen powers of observation have no doubt brought you to a clear understanding of the Great Basin's geography. Rather than forming a single giant bowl, it is in fact comprised of the topography before you: a "sea" of many basins separated by an "archipelago" of parallel mountain range "islands." On the east side of Pine Valley, the road rises quickly into another picturesque, mildly twisty climb through the narrow Wah Wah range. The road summits this time over 6,400 ft. and quickly dumps you into yet another high desert basin.

Wah Wah Valley, into which you now descend, is a virtual repeat of Pine Valley. The vegetation here strikes me as subtly different from the last valley, but this may have only been a seasonal effect the last time I rode this trail. Like Pine Valley, broad, striking vistas present themselves as you race towards the San Francisco Mountains ahead. A bit of caution is in order as you traverse Wah Wah Valley. Ranching activity is greater here than at other points on our ride, with cattle on or near the highway. Be careful crossing this open range.

Climbing into the San Francisco Mountains brings you to the last mountain passage on our ride. The road gently loops through the southern end of this range as it climbs to Frisco Summit at 6,500 ft. Like the previous passes, this mountain crossing is as delightful as it is short.

Just before Frisco Summit, look for a historical site marker on the left (northwest) side of the highway. This marks the location of the town of Frisco, a mining settlement with a fascinating story.

In September 1875 a silver ore deposit was discovered in these hills. The Horn Silver Mine quickly became the largest producer in the area, and just as quickly, the town of Frisco sprung up around it. By 1877, a smelter was constructed, a railroad spur from Milford was in operation, and the town had a post office and thriving commercial district. In 1879, the United States Annual Mining Review and Stock Ledger declared the Horn Silver Mine to be "the richest silver mine in the world now being worked."

At its peak, Frisco was a wild boom town with a population of 6,000 and was home to over 20 saloons, as well as several gambling parlors and brothels. Vice and crime were commonplace and murder was rampant, with daily shootings (and killings) reported. At one point, the city contracted a wagon to pick up the bodies and haul them to the cemetery. In an effort to get a lid on the problem, the city fathers hired a marshal out of Pioche, NV to clean up the town. He was reportedly offered anything he needed — including the construction of a jail and courthouse — but according to legend, he refused, saying he had no intention of making arrests and thus no need for a jail. His message to the lawless: get out or die. To make his point, the same legend tells of him killing at least three and as many as six (depending on the version) miscreants on his first night in town. Needless to say, things quickly began to settle down.

In February 1885, the Horn Silver Mine collapsed in a massive cave-in and with it, so began the gradual collapse of Frisco. At that point the mine had produced $60,000,000 worth of zinc, copper, lead, silver and gold. Within a year, the mine was producing again, but never on the previous scale. By 1900, the town's population was down to 500 with just 14 businesses. In 1912, only 150 inhabitants and a dozen businesses remained. By 1920, Frisco was a ghost town.

Used by permission, Utah State Historical Society, all rights reserved.　　　Frisco, Utah – ca.1880

Today, the charcoal kilns from the smelter and the cemetery remain and are accessible. Numerous derelict buildings and structures recently remained as well, but in 2002 mining operations resumed in the area and these ruins became inaccessible on private property. They may have disappeared as of this writing, or could in the near future, as mining operations progress.

After cresting Frisco Summit, SR 21 takes us on a gentle 15 mile descent into Milford. The granite peaks of the Mineral Mountains jut up in the distance and beyond them, the grand Colorado Plateau rises on the eastern edge of the Great Basin — two massive geographic features on a continental scale, juxtaposed in a vivid contrast that gives Utah its unique character.

Rolling into Milford, SR 21 meets SR 257. Turn left (north) at this intersection to continue the loop, but first consider if a rest stop is in order. Fuel, food and refreshment are all available in Milford. Turn right (south) at the intersection to execute a pit-stop.

SR 257 between Milford and Delta is a well-maintained highway that sees little traffic. Except for a broad bend around the foothills of the Cricket Mountains, this trail is very straight and relatively flat. It's a speed run, no doubt, and as such, it forms the basis for a trail I call the "Western Corridor" (see the "Riding Through" section, page 290). This has become my preferred route (hell, let's be honest — my only route) when riding to Cedar City or St. George from the Wasatch

Front. For the next 75 miles you'll see why as you open up the throttle and blow out the pipes.

Rolling north across the Beaver Bottoms, you'll be in another broad basin with the San Francisco and Cricket ranges forming the western wall and the Mineral Mountains on the east. Not far out of Milford, a wind farm has sprung up in recent years and it seems to grow bigger every time I ride through. These giant power-generating windmills are mesmerizing, and I often have difficulty keeping my eyes on the road as I ride by.

The road runs in close tandem with a Union Pacific / Amtrak rail line all the way to Delta, and frankly I think I've encountered more trains on this road than auto traffic. If you flash your lights or wave when you pass a train, the engineer will usually answer with a blast of his horn. Everyone loves bikers!

Except for the occasional cattle guard and a railroad crossing at a lime plant halfway up the highway, there is little to slow you down for 66 miles until you reach Deseret. These obstacles are bone-jarring if you hit them at full speed, though, so watch out.

As you roll into the community of Deseret, you'll notice another historical marker on the left (west) side of the highway. This is Fort Deseret, an adobe fort built in 1865 by Mormon pioneers to address security concerns stemming from the Blackhawk War. The walls of the 550-foot square fort are still there. Originally ten feet high with a thickness of three feet at the base, the walls enclosed bastions at the northeast and southwest corners and presented firing ports on all sides. The fort was completed in just 18 days. Never actually used as a fighting redoubt, its main use was to pen livestock to prevent theft by the Indians. In 1866, Blackhawk himself did indeed show up looking for cattle to appropriate. The fort was put to good use, securing the town's livestock while negotiations facilitated a peaceful resolution to the confrontation.

Just north of Deseret, SR 257 comes to an end when it meets US 6/50. Turning right (east) will take you back to Delta, about six miles away, and so too, the end of our ride. Ideally, you've filled up a whole day riding and exploring and have left yourself just enough time to beat the setting sun home. As I have, I think you also will come away from this ride with a renewed appreciation for the beauty of the desert — different, yes, from the alpine forests of the north or the color country of the south, but every bit their equal. Is Utah a great place to ride, or what?!

Great Basin Loop – Notes

Pit Stops:

Delta:
Sinclair
111 W Main St.
(435) 864-4461

Sinclair
777 W Main St.
(435) 864-3510

7/11
17 E Main St.
(435) 864-4017

Border / Baker, NV:
Border Inn
US 6 (Utah/Nevada border)
(775) 234-7300

Baker Sinclair
NV Hwy 487
(775) 234-7316

Milford:
KB Express / C-store
238 S Main St.
(435) 387-2890

Chevron
402 S. Main St.
(435) 586-6931

Accommodations & Camping:

CAMPGROUNDS:

National Park Campgrounds: info (775) 234-7331 or www.nps.gov/grba

HOTELS:
Delta:
Days Inn
527 Topaz Blvd.
(435) 864-3882

Budget Motel
75 S 350 E
(435) 864-4533

Baker NV:

Hidden Canyon Ranch B&B
2000 Hidden Court Pkwy
(775) 234-7172

Silver Jack Inn
14 Baker Ave
(775) 234-7323

RECOMMENDED DINING:

Delta:

Rancher Cafe
171 W Main St.
(435) 864-2741

Delta Freeze
411 E. Main St.
(435) 864-4790

Mi Rancherito Mexican Restaurant
540 Topaz Blvd.
(435) 864-4245

Baker NV:
LectroLux Café
14 Baker Ave.
(775)234-7323

Milford:
Penny's Diner
777 Hwy 21
(435) 387-5266

How cold is it?

Anyone who has ever ridden a motorcycle understands the effect wind has on temperature. But how much effect? What is wind chill?

In late 2000, the Office of the Federal Coordinator for Meteorological Services and Supporting Research – OFCM (I'm not making that up—that's your tax dollars at work!) formed a group of government agencies and academics called the Joint Action Group for Temperature Indices, or JAG/TI (really, I swear—I couldn't make this stuff up if I tried). This group consisted of people who actually paid attention in science classes back in high school while the rest of us were drawing sketches of radical choppers in our notebooks. They applied current science and technology to an old formula, in use since 1945, and created a more accurate and useful formula for understanding the dangerous effects of winter winds and freezing temperatures. I then took their formula and created the accompanying chart, which gives us a tool for planning off-season rides and validates my theory that it isn't really necessary to pay attention in science class as long as one or two eggheads do to insure the continued survival of the species.

Wind chill temperature, simply defined, is how cold living creatures feel outside in the wind. The idea is based upon the rate of heat loss from exposed skin caused by temperature and wind. As wind velocity increases, it draws heat from the body much quicker, making it feel much colder. It's important to note that wind chill only affects humans (and animals), not inanimate objects. In a 50-mph wind, for example, at an air temperature of 40°F it will feel like 26°F. Your bike however will still think that it's 40°F (assuming that your bike can think—I know mine can). The only effect of the wind on your bike will be to decrease the time the engine takes to cool, but it will never cool below the ambient air temperature. The wind makes it feel colder but doesn't actually make the air temperature colder.

So, what does this mean to you, the biker? It means that you must consider more than just the nominal air temperature when planning a ride in late fall, winter and early spring. How fast will you be going on your intended route? As the accompanying chart illustrates, even a 60-mph ride can have a dramatic wind chill effect. This increases your chance of frostbite on exposed skin and, more importantly raises the risk of hypothermia. Plan your route with care, dress appropriately in layers, and be mindful of the dangers of frostbite and hypothermia. Bear in mind also, that even before hypothermia sets in, the cold has a tendency to sap your strength when you ride. Fatigue will be a factor, so take it easy and stop often to rest. With these things in mind, if there's no snow on the road, fire 'er up and let's ride!

Note: The National Weather Service only defines wind chill for temperatures at or below 50°F and wind speeds above 3 mph. For the sake of curiosity, I have applied their formula to temperatures up to 60°F in the chart. For more information on wind chill and weather see www.nws.nooa.gov.

Wind (mph)	\multicolumn{12}{c}{Temperature (°F)}
	60	55	50	45	40	35	30	25	20	15	10	5	0
5	60	54	48	42	36	31	25	19	13	7	1	-5	-11
10	58	52	46	40	34	27	21	15	9	3	-4	-10	-16
15	57	51	45	38	32	25	19	13	6	0	-7	-13	-19
20	57	50	44	37	30	24	17	11	4	-2	-9	-15	-22
25	56	49	43	36	29	23	16	9	3	-4	-11	-17	-24
30	56	49	42	35	28	22	15	8	1	-5	-12	-19	-26
35	55	48	41	35	28	21	14	7	0	-7	-14	-21	-27
40	55	48	41	34	27	20	13	6	-1	-8	-15	-22	-29
45	54	47	40	33	26	19	12	5	-2	-9	-16	-23	-30
50	54	47	40	33	26	19	12	4	-3	-10	-17	-24	-31
55	54	47	40	32	25	18	11	4	-3	-11	-18	-25	-32
60	54	46	39	32	25	17	10	3	-4	-11	-19	-26	-33
65	53	46	39	32	24	17	10	2	-5	-12	-19	-27	-34
70	53	46	38	31	24	16	9	2	-6	-13	-20	-27	-35
75	53	46	38	31	23	16	9	1	-6	-13	-21	-28	-36
80	53	45	38	30	23	16	8	1	-7	-14	-21	-29	-36

Section III

Southern Utah

This region is comprised of nine southern counties and runs the breadth of the state from Nevada to Colorado. I-15 runs through the corner of Arizona to Nevada in the west and a cornucopia of state and federal highways provide ample pavement from which to explore the wonders of the area.

This section of Utah is home to five national parks and four national monuments. The stunning red rock landscapes, the bold natural sculptures in sandstone, the stark deserts and forested snow-capped mountains of Southern Utah draw visitors from all over the world to marvel at its beauty. Here, you'll ride amidst the spectacular panoramas of the Colorado Plateau and watch eons of geologic history unfold before your eyes as you climb the Grand Staircase. Saddle up! Some of the best rides in the world await you in Southern Utah.

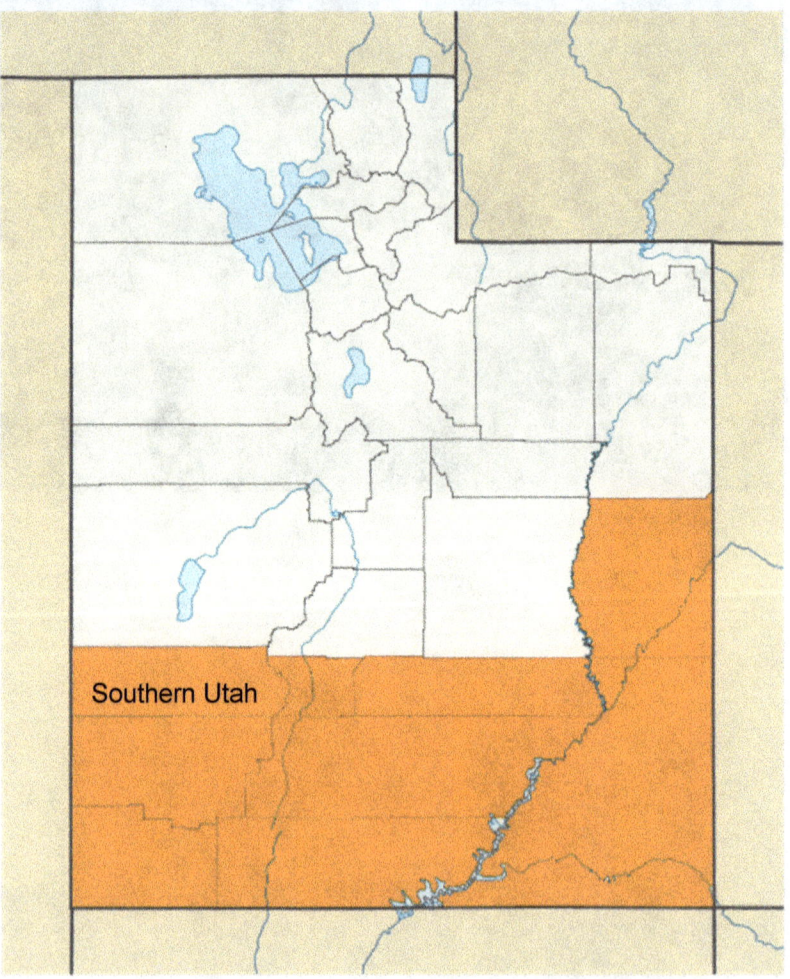

Cedar Breaks Loop

Cedar Breaks National Monument

Cedar Breaks is a stunning natural amphitheater carved from the Pink Cliffs on the west face of the Markagunt Plateau. Millions of years of sedimentary deposits provided the colorful building material from which the forces of uplift and erosion sculpted this natural wonder. Spanning three miles and plunging 2,000 feet from the rim of the escarpment to the valley floor, Cedar Breaks presents a grand panorama of jagged fins, columns and spires.

This awesome spectacle is but one of the many treats on this ride. Riding the loop will carry you over a vertical span of 5,000 feet through cool high country forests and warm desert valleys. Truly a ride for all the senses, on this one you'll see the full spectrum of nature's pallet, smell the intoxicating scent of spruce, cedar and wildflowers, taste the crisp, clean rarified mountain air, feel the temperature change as you climb and descend from the plateau and revel in the symphony of motorcycle pipes reverberating off the canyon walls. Enjoy!

Cedar Breaks Loop
Route Map

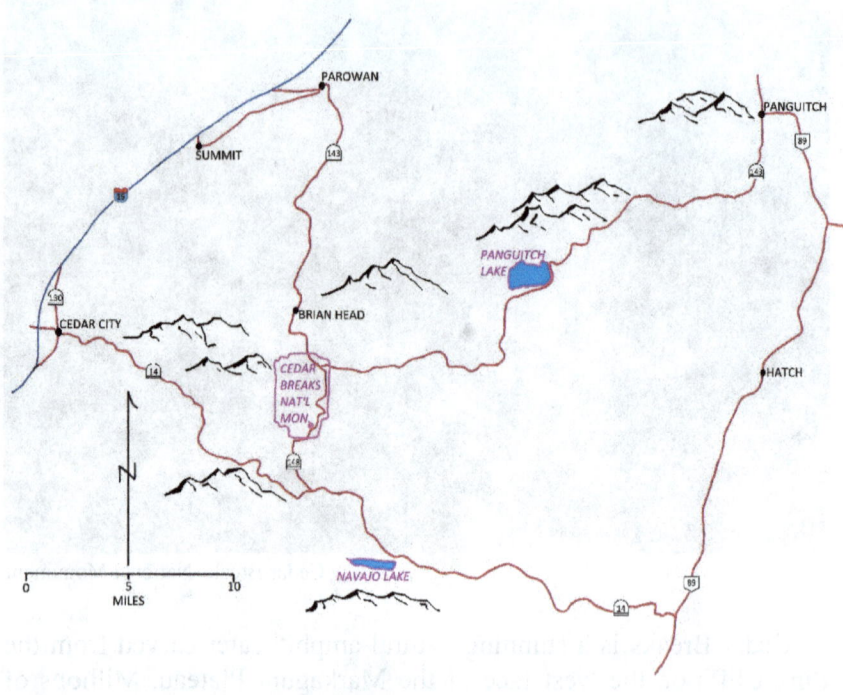

ROUTE: From Panguitch, take SR 143 south out of town. Ride southwest to junction with SR 148 at Cedar Breaks Nat'l Monument. Continue on SR 143 north to Parowan. Take I-15 or frontage road southwest to Cedar City. Go east on SR 14 out of Cedar City to US 89 at Long Valley Junction. Turn north on US 89 to return to Panguitch.

Section III: Southern Utah

On the road...

It's been said that if Cedar Breaks were anywhere else but in Southern Utah, it would be considered one of the greatest scenic wonders of the world. In fact, it is one of the greatest scenic wonders of the world, in a region so full of natural beauty that it overwhelms the senses. Competing with heavy hitters like Zion and Bryce Canyon National Parks, Cedar Breaks doesn't get the attention it deserves, but as motorcyclists, this is to our advantage. We get to enjoy this delightful loop almost all to ourselves.

There are three good base points on the loop from which to jump in: Cedar City, Parowan and Panguitch. In this narrative, we'll begin in Panguitch (a town ideally situated as a hub for multiple rides), but it really doesn't matter where you launch. Cedar City and Parowan have the advantage of proximity to I-15 for fast accessibility. This route of roughly 125 miles will take up at least half a day (3–4 hours), but can be easily stretched beyond that.

At the junction of US 89 and SR 143 in the center of Panguitch, take SR 143 westbound. Labeled as a westbound route because it runs generally east–west, this highway actually departs due south from the intersection, where US 89 makes an abrupt ninety-degree bend to the east. Not too far out of Panguitch, you'll see an amusing road sign that reads, "This is not US 89". This sign always cracks me up. It is the only highway marker I've ever come across telling me what road I'm not on. I've often wondered how many idiots had to complain, how many times and to whom in order to get such a sign posted. And why stop there? Shouldn't UDOT tell me what other roads I'm not on?

Of course, with your finely tuned biker navigation skills, you'll quickly come to grips with traveling south on a westbound route and just enjoy the ride. SR 143 is a scenic route right from the start. The road climbs out of Panguitch into foothills dotted with sage and cedar and soon becomes amusingly twisty as it runs through a mountain canyon. This charming little gorge is called South Canyon.

After a few miles, the landscape opens up briefly to reveal a meadow and ranches. The highway then meets Panguitch Creek for a second canyon segment, hugging the stream tightly through a stretch of fun curves.

Again the terrain opens up into broad meadows as you come upon Panguitch Lake. This lovely little resort area has lodging, food, recreational rentals and a convenience store. Though not very far into the ride, it's a cool place to stop for a break. At this point, you've climbed almost 2,000 feet to an elevation of nearly 8,400 feet. With 2,000 feet yet to go, you may think about having a jacket handy.

From Panguitch Lake, the road climbs quickly into the mountains, again becoming pleasantly twisty. Evergreen forests of Englemann spruce and fir mix with liberal quantities of aspen to frame a road winding through broad curves and fun tight turns. At around the 9,000 foot level, the aspens become dominant and open meadows appear, making a colorful landscape in early fall. At about 10,000 feet the aspens thin out and almost disappear, giving way to the wide open meadows on top of the Markagunt Plateau. In springtime, these meadows burst to life in a colorful explosion of wildflowers.

Riding across the top of the plateau you'll encounter cool temperatures even in the height of summer and downright cold ones in the early and late season. This is part of the appeal, in my opinion. I love to beat the heat by climbing above it. It's a good idea to have a jacket along nonetheless. A word about the riding season is in order as well. Early season here means June, late season is September. Snow usually lingers (and the road can remain closed) well into May. By the end of September time is running out. Snow flies in October and the road can be closed again by the middle of that month. The visitor center at Cedar Breaks is closed from October to the end of May, a good indicator of riding season.

On top of the plateau, SR 143 meets SR 148, the road into Cedar Breaks National Monument. The elevation at this highway junction is 10,545 feet, a good 4,000 feet above our start point in Panguitch and nearly 5,000 feet over the low spot on the loop. Up here I get winded just putting up my kickstand! Turn left (south) at the junction to visit the park.

SR 148 is a short road that runs along the rim of the bowl and joins SR 14 on the other side of the loop. The visitor center lies a few miles down the road. Not far past the junction you'll find Chessman Ridge Overlook, presenting a marvelous view of Cedar Breaks. Take the time to visit this overlook. The view from here is truly spectacular. This is Utah at its best!

Cedar Breaks is an amazing natural wonder. Red, white, yellow and purple layers of rock are chiseled in bold columns and fins into the Claron Formation, the highest, and in geologic terms, the most recent of a series of escarpments ranging across Southern Utah known as the Grand Staircase. Bristlecone Pine trees, some of the oldest trees

Chessman Ridge Overlook –Cedar Breaks Nat'l Monument

known, live in this grand coliseum. One specimen living within the monument's boundaries has been found to be over 1,600 years old. Designated as a national monument in the 1930s, Cedar Breaks has never garnered the level of attention that other area attractions enjoy. While Zion and Bryce Canyon can draw roughly 4.4 million combined visitors a year, fewer than one in six of those find their way to Cedar Breaks.

After experiencing the view from the rim, return to SR 143 and continue westbound. (This time you'll go westbound by traveling north, but we've already established that you can deal with that.) A short distance from the SR 143/SR 148 junction you'll find North Face Overlook, another grand vantage point from which to view the Breaks.

Two miles down the road you'll come to Brian Head ski resort. Cabins and ski lodges dot the hills and you can find gas and food here.

Past Brian Head, the road plunges down a very steep grade of 10% or more. This stretch is a slow road as it follows Braffit Ridge, with double S curves and 180° switchbacks, but it's a fun ride nevertheless. Eventually the road straightens somewhat and makes a gentler descent through Parowan Canyon, a very lovely ride. Before you know it, the road bursts from the Hurricane Cliffs into Parowan Valley, depositing you in the town of Parowan. The elevation here is about 6,000 feet. You've just descended about 4,500 feet very quickly. Take a deep breath, for we won't linger down here very long. We're going back up soon.

Parowan is a neat little city with the feel of small town America. Coming into town, follow the SR 143 highway markers. This road becomes Main Street and you'll find gas here, as well as places to pull over for a cold drink or something to eat. SR 143 turns off of Main Street onto 200 South and runs due west to I-15 at exit 75. You can go to the freeway here and head south towards Cedar City or continue south on Main Street for another block where it bends to the southwest and parallels the freeway. This is Old Highway 91 and it shadows the freeway through rural country along the face of the Hurricane Cliffs down to the community of Summit where it joins I-15 at mile 71. Again, you can jump on I-15 southbound to Cedar City or stay on Old 91, which fronts the freeway. Either way, go south.

At Cedar City, jump off the freeway at exit 59. This off ramp puts you on SR 56, which is 200 North in Cedar City. Go east on 200 North to Main Street (SR 130) and turn right (south). Two blocks south, you will come to Center Street, which is SR 14. Turn left here and head east on SR 14.

Cedar City has the charm of a small college town, perhaps because it is a small college town. Along the route through town just described, you'll find plenty of gas as well as ample food and drink.

SR 14 climbs out of Cedar City through Cedar Canyon, running along Coal Creek. This road too becomes immediately scenic. Cedar Canyon is a colorful gap in the jagged red rock cliffs. You'll be treated to a kaleidoscope of desert southwest colors. Pastels of pink and gray reveal layers of time in the striped cliffs. Tan, green and black highlights round out the pallet. Riding through the canyon just a short way out of town you'll find a couple of fine eateries, should the urge for steak or seafood grab you.

The highway climbs a grade which varies between 4 and 8% into a narrower canyon with solid vertical rock walls that appear to be granite. Here the acoustics are great, especially on a cool day. Those of you riding V-twins will enjoy playing the pipes through this narrow breach. Go ahead and enjoy the music.

Near the top of the canyon the road twists through a couple of aggressive switchbacks. Just as you come out of the second curve you'll get smacked in the face by a bold view of a large pink and

Section III: Southern Utah

View from Zion Overlook

orange escarpment scooped out of the mountain face. This view looks much like Cedar Breaks, as well it should. These are the same Pink Cliffs from which the Breaks are carved, just a few miles to the north.

Shortly past the Pink Cliffs you'll find a roadside turnout called Zion Overlook. This viewpoint presents a panoramic vista of the dramatic geography to the south. On a clear day you can see across Kolob Terrace into Zion National Park beyond.

Not far from the overlook the road tops out back on the Markagunt Plateau. Once again the ride has brought you to an elevation of 10,000 feet. As you roll onto the plateau, you'll find the junction with SR 148 which leads back to Cedar Breaks.

Here SR 14 begins a long run across a relatively flat landscape of mountain meadows bordered by thick evergreen forests. Soon, you'll come upon dramatic lava flows, bearing frozen witness to this area's recent volcanic history. These lava formations appear on both sides of the highway, but predominantly on the left (northeast) side. At one point a broad open meadow abruptly ends at the base of a large black lava flow, presenting a stark lunar-like landscape in harsh juxtaposition with the green mountain pasture. As the road continues, scattered lava formations dot the route but the forest begins to

Navajo Lake – off of SR 14

encroach. Here and there you'll spot a lone tree taking tentative hold amongst the harsh barren rocks.

Near these lava formations you can find another roadside overlook offering a pleasing view of Navajo Lake. While the view is not as far reaching as you may have come to expect on this ride, this turnout makes a pleasant spot to stop and stretch.

For about five miles past Navajo Lake the road makes a gradual, almost imperceptible, decent after which you'll come to the village of Duck Creek. This is a small community of cabins and recreational property lying in a pastoral setting of mountain meadows surrounded by thick forest. Duck Creek has gas and a C-store, and you could probably even scrounge up something to eat here as well.

After Duck Creek the highway descent becomes more noticeable as it continues to roll through the cool evergreen forest. Soon, however, the forest opens up across Harris Flat and the road drops down a steep 8% grade with very tight, winding curves. Coming rapidly off the plateau, SR 14 meets US 89 at Long Valley Junction. Gas is available at this junction.

At the junction turn left (north) onto US 89. This last segment of the ride is a short dash up Long Valley back to Panguitch.

As the name implies, Long Valley is a long, yet relatively narrow mountain dale, spotted with ranches and offering the occasional distant view of the steps of the Grand Staircase-Escalante and the bold colors of Bryce Canyon country. This segment of the Heritage Highway (US 89) meanders along the Sevier River in a gentle, relaxing run up the valley.

About thirteen miles from Long Valley Junction, the road rolls into Hatch, another small community where you can find gas, food and lodging. Roughly 15 miles beyond Hatch you'll find yourself back in Panguitch to close the loop and end the ride.

Cedar Breaks loop is definitely a "tall" ride. Even the low parts are over a mile high. Riding the high country is always a treat, of course, but the best part about this ride for me is the dramatic and rapid elevation changes.

This loop is a versatile ride as well. It is one that you can blast through in less than half a day on a single tank of gas or one that could be stretched out into a lazy day in the saddle. With a little forethought, it makes a great lunch or dinner ride.

It is probably redundant to point out the unique character of this ride, but it is no less true. Each ride I take in Utah has its own subtle variations that make it special and the Cedar Breaks loop is no exception. Aren't you glad you're not in Kansas anymore, Toto?

Cedar Breaks Loop – Notes

Pit Stops:

Panguitch:
Leland's Chevron
10 E. Center
(435) 676-2718

Silver Eagle
595 N. Main (US 89)
(435) 676-2790

Panguitch Lake:
Panguitch Lake Gen. Store
53 W. Hwy 143
(435) 676-2859

Parowan:
Burton's (Chevron)
200 S. Main (SR 143)
(435) 477-3646

Maverik
210 S. Main (SR 143)
(435) 477-3310

Cedar City:
Color Country Chevron
1100 W. 200 N. (SR 56)
(435) 586-6600

Maverik
809 W. 200 N. (SR 56)
(435) 586-4737

Long Valley Junction:
Tesoro
US 89 & SR 14
(435) 648-2185

Accommodations & Camping:

CAMPGROUNDS:
National Forest Campgrounds: info (877) 444-6777 or www.reserveusa.com.
White Bridge – SR 143
Cedar Canyon – SR 14
Navajo Lake – SR 14

Spruces – SR 14
Te-ah – SR 14

National Park Campgrounds: info (435) 586-9451 or
www.nps.gov/cebr
Cedar Breaks Nat'l Monument
Point Supreme Campground

Commercial Campgrounds:
KOA
555 S. Main, Panguitch
(435) 676-2225

HOTELS:
Panguitch:

New Western
180 E. Center St. (US 89)
(435) 676-8876

Purple Sage Motel
132 E. Center St. (US 89)
(435) 676-2659

Bryce Canyon Motel
308 N. Main St. (US 89)
(435) 676-8441

Bryce Way Motel
429 N. Main St. (US 89)
(435) 676-2400

Panguitch Lake:
Bear Paw Lakeview Resort
905 S. Hwy 143
(435) 676-2650

Panguitch Lake Resort
796 Lake Shore Dr.
(435) 676-2657

Brian Head:
Brian Head Reservations Center
356 S. Hwy 143
(435) 677-2042 /800-845-9781

Parowan:
Day's Inn
625 W. 200 S.
(435) 477-3326

Cedar City:
Comfort Inn
250 N. 1100 W.
(435) 586-2082

Crystal Inn
1575 W. 200 N.
(435) 586-8888

Abbey Inn
940 W. 200 N.
(435) 586-9966

Best Western
80 S. Main
(435) 586-6518

Hatch:
Bryce-Zion Midway Resort
244 S. Main (US 89)
(435) 735-4199

Hatch Station
177 S. Main (US 89)
(435) 735-4265

RECOMMENDED DINING:
Panguitch:
Flying M Restaurant
614 N. Main
(435) 676-8008

Cowboy's Smokehouse
95 N. Main
(435) 676-8030

Harold's Place
3066 E Hwy 12
(435) 676-2350

Parowan:
La Villa Fine Mexican
13 S. Main
(435) 477-1541

Cedar City:
The Pizza Factory
131 S. Main
(435) 586-3900

Rusty's Ranch House
2275 Hwy 14 (2 mi. up Cedar Cyn.)
(435) 586-3839

Milt's Stage Stop
3560 E. Hwy 14 (5 mi. up Cedar Cyn.)
(435) 586-9344

Hatch:
The Galaxy of Hatch
216 N. Main (US 89)
(435) 735-4037

Cactus Cowboy
594 US 89
(435) 735-4500

Legacy Loop Highway

Extinct volcano overlooks the town of Veyo

This ride is the long way between Cedar City and St. George. Now that statement would probably turn most travelers off. But as a motorcyclist, like me you're probably thinking, "Cool! Let's go".

The Legacy Loop Highway will take you miles off the beaten path on a fun ride down secondary highways. Along the way you'll see some history and enjoy a relaxing roll through rural southwest Utah. You'll find twisty roads, mountains, desert valleys, volcanoes, plenty of warm sunshine and the striking colors of red rock country.

If you look for every opportunity to avoid the freeway; if how you get there is more important than when you get there; if the shortest distance between two points makes you think of your car rather than your motorcycle; ride the Legacy Loop Highway. If, "I wonder what's down this road", is the first thing that goes through your mind at an intersection; if you've got $20 and an empty gas tank; if you've got a couple of hours to kill and you're trying to decide between the lawnmower and your bike; ride the Legacy Loop Highway.

This ride is an enjoyable diversion. Freeways are for people that just don't get it. Here's to taking the long way around. Enjoy!

Legacy Loop Highway Route Map

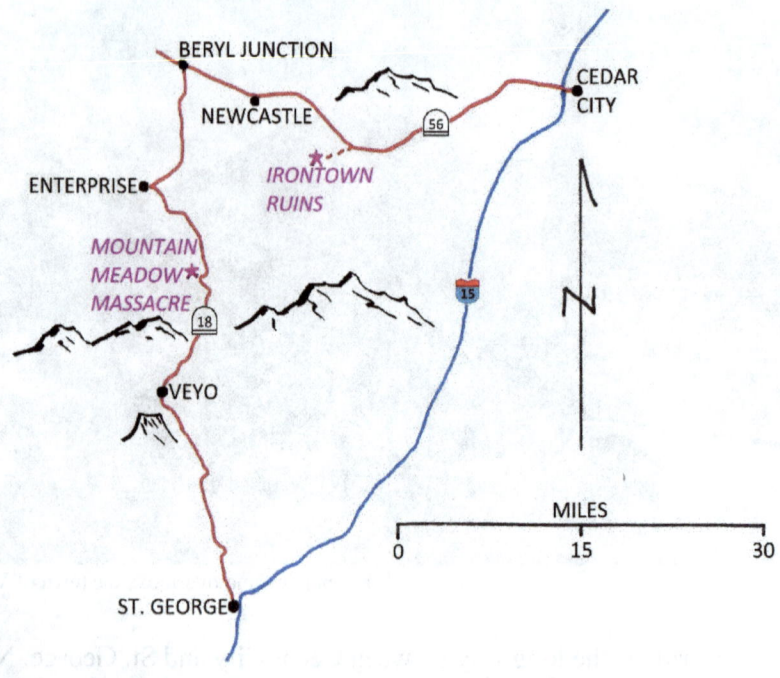

ROUTE: From Cedar City, take SR 56 westbound to Beryl Junction. At Beryl Junction, take SR 18 south to St. George.

Section III: Southern Utah

On the road...

Winding through southern Utah one day, I pulled open a map to see if I could find a way from Cedar City to St. George without taking the freeway. Some people don't mind "slabbin' it" once in a while, but I try to avoid it. It just seems unimaginative to me. What I found is a delightful little detour that is well known to locals but far less so to riders from the north, such as me.

Far from being just a means to an end, I was pleased to discover a route that makes a worthy ride in itself, regardless of destination. I was treated to a ride through the forests of cedar and juniper in the mountains west of Cedar City, experienced the history of Iron Mountain and Mountain Meadows, found volcanoes I had no idea existed and thrilled to the beauty of brilliant red rock cliffs surrounding St. George.

Later, as I sat and pondered a name for this run, I happened to glance at a detailed atlas and noticed the label "Legacy Loop". Curious, I did a little digging. It seems that back in the mid-'90s, state senator Dixie Leavitt (father of then governor Mike Leavitt) sponsored and passed legislation to give this route special name designation. Apparently his intent was to increase travel and tourism by encouraging this route as an alternative to the freeway. Bearing in mind that the route is longer in both time and distance than I-15, you've really got to give the good Senator credit for thinking like a biker. I wonder if he rides.

We'll begin in Cedar City. This a good ride to segue from riding the Cedar Breaks Loop to touring St. George and Zion National Park.

Take SR 56 westbound out of town. It can be found on 200 N. or exit 59 off of I-15. The highway runs due west out of town along the railroad tracks then bends slightly to the south for a straight, flat seven mile run to the hills. Reaching the foot of the mountains the course remains fairly straight but the ride begins to climb into forests of juniper and cedar. The aroma of these trees combined with ample sage is quite pleasant, especially after a summer rain.

About fifteen miles from Cedar City you'll come to a cutoff to Old Iron Town State Park at Iron Mountain. This site contains the ruins of a mid-nineteenth century iron smelting operation and mining camp. The park lies about three miles off the highway on an unpaved hard-pack dirt road. This trail is passable on a heavy road bike and the short distance makes the historic site an accessible and worthwhile detour.

Charcoal Kiln at the Old Iron Town ruins

About ten years after the Iron Mission in Cedar City folded, Peter Shirts discovered the site that became Iron City. In 1868, the Great Western Iron Manufacturing Co. was organized by Ebenezer Hanks and the little operation was off and running. By 1870, the camp's population was nearly 100 and had a brick schoolhouse, a foundry, machine shop, pattern shop and a blacksmith. Their enterprise struggled, however, and by 1877 the company had shut down. In 1882 the operation was taken over by the Iron Manufacturing Company of Utah and the town site became known as "Little Pinto". That firm ultimately failed as well. Today, remarkably well-preserved remnants of the derelict smelter remain as silent witness to this venture.

After Iron Mountain, the road bends slightly northwest and drops into the Escalante Valley. At the edge of the valley lies the small town of Newcastle. Gas is available at the intersection of the highway and Main Street.

A straight, flat six mile run across Escalante Valley from Newcastle brings you to Beryl Junction, the intersection of SR 56 and SR 18. At the crossroads you might find a cold drink or a snack.

Section III: Southern Utah

Monument overlooking the Mountain Meadows Massacre site

At the junction, turn left (south) onto SR 18. This highway runs due south down the Escalante Valley through farm country. The farms along the roadside make great heat exchangers, seeming to cool the desert air as you ride by. Catching the mist from irrigation sprinklers is a refreshing treat on a hot summer day.

Racing down the valley, the road runs straight at the mountains as if on a collision course. Then at the base of the hills, it bends west towards the town of Enterprise. Gas, food and drink are available in town.

Climbing out of Enterprise, the highway begins a twisting run back into the mountains. About nine miles from town you'll come upon the Mountain Meadows Massacre site.

In August of 1857, a wagon train led by Alexander Fancher, comprised of Arkansas emigrants bound for California, arrived in Salt Lake City. Their timing could not have been more unfortunate. President Buchanan had recently dispatched a military expedition to Utah to put down a perceived rebellion. Utah governor Brigham Young responded by issuing a proclamation of martial law, which forbade people from traveling through Utah without a pass and discouraged Utah citizens from trading with outsiders.

Stone cairn marks the mass grave of Mountain Meadows Massacre victims

War hysteria filled the air. In need of re-supply before continuing their journey, the Fancher party was met with a cold shoulder from the Mormons, who typically greeted visitors with open arms and were usually eager to trade. Moving south without a pass and without the provisions they needed, contact with the local population became more abrasive on both sides. By the time the wagon train reached southern Utah, inflammatory accusations and innuendos by both factions had been wildly exaggerated and accepted as truth.

Pissed-off and hungry, the Fancher train moved west from Cedar City to Mountain Meadows, an established campsite on the old California Road, to rest for a few days. Here, on September 7th, 1857 they were attacked by a group of local Mormons (some masquerading as Indians) accompanied by a band of Piute Indians. A siege ensued, lasting for four days. On September 11th, Mormon militia leaders approached under a flag of truce and offered to escort the Fancher party safely to Cedar City if they would leave their weapons and wagons behind. Believing they were being rescued, the emigrants surrendered their arms and abandoned their property to the Mormons. One and a half miles from the siege site, the militia escort fell upon the helpless travelers and slaughtered one hundred and twenty men, women and children. Only seventeen children, too young to tell the tale, were spared. In a painful irony, a messenger arrived two days later with orders from Governor Young to allow the wagon train to pass unmolested. Some Arkansas partisans believe this order was issued *ex post facto* as part of a cover-up, yet many historians believe the order was genuine and was simply a case of bad timing.

Controversy and cover-up have persisted for over 150 years. Mistrust and hurt feelings linger on both sides to this day. This is undoubtedly the darkest and most painful moment in Utah's history. It is a story that must be told, openly and honestly, for the healing to become complete. Don't ride by without stopping here to investigate this incident and pay your respects.

About five miles past the Mountain Meadows site you'll see the cutoff to Central and Pine Valley. Several campgrounds lie down this road in the mountains east of Pine Valley.

Eleven miles south of Mountain Meadows you'll roll into the town of Veyo. The most striking feature of this little burg is the Veyo Volcano, a silent sentinel standing watch over town at the south end of Main Street. Veyo offers you a chance to pull over for gas, food or a much needed cold drink.

Rolling out of Veyo to the south you'll pass by the volcano for a closer look and climb up onto a plateau running south to Diamond Valley. You're in volcano country now; the one at Veyo is one of several extinct fire-breathers in a volcanic field that formed the surrounding landscape. Note the lava flows as you pass south through the community of Dammeron Valley. At the south end of this straightaway, near the edge of Diamond Valley you will come upon another volcano in the Santa Clara lava flow. This one and the one at Veyo are of the cinder cone variety. This second one has a particularly well defined crater at the top, is etched with vertical lines and is surrounded by jagged cinders and lava rocks. Close your eyes (no, wait...don't close your eyes if you're riding) and you can easily imagine this mountain blowing its top in a fiery explosion.

At the Diamond Valley volcano, the road bends west and almost knocks you off your bike with a bold view of brilliant white cliffs set against a backdrop of red rock mountains. Coming around a second sweeping curve to the south treats you to an expansive view of the Red Cliffs Desert Reserve. Lava from the nearby volcanoes once flowed through the gorge before you, helping to excavate and form this stunning landscape.

Here the highway gradually descends through a vista of brilliant colors into St. George. Near the top of this final stretch you'll pass the cutoff to Snow Canyon, a magnificent scenic road we'll explore in the next chapter. The bottom end of SR 18 deposits you on Bluff Street in the northwest corner of town, bringing an end to this run.

The Legacy Loop Highway is not only a wonderful detour from the monotony of the freeway between Cedar City and St. George, it is a great two-wheeled escape in its own right. The route even has a cool name but don't be surprised if few people know it. While this run has been officially designated as the Legacy Loop for nearly twenty years, only recently has the name appeared on UDOT's official highway map and have highway markers been placed. Most travelers still seem to be unfamiliar with the name. I guess it's up to bikers to spread the word.

Legacy Loop Highway – Notes

Pit Stops:

Cedar City:
Color Country Chevron
1100 W. 200 N. (SR 56)
(435) 586-6600

Freeway Sinclair
1495 W. 200 N. (SR 56)
(435) 586-1531

Newcastle:
Silver Peak Supply (C-store)
21 E. Hwy 56
(435) 439-5411

Enterprise:
Cottonwood Inn C-store (Sinclair)
855 E. Main
(435) 878-2603

Veyo:
Spanish Trail Supply (Sinclair)
21 S. Main (SR 18)
(435) 574-0808

St. George:
Fabulous Freddy's
806 N. Bluff St. (SR 18)
(435) 674-0109

Mira Monte Sinclair
386 N. Bluff St. (SR 18)
(435) 674-0012

Accommodations & Camping:

CAMPGROUNDS:
National Forest Campgrounds info: (877) 444-6777 or www.reserveusa.com.
Pine Valley Area Group sites – off SR 18

HOTELS:
Cedar City:
Quality Inn
250 N. 1100 W.
(435) 586-2082

Crystal Inn
1575 W. 200 N.
(435) 586-8888

St. George:
Lexington Hotel
850 S. Bluff St.
(435) 628-4235

Best Western Abbey Inn
1129 S. Bluff St.
(435) 652-1234

RECOMMENDED DINING:
Cedar City:
The Pizza Factory
131 S. Main
(435) 586-3900

St. George:
Jazzy Java Rock'n Roll Grill
285 N. Bluff St.
(435) 674-1678

The Pizza Factory
2 W. St George Blvd., #8
(435) 628-1234

Pancho & Lefty's
1050 S. Bluff St.
(435) 628-4772

Snow Canyon Loop

Riding Snow Canyon

Snow Canyon is a natural wonder of breathtaking beauty situated less than ten miles from St. George. For centuries people have marveled at this scenic treasure of sculpted sandstone cliffs, lava flows and vibrant color. Today, it is our good fortune that this canyon lies along a loop of paved highway, making it a delightfully quick riding getaway.

In addition to the spectacular scenery of Snow Canyon, this loop takes you through another amusing canyon run past Gunlock Reservoir. Best of all, the entire ride can be accomplished over a long lunch hour, as a quick after-work escape, or a short dinner ride.

Two state parks, multiple canyons, a river, reservoir, and a couple of volcanoes are a lot to cram into a quickie. But that's what makes this one so fun. Enjoy!

Snow Canyon Loop Route Map

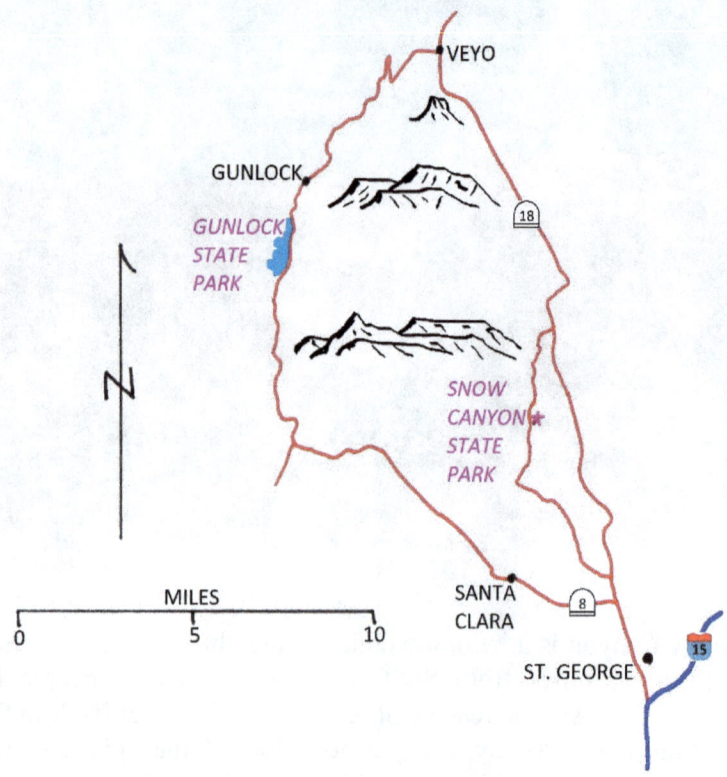

ROUTE: From St. George, take Bluff St. (SR 18) north to Sunset Blvd. (SR 8). Turn left (west) on Sunset Blvd. to Santa Clara. At the end of SR 8, take Old Highway 91 northwest out of town. At the road fork just past Shivwits, go right (north) towards Gunlock. Stay on this road to Veyo at the junction with SR 18. Turn right (south) on SR 18 to Snow Canyon State Park. Turn right on Snow Canyon Rd. and ride south through park. At south end of park, turn left (east) on Snow Canyon Parkway to Bluff St. (SR 18). Turn right on Bluff St. to St. George.

On the road...

There are a few places in Utah with that special combination of good roads, close proximity to an urban center, being arranged in a loop so that one may start and end in the same place without backtracking, ranging between 50 and 100 miles in length and endowed with scenic appeal or aggressive road characteristics or both. These loops are tailor made for the motorcycle enthusiast wishing to squeeze a quick ride into a busy schedule.

I affectionately call these rides "quickies". Be careful throwing the term around too loosely, though. I learned this lesson the first time I told my wife I was going out for a quickie. Since then, I always ask her if she would like to do a quickie. Regardless of how she responds, I win.

Snow Canyon Loop is a quickie and boy is it ever a good one! At just about 50 miles, it is the perfect distance to sneak away from work on a lunchtime ride, or to do in the evening before dinner.

Starting in St. George, take Bluff Street north to Sunset Blvd. At Sunset Blvd., turn left (west). This puts you on SR 8, westbound to Santa Clara. In Santa Clara, SR 8 ends, which is to say that state responsibility for the road ends. The road itself continues and about this point becomes Santa Clara Blvd. Stay on this road westbound out of town.

At the west edge of Santa Clara, you'll pass the Jacob Hamblin Home. Hamblin was a Utah pioneer of some note. Mormon missionary, Indian Agent, frontiersman and explorer, he figured prominently in the settlement and development of the area. This beautiful home, built for Jacob and his two wives in 1862, is a lovely and magnificently well-preserved example of nineteenth century pioneer architecture.

Just past the Hamblin Home, the road turns to the right (north) and becomes Old Highway 91. In spite of all the name changes, you're on the same ribbon of pavement that began with Sunset Blvd. Here the road runs flat and straight to the northwest away from the city, skirting the edge of Ivins on the way. On this stretch of rural highway you can see the brilliant red Santa Clara bench and the escarpments of the Red Mountains to the north. Rolling through this wide valley in early evening, the cliffs of the bench are almost aflame as the setting sun reflects off the red rock.

Less than five miles from Santa Clara, the road enters the Shivwits Indian Reservation and quickly joins alongside the Santa Clara River. As the road meets the river, both run through a dramatic rock gorge.

About a mile or so past this gorge, the road forks. To the left, Old Highway 91 runs over the Beaver Dam Mountains into Arizona. Take the right fork to the north towards Gunlock. The last time I rode this route, the road was not clearly marked. This may have changed since then, but it really matters little. You've only got two choices so there's a fifty-fifty chance you'll get it right. If you find yourself in Arizona, you chose wrong.

This local road runs along the Santa Clara River through a pleasant canyon. It's a fun bike road, with plenty of entertaining curves and hills, but a slow ride, due to poor road condition. The posted speed limit is 40 mph and this is really the practical limit as well. It's a shame this road is not in better shape, for it could support a higher practical speed on a motorcycle. Until the road is completely resurfaced to improve its poor condition (which may already be the case by the time you read this), I believe you too will find 40 to 50 mph to be the comfortable limit. Any faster is a real kidney bruiser.

A few miles past the fork you will come to Gunlock Reservoir and State Park. Gunlock Reservoir is a cute little lake tucked into the folds of the rock. Only about one and a half miles long and a half-mile wide, it nonetheless supports a wide variety of water recreation, from water-skiing to fishing.

Just past the reservoir, the road runs through the river bottoms, thick with trees and bushes. On this short stretch, the shade provides a cool green refuge from the heat. Suddenly, you'll spot a gravel quarry ahead that appears to sit in the middle of the road. The illusion is almost complete, as if the road has come to a rocky end, but as you proceed, the path veers around this obstacle and happily continues.

A little over a mile from the reservoir, you'll roll into the town of Gunlock. This is a quiet, peaceful little community with a rural mountain atmosphere – the kind of place where people wave as you pass, just because it seems the natural thing to do.

Outside Gunlock, the road continues to trace the Santa Clara River upstream and then quickly comes to a sharp switchback where it climbs up onto the bench. Here, you'll find yourself in the "suburbs" of Veyo. A short roll through the farms and ranches on the outskirts brings you into town, where the road becomes Center Street. This street runs to the east until it comes to a T-intersection with SR 18.

Gunlock Reservoir

At SR 18, turn right (south). Here, the road climbs out of town past the Veyo Volcano, one of several extinct cinder-cones in a volcanic field that helped shape the surrounding area as recently as the last 10,000 years.

Rounding the volcano, the road runs straight for five miles or so down a broad shallow valley on top of a plateau. This scenic stretch of road brings you back into the Red Mountains. Hints of red appear on the cliffs as you roll through a landscape of lava. At the south end of this stretch, the highway bends abruptly to the west at the base of another cinder-cone. This well-defined volcano looks much more recent than the Veyo cone, and may well be.

Curving through the lava flow at the base of this volcano, the highway suddenly presents a spectacular view of the white and red cliffs of Snow Canyon. Brilliant white rock cliffs and what appear to be petrified sand dunes are set against the backdrop of a bold red ridge. Quickly bending again to the south, the highway here opens into four broad lanes. This is a good thing, for the stunning change of scenery makes it hard to keep your eyes on the road.

Gradually descending into a valley of brilliant red cliffs, you'll marvel at the vivid color, especially at sunrise or sunset when low sun

Snow Canyon

angles set the mountains ablaze with light. About a mile past the cinder-cone, you will come upon the road into Snow Canyon State Park. Turn right here to ride through the park.

Used by Indians since pre-Columbian times, Snow Canyon was discovered by white settlers looking for lost cattle in the 1850s. I think it's fortunate that these disoriented bovines wandered here, but I've got to believe we would have found this place anyway, eventually. In more recent times, the canyon has been featured in Hollywood movies, like *Butch Cassidy and the Sundance Kid*, *Jeremiah Johnson*, and *The Electric Horseman*. The park gets its name, not from the weather, but from Lorenzo and Erastus Snow, prominent Utah pioneers.

Snow Canyon is the result of the deposition and concretion of quartzite sand over millions of years, scraped and carved by erosion, then reshaped by lava and further erosion. The majestic views in the park are truly inspiring. You'll witness a panoply of color in the sandstone sculpture, enhanced by the delicate dance of light and shadow. The park is a fee area, but well worth the price of admission. While I don't know if it is park policy, I have been allowed to pass free of charge after indicating my intent to simply ride through without stopping.

The road through the park is less than four miles and empties at the south end onto Snow Canyon Parkway near Ivins. Turn left on Snow Canyon Parkway to travel southeast back to SR 18.

At the south end of Snow Canyon Road and on Snow Canyon Parkway, you'll ride through several high-end residential developments filled with cookie cutter homes in a desert southwest motif, intended to blend in with the surrounding landscape. This, my friends, is the tragic result of yuppies with too much money. Sarcasm aside, the architecture is interesting and well executed.

At the intersection of Snow Canyon Parkway and SR 18, turn left (south) to return to St. George. SR 18 becomes Bluff Street in this area and deposits you back in the northwest corner of town where you began.

Now satisfied with a healthy dose of wind and sunshine, if you hustle you can be back where you're supposed to be before your boss or your spouse notices you've been missing. Snow Canyon loop is the quickie that never gets old. Don't be surprised to find yourself riding it every chance you get.

Snow Canyon Loop – Notes

Pit Stops:

St. George:
Chevron
927 W. Sunset Blvd. (SR 8)
(435) 628-6574

Mira Monte Sinclair
386 N. Bluff St. (SR 18)
(435) 674-0012

Santa Clara:
Snow Canyon Chevron
2275 W. Santa Clara Dr.
(435) 628-3778

Veyo:
Spanish Trail Supply (Sinclair)
21 S. Main (SR 18)
(435) 574-0808

Accommodations & Camping:

CAMPGROUNDS:
Utah State Parks Campgrounds info: (800) 322-3770 or www.stateparks.utah.gov .
Gunlock Reservoir & State Park – Gunlock
Snow Canyon State Park – St. George

HOTELS:
St. George:
Lexington Hotel
850 S. Bluff St.
(435) 628-4235

Best Western Abbey Inn
1129 S. Bluff St.
(435) 652-1234

RECOMMENDED DINING:
St. George:
Anasazi Steakhouse & Gallery
1234 W. Sunset Blvd.
(435) 674-0095

Pancho & Lefty's
1050 S. Bluff St.
(435) 628-4772

Zion Park Run – SR 9

Riders pause for group photo at Zion Nat'l Park

In 1880, geologist Charles E. Dutton wrote, "Nothing can exceed the wondrous beauty of Zion … in the nobility and beauty of the sculptures there is no comparison." Riding into Zion today, one might almost consider this an understatement. There is but one word that comes to mind upon seeing Zion Canyon for the first time – majesty. This is where Nature's throne resides, resplendent in all her grandeur.

SR 9 is a splendid route linking the St. George area with the US 89 corridor. Though short in length, this ride can take the better part of a day to complete. It's just hard to hurry. It will be, however, one of the most enjoyable days spent on a motorcycle that you could ever imagine.

So saddle up and we'll hop over the Hurricane Cliffs, trace the Virgin River upstream and leave you awestruck and speechless at Zion Canyon. Then we'll go through, not over the mountain to twist our way past the White Cliffs of the Grand Staircase and dash across a high plateau to Long Valley. This one is a real treat. Enjoy!

Zion Park Run – SR 9 Route Map

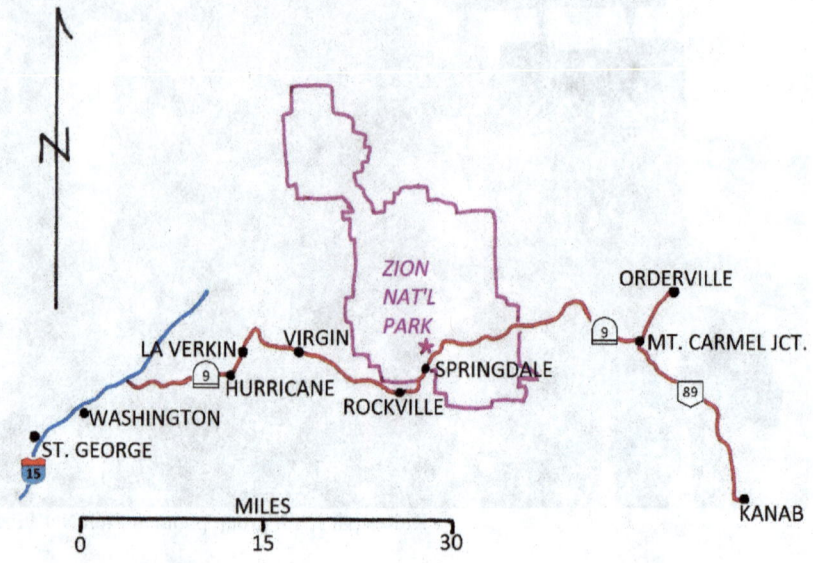

ROUTE: At exit 16 from I-15, take SR 9 eastbound to US 89 at Mt. Carmel Junction.

Section III: Southern Utah

On the road...

To Ancestral Puebloans, Piutes, Mormon pioneers and early explorers, Zion Canyon was no secret. Yet when reports of this marvel began to circulate widely at a time when southern Utah was still a rugged and remote mystery, many doubted such a place could be real. In 1909 Zion National Park was established, at once preserving this masterpiece while making it accessible to all. Today, no doubt can remain about its reality, yet it still must be seen to be believed.

And see it you will for this ride takes us right into the mouth of Zion Canyon and across the south end of the Zion National Park. SR 9 is a thoroughly enjoyable road from end to end, but it is nothing short of spectacular through the park. While this is a route you could dash across in a couple of hours, I can't imagine why anyone would. It's likely that you'll need to stop repeatedly upon swallowing a bug or two as you roll, mouth agape, through this grand display of nature at its finest.

We'll start at exit 16 off the I-15 freeway near St. George. This is the Hurricane exit just north of the town of Washington and it puts you on the beginning of SR 9. Go eastbound on SR 9 and you'll climb quickly through a saddle onto the Harrisburg Bench where you will cross the Virgin River and find a sweeping desert southwest landscape before you. Here, square mesas stand watch over a desert valley, calling to mind the rectangular landscape of Glen Canyon, though on a smaller and less colorful scale.

A straight, flat dash of seven miles through this desert valley brings you to the town of Hurricane. If you hail from outside southwest Utah, you may be tempted to pronounce this name as 'hərɪˌkeɪn. After even the briefest contact with the natives however, you will quickly learn that the correct pronunciation in the local dialect is 'hərˌkən. Now if you really want to have fun with this charming linguistic idiosyncrasy, ask a local what kind of tropical storm is common along the southern Atlantic coast in late summer and see how many tell you it's a 'hərɪˌkeɪn. This will leave you scratching your head. Either way you say it, all services can be found in Hurricane.

On the eastern edge of town the highway bends north at the junction with SR 59 and brings you almost without interruption to the town of La Verkin (rhymes with 'hərˌkən). Here too you will find most necessary services, with the exception of United Nations facilities. This charming little community voted to ban the UN a several years ago, courageously leading the charge against globalization. Hey, you've got to admire them for taking a stand.

On the north end of La Verkin, SR 9 makes a sharp right turn (east) at the junction with SR 17. Here the route climbs up the Hurricane Cliffs and begins another scenic canyon run, better than before. A bold panorama lies before you, where the Virgin River paints a swath of green down the middle of a broad desert canyon. Again the landscape calls to mind more famous landmarks. Could this be another Grand Canyon under construction? Check back in a couple of hundred million years to find out.

The road winds lazily, rising and falling, to bring you to the town of Virgin. Beyond, more of the same desert canyon run makes for a relaxing ride. The road here is broad and well maintained. Even heavy summertime tourist traffic won't be cause for stress.

About 10 miles beyond Virgin you'll come upon a lovely oasis in the desert called Rockville. This tiny locale flows almost seamlessly into the town of Springdale. Together they form an enchanting enclave of quiet homes in a pastoral green setting amidst the stark desert surroundings. Rockville is the smaller of the two, more of a quiet residential community. Springdale, which sits at the mouth of Zion Canyon, has the feel of a resort town, due to its proximity to Zion National Park.

Springdale offers a variety of food, lodging and gas. It's a good place to stop and fuel up or grab a bite to eat before beginning your tour of the park. You might also consider leaving your ride in town and catching the free park shuttle which takes you all the way up Zion Canyon. You can also catch the shuttle inside the park at the visitor center. This is the only available transportation on the Zion Canyon Scenic Drive.

The entrance to Zion National Park lies on the north edge of Springdale. Here you'll get your first look at the towering monoliths forming the walls of the Zion Canyon. Upon entering the park, you'll find the visitor center just inside the gate. This facility is a first class affair, just as one might expect from the National Park Service. Stop in for information about the park and, while there, check out their innovative cooling system. Large openings that look like fireplaces lead to wide chimneys, drawing hot air from the building. Inside, a pleasantly cool temperature, that you would swear was artificial, provides welcome refuge from the summer heat.

The Three Patriarchs - Zion Canyon

Here at the visitor's center you have a decision to make. If you wish to see Zion Canyon, the park's centerpiece, you must leave your bike behind and jump on one of the free park shuttles. As indicated above, this is the only available means to travel Zion Canyon Scenic Drive. Due to traffic and parking problems, this road is closed to private vehicles from April to October. The shuttle makes nine stops in the canyon and the round trip will take a minimum of 90 minutes. Two hours is a more practical average for planning purposes. This trip is well worth the time spent and I highly recommend it. You can park and catch the shuttle at the visitor center or back in Springdale. The visitor center parking lot is generally packed by mid-morning, making Springdale an attractive alternative. Of course, on a motorcycle it is much easier to find a place to park creatively than it is for those unenlightened travelers silly enough to have brought their automobiles.

The Zion Canyon shuttle will take you to Zion Museum, with interpretive displays on the park's geology and history. Other stops include Court of the Patriarchs where you can view the mountain peaks known as the Three Patriarchs and the Zion Lodge, with food, lodging and a gift shop. At Zion Lodge you can take a footpath to the

The Great Arch

Emerald Pools or The Grotto Trail, which leads to the next shuttle stop with the same name. At the Weeping Rock you will witness runoff from the rain and snow on the plateaus above seeping from the porous rock wall of the canyon. At the top of the shuttle route, the Temple of Sinawava is a wide amphitheater enclosed by towering vertical rock walls. Here, another footpath leads deeper into the canyon to The Narrows.

After touring the canyon and recovering your bike, proceed north from the visitor's center about a mile and a half to the point where SR 9 separates from the Zion Canyon road. Here, you'll turn to the east for a short, but amusing frolic over a wonderfully twisty road to the park's East Gate. The scenery you'll encounter along the way is nothing short of spectacular.

From the canyon floor, the road quickly begins a steep climb, traversing the mountain through a series of tight switchbacks. The road here is shaped like a couple of giant paperclips laid end to end. Climbing through the curves, you'll be treated to a series of panoramic views of the canyon. Along the way you will find The Great Arch, still under construction, taking shape in the red rock wall. This is another feature that you'll have to check back on in a hundred million years or so to see how it turns out. The ride up the canyon is dazzling and there

Vent hole for the Zion-Mt. Carmel tunnel cut into the sheer rock wall

are several turnouts at which you can stop to examine the unbelievable scenery.

At the top of the climb you'll come to a fun engineering marvel, the Zion/Mt. Carmel tunnel. This hole in the mountain is over a mile long and connects the canyon highway with the high plateau to the east. The longest tunnel in the US at the time, it was considered an almost impossible feat when it was completed in 1930 and is still fairly impressive today. Here, you must be prepared to stop and wait your turn to pass through the tunnel. While the road looks like it will easily support two-way traffic, the NPS limits the flow to one-way at a time. I find this gives the trip an almost amusement park quality as you wait in line for your favorite ride. Running the tunnel on a motorcycle is great fun. The acoustics inside are great and the urge to rev your engine is irresistible.

The other side of the tunnel deposits you into a strikingly different landscape from that through which you just passed. Here you will find yourself amidst the time worn sandstone, the countryside painted with desert pastels of white, pink and orange. This stretch of road is literally chiseled into the "slickrock" and leads you through colorful vistas on a playfully twisty romp across the high plateau. As the highway beckons you to give chase, Nature invites you to stop and admire her handiwork with a display of fascinating shapes carved from the rock.

Riders pause to enjoy the stunning view outside the west end of the tunnel

Just before the park's East Gate, the ride brings you to Checkerboard Mesa, a mount of buff-colored sandstone etched with a fascinating pattern of crisscross grooves. The roadside turnout here is the last before exiting the park.

Shortly after passing through the park's East Gate you'll come upon a roadside trading post where you can find gas and refreshment. Beyond, the highway stretches across an open plateau of forests and meadows in a relatively straight, flat run that invites you to open the throttle to tease the wind. If you look carefully, you may notice that you are riding on top of the White Cliffs, one of the formations that make up The Grand Staircase. The ride becomes mildly twisty as the highway bends to the southeast and drops gently to US 89 at Mt. Carmel Junction.

At the highway junction, facilities for gas, food and lodging mark a comfortable end to the ride. To the left (north), US 89 winds through Long Valley up to Panguitch and Bryce Canyon National Park. Turning right (south) takes you over the Sand Hills and through a delightful red canyon to the town of Kanab, beyond which lies the North Rim of the Grand Canyon in Arizona.

If you took the time to tour Zion Canyon, this little joyride has taken up most of your day and left you with a camera full of stunning images, a treasure of motorcycling memories and a broad grin plastered across your face. A hundred years ago, people were incredulous that such a place existed. Today, it is incredible that so many rides such as this abound throughout southern Utah. Well, believe it, for down here it seems that the next mile is always better than the last.

Zion Park Run – Notes

Pit Stops:

St. George:
Conoco
995 E. St George Blvd (exit 8, I-15)
(435) 673-4316

Hurricane:
Quail Lake Quick Stop (Chevron)
4390 W. State (SR 9)
(435) 635-2243

Zion Food Mart (Shell)
309 State (SR 9)
(435) 635-9034

La Verkin:
Maverik
460 N. State (SR 9)
(435) 635-4658

Springdale:
Chevron
1593 Zion Park Blvd. (SR 9)
(435) 772-3677

Mt. Carmel Junction:
Shell
Jct. SR 9 & US 89
(435) 648-2326

Accommodations & Camping:

CAMPGROUNDS:
National Park Campgrounds / Zion Nat'l Park
info: (435) 772-3256 or www.nps.gov/zion .

HOTELS:
St. George:
Ramada Inn
1440 E. St George Blvd.
(435) 628-2828

Hampton Inn
53 N. River Rd.
(435) 652-1200

Hurricane:
Comfort Inn
43 N. 2600 W.
(435) 635-3500

Days Inn
40 N. 2600 W.
(435) 635-0500

Springdale:
Best Western Zion Park Inn
1215 Zion Park Blvd. (SR 9)
(435) 772-3200

Bumbleberry Inn
97 Bumbleberry Lane
(435) 772-3224

Quality Inn
479 Zion Park Blvd. (SR 9)
(435) 772-3237

Zion Nat'l Park:
Zion Lodge
1 Zion Canyon Scenic Dr.
(435) 772-7700

Mount Carmel Junction:
Best Western
Jct. SR 9 & US 89
(435) 648-2203

RECOMMENDED DINING:

St. George:
Jimmy John's
42 S. River Rd., #11
(435) 656-3900

Hurricane:
Lupitas Mexican Food
70 E. State (SR 9)
(435) 635-0206

Springdale:
Bit & Spur Saloon
1212 Zion Park Blvd. (SR 9)
(435) 772-3498

Whiptail Grill
445 Zion Park Blvd. (SR 9)
(435) 772-0283

Spotted Dog Café
428 Zion Park Blvd. (SR 9)
(435) 772-0700

Oscar's Café
948 Zion Park Blvd.
(435) 772-3232
cafeoscars.com

Riding Safe

Don't assume that you are visible to other motorists on the road; in fact, assume the opposite and make your presence known.

- Make yourself visible. Consider choosing bright clothing, even a florescent vest. Consider reflective gear, especially at night.

- Make your bike visible. Always ride with your headlight on and use high beams rather than low beams. Consider a modulating headlight – Utah allows them!

- Ride where you can be seen. Avoid the blind spot on other vehicles. Use lane positioning to your advantage and provide sufficient space for emergency braking or avoidance maneuvers. Never share a lane with a car.

- Clearly signal your intentions to other motorists. Never change lanes without looking over your shoulder – don't rely solely on your mirrors.

- Make liberal use of your horn (without being obnoxious).

Risky situations to be aware of:

- Cars making left turns in front of you. This is the number one cause of car – motorcycle crashes. Be prepared to react when you see an oncoming car signaling a left hand turn.

- Riding in a driver's blind spot. Drivers may fail to adequately check blind spots before turning or changing lanes.

- Hazardous road conditions, such as potholes, wet leaves, sand and gravel, railroad tracks or road obstructions. Be aware that these things may dictate maneuvers or actions on your part that other drivers may not anticipate.

- Obstructed line of sight. Large vehicles, forward visible road horizon or curves may conceal obstacles.

Be seen, be aware and be safe.

Escalante Run – SR 12
"All-American Road"

Riders on SR 12 near Escalante

With so many magnificent motorcycle roads in Utah, it's easy to run out of superlatives to describe them. It's quite difficult, on the other hand, to pick the single best. You can be certain, though, that SR 12 is always on the short list when riders discuss the absolute best roads in Utah.

"All-American Roads" are scenic byways that are so unique, so exceptional, that they qualify as a destination unto themselves. SR 12 has received this designation from the Federal Highway Administration, identifying it among the top scenic drives in the United States. *Car & Driver* rates it as one of the top ten drives in the nation.

SR 12 runs 124 miles across such a grand diversity of terrain that it defies description. You'll ride through the brilliant colors of Red Canyon, over the top of the Paunsaugunt Plateau and roll through Bryce Canyon country to skirt the north edge of the Grand Staircase-Escalante National Monument, then cross a high narrow ridge called the Hogback before climbing over Boulder Mountain into the colorful Fremont River basin.

Maybe there are no superlatives adequate to describe this run. Enjoy!

Escalante Run – SR 12 Route Map

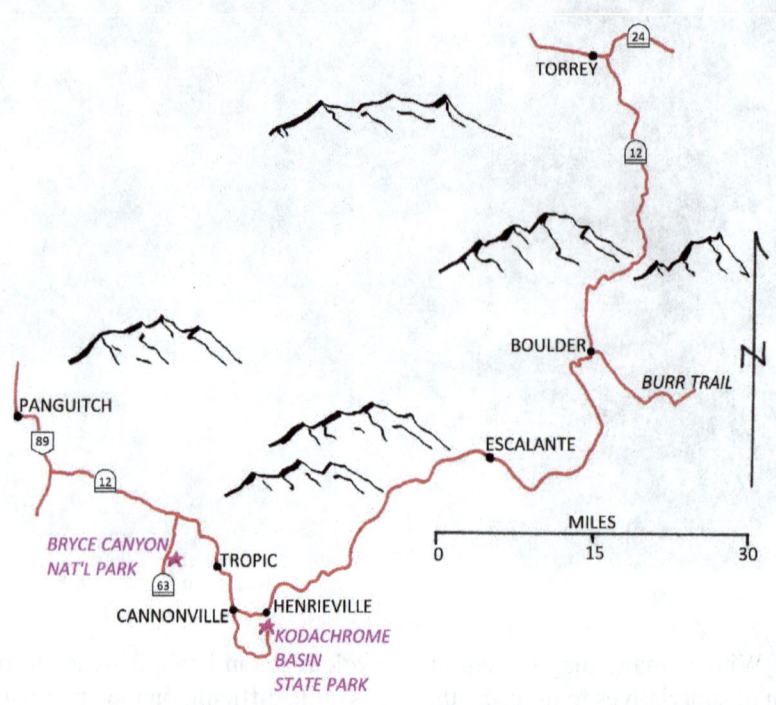

ROUTE: From the junction of US 89 & SR 12 seven miles south of Panguitch, take SR 12 eastbound to the junction with SR 24 in Torrey.

On the road...

Garfield County, in the heart of southern Utah, contains some of the best riding opportunities in the state, and by extension, the entire country. Seven highways crisscross the county, six of which are featured in this book. Two national parks, three state parks, America's largest national monument and a national recreation area are found within its borders. If that weren't enough for the haggard urban refugee seeking escape, the county's tourism website boasts that Garfield contains less than one person per square mile, no stoplights and only one attorney! (www.brycecanyoncountry.com)

From the rider's perspective, the crown jewel of Garfield County is undoubtedly SR 12. In a region full of overwhelming scenic beauty, this is a road you can really sink your teeth into.

We'll examine this run from west to east. Our ride begins at the junction of SR 12 with US 89 just seven miles south of Panguitch and eight miles north of Hatch. As you head eastbound on SR 12 from the junction, you'll ride past a cluster of motels, eateries and a trading post. If you didn't gas up in Panguitch or Hatch, this is a good opportunity to top off the tank or grab something to eat. Keeping the tank full is not a worry on this ride, however. Gas, food and refreshment are plentiful along the entire route.

Only a short distance into the ride, you'll come to the mouth of Red Canyon You'll quickly see that it didn't take much imagination to come up with this name. The cliffs in the canyon are bright vermilion, shaped by the forces of erosion and draped with a blanket of evergreen forest – a real scenic treat. A visitor center near the mouth of the canyon offers insight into the geology and history of the canyon, as well as travel info for the surrounding area. The road through Red Canyon is pleasantly twisty but slow. Speed limits range from 35 to 50 mph and summertime automobile traffic can be heavy. Sit back and enjoy the splendid colors. You'll soon have the opportunity to get around any vehicles slowing your progress when you come out of the top of the canyon. From there on the road is wide open and traffic is a minor consideration.

Red Canyon is a short run and the road quickly climbs out of the eastern end onto the Paunsaugunt Plateau, where it summits at over 7,600 feet. Here you'll find yourself on a straight dash across the top of the plateau. The terrain is wide open and the highway flat and straight. This is where you give your mount the spurs and put those

Red Canyon

timid souls in their four-wheeled cages behind you. Gas, food and refreshments are available on this stretch near the highway summit.

A short five miles or so from the eastern mouth of Red Canyon brings you to Ruby's Junction at SR 63. This is the road to Bryce Canyon National Park. Gas, food and lodging are available at Ruby's Junction and the park entrance lies just three miles south of SR 12 on SR 63.

Bryce Canyon is one of the best scenic treasures along the Escalante Run. Pink, red and orange spires fill grand amphitheaters carved out of the sandstone. Viewpoints along the canyon's forested rim present spectacular views and the park's visitor center holds a wealth of information on this fascinating geology. A detour into the park is time well spent.

Back on SR 12, the road twists through a colorful sculpted canyon as it moves east from SR 63. The landscape looks much like that of Bryce Canyon, no coincidence since this stretch of road through the Pink Cliffs is within the park boundary. Coming out of the canyon, the highway drops you into Tropic Valley and the community of Tropic, where basic services are available.

Section III: Southern Utah

Kodachrome Basin

Beyond Tropic the road carries you south along the Paria River, winding gently into another tiny town called Cannonville. Gas, food and lodging are likewise available here. This point in the ride offers another scenic detour as well. Turning south at the road junction takes you on a short side trip to Kodachrome Basin State Park. A BLM visitor center can be found about a block south of the highway with more info on the area.

Kodachrome Basin gets its name from a 1948 expedition by the *National Geographic Society* (featured in the September 1948 issue of *National Geographic Magazine*) to explore the area. Impressed by the vivid colors of the spires, arches and sandstone chimneys they found, these explorers named the site for the new color film they used to record their expedition. The Kodak Corp. later graciously consented to lend the name to Utah for the state park. Kodachrome Basin lies just seven miles off of SR 12 on a paved road. Camping and lodging are available within the park and guided horseback or stagecoach rides allow you to park your bike and visit the more remote and scenic areas. Call Trail Head Station at (435) 679-8787 to schedule a trip.

Powell Point

Back on SR 12, a short hop east brings you to Henrieville, the third tiny community in rapid sequence east of Bryce Canyon National Park. Henrieville too has basic services: gas, food, liquid refreshment and shelter.

After Henrieville, the road bends to the north and climbs into an enjoyable mountain canyon while taking you within the borders of the Grand Staircase–Escalante National Monument. Grand rock cliffs of tan and gray enclose the route, and a swath of green lines the canyon floor as the road winds its way up to Powell Point overlook.

Powell Point is a historic geographic reference and survey point, its unmistakable profile making it ideal as such. This rock is named for explorer John Wesley Powell and sits atop a stratum of steel-gray escarpments, called The Blues.

From Powell Point, the road drops down into the open ranch country of Upper Valley and traces Upper Valley Creek up to the Escalante River. Here, you'll roll into the town of Escalante, named for Franciscan priest Silvestre Velez de Escalante who led the first recorded exploration of southern Utah in 1776. Of course, having failed to familiarize himself with the (yet to be devised) doctrine of Manifest Destiny, he had the ridiculous idea that he was in Mexico at

Section III: Southern Utah

Riding the twisties below Head of Rocks Overlook

the time. Like the other outposts on this trek, all services are available in this desert burg. Escalante marks roughly the midpoint of the ride, making it a well-placed rest stop for gas or a cold drink.

A mile and a half west of Escalante (just before you roll into town), look for Escalante State Park. Colorful petrified wood and dinosaur bones are found within the park, which lies on the shore of Wide Hollow Reservoir.

Moving east from Escalante, you'll cross Big Flat and come around a corner to a stunning view that will virtually knock you out of your saddle. This is Head-of-Rocks Overlook, a must-stop viewpoint overlooking the northern tip of the largest national monument in the United States.

The Grand Staircase–Escalante National Monument is a colossal reserve that is comprised of three discrete regions. The Grand Staircase, a great geologic ladder, has five distinct steps, each with its own unique ecosystem ranging from Sonoran desert to evergreen forests. These steps begin in the Grand Canyon and are comprised of the Chocolate, Vermilion, White, Gray, and Pink Cliffs. The middle region is a wedge shaped zone formed by the Kaiparowits Plateau, bordered by The Cockscomb in the west and the Straight Cliffs of the

Fifty Mile Mountains in the east. The third region to the northeast is known as The Canyons of the Escalante, characterized by the gorges cut in sandstone by the Escalante River. Between Tropic and Escalante, you skirted the northern boundary of the Kaiparowits region. Between Escalante and Boulder, you'll be riding through the third region, the Escalante Canyons region.

Below Head-of-Rocks Overlook the road bends like a giant pretzel. Gazing down at the road through the valley below, you'll undoubtedly feel eager anticipation at hitting its twists and turns. In the height of the season, mid to late summer, you will likely be able to watch several sets of riders wind through the curves while you take in the view from the overlook.

After running the pretzel below the overlook, you'll come into red-rock country. About three miles up the highway is another roadside turnout called Boynton Lookout. This viewpoint overlooks Phipps-Death Hollow, named for Washington Phipps. There's an interesting story here, as well. It seems that Phipps and John F. Boynton were partners in a rather successful horse enterprise. They used the hollow you see below to corral and graze their animals. One night, however, the two found themselves in a dispute over the affections of a young lady. Boynton ended up shooting Phipps dead. The next morning, racked with guilt, he turned himself in to the authorities in Escalante. They gave him $10 and instructed him to ride to Parowan, the county seat at the time, for trial. Boynton took the cash and – big surprise – disappeared, never to be seen or heard from again. I'm told that law enforcement in Garfield County is considerably tighter today.

Below Boynton Lookout the road takes you through a beautiful red-rock canyon carved by the Escalante River. The landscape here looks strikingly like the Moab area and the road is somewhat reminiscent of SR 128 along the Colorado River. After a short, twisty run along Calf Creek through the canyon, the road climbs up to Haymaker Bench.

From here you'll cross a narrow ridge called The Hogback, where the terrain drops off steeply on both sides of the road. You'll be treated to bold views of the deep sandstone ravines below. Another roadside turnout here allows you to examine this dynamic landscape.

After crossing The Hogback you'll ride over a slightly broader bench before dropping down into the town of Boulder. This is a quaint little community where you will find all basic services, as well as one of my personal favorite rest stops, The Burr Trail Grill. If it's time to

Section III: Southern Utah

The Burr Trail Grill - a favorite of bikers of all persuasions

take a break, treat yourself to lunch at this charming café found at the junction of the highway and the Burr Trail. The food is great and the atmosphere is friendly and relaxing.

Speaking of the Burr Trail, this short spur of paved road is one worthy of exploration before you leave Boulder. Many riders I know like to take a detour from SR 12 to ride this historic trail before continuing on. While the pavement ends about 28 miles from Boulder, making it a short in-and-out affair, the road will take you on a marvelously scenic run across the top of the Escalante National Monument to the Waterpocket Fold at the edge of Capitol Reef National Park.

Also while in Boulder, you may want to take a look at Anasazi State Park & Museum. Here you'll find one of the largest ancient Puebloan villages west of the Colorado River. The village is partially excavated and the museum contains many prehistoric artifacts uncovered there.

Leaving Boulder you'll ride SR 12 north, beginning a climb of almost 3,000 feet over Boulder Mountain. Outside of town, the landscape begins to shift in a gradual but dramatic change. You'll cross a broad, open plateau as you leave the arid heat of the desert behind and climb into the cool green of the Dixie National Forest. Here, you'll enjoy a twisty mountain run of over 20 miles through cool forests of evergreen and aspen, much like riding the mountains of northern Utah. Occasionally, the road opens up at overlooks offering sweeping vistas of the surrounding landscape. Before coming to the highway summit at 9,400 feet, you'll find Homestead Overlook and Steep Creek Overlook where you can examine the Escalante behind you and gaze across the landscape you saw at Head-of-Rocks Overlook from the opposite perspective. On the north side of the summit you'll find Larb Hollow Overlook, as well as several other nameless turnouts where you can look across the mountain landscape to the east and glimpse the rugged terrain within Capitol Reef National Park beyond. Each of these turnouts offers spectacular views, all worth stopping to enjoy.

A note of caution about Boulder Mountain: the road travels through open range. Take note of warning signs, such as highway markers and manure on the pavement. I have often encountered livestock on the road and on a recent ride, found a surprising number of deer on or immediately beside the highway.

After a moderately steep descent from the north side of the summit which, by the way, is a thoroughly amusing and twisty romp, the road begins to level off to a gently winding roll through ranch country. Soon the red cliffs near Torrey come into view, signaling the end of the ride.

SR 12 lopes out of the ranch land and hay farms from the south to join with SR 24 on the east end of Torrey. At the highway junction, you'll find gas, food, lodging and travel info. To the left (west) lies the main part of town, with more food and lodging. Going right (east) takes you to Capitol Reef and more great riding beyond.

Upon completing the Escalante Run, you'll no doubt agree that this has been a spectacular ride, certainly among the best in Utah. This route has all the requisite ingredients for a perfect ride: outstanding road character; ideal length; diverse geography; overwhelming scenic beauty; plenty of services, excellent recreational destinations, and perfect location linking Utah's magnificent national parks. Makes you glad you ride a motorcycle, doesn't it?

Escalante Run – Notes

Pit Stops:

Panguitch:
Leland's Chevron
10 E. Center
(435) 676-2718

Owens Travel Center
455 E. Center
(435) 676-8986

Bryce Canyon:
Bryce Canyon Pines (Chevron)
Hwy 12, Milepost 10
(435) 834-5441

Ruby's General Store
26 S. Main
(435) 834-5341

Tropic:
Clarke's Country Market (Phillips 66)
141 N. Main St.
(435) 679-8383

Escalante:
Sinclair
85 W. Main
(435) 826-4257

Canyon Country Gas
Hwy 12
(435) 826-4259

Boulder:
Hills & Hollows (Sinclair)
Hwy 12
(435) 335-7349

Boulder Exchange
Hwy 12 (north)
(435) 826-4232

Torrey:
Phillips 66
Jct. Hwy 12 & Hwy 24
(435) 425-3302

Texaco
Jct. Hwy 12 & Hwy 24
(435) 425-3345

Accommodations & Camping:

CAMPGROUNDS:
National Forest Campgrounds info: (877) 444-6777 or www.reserveusa.com.
Red Canyon – SR 12
Oak Creek – SR 12 (Boulder)
Pleasant Creek – SR 12 (Boulder)
Single Tree – SR 12 (Boulder)

Nat'l Park Campgrounds/Bryce Canyon Nat'l Park info: (435) 834-5322 or www.nps.gov/brca

Utah State Parks Campgrounds info: (800) 322-3770 or www.stateparks.utah.gov .
Kodachrome Basin State Park – Cannonville
Escalante State Park - Escalante

Commercial Campgrounds

KOA
555 S. Main
Panguitch
(435) 676-2225

Bryce Pioneer Village
80 S. Main
Tropic
(435) 679-8546

KOA
250 Red Rock Dr.
Cannonville
(435) 679-8988

Canyons of Escalante
495 W. Main
Escalante
(435) 826-4959

HOTELS:
Panguitch:
New Western
180 E. Center St. (US 89)
(435) 676-8876

Bryce Canyon Western Resort
3800 US 89
(435) 676-8770

Harold's Place
3090 Hwy 12
(435) 676-8886

Bryce Canyon:
Bryce Canyon Pines
Mile 10, Hwy 12
(800) 892-7923

Best Western Ruby's Inn
26 S. Main St.
(435) 834-5341

Tropic:
America's Best Value Inn
200 N. Main (SR 12)
(435) 679-8811

Bryce Canyon Inn
21 N. Main (SR 12)
(435) 679-8502

Cannonville:
Grand Staircase Inn
105 N. Kodachrome Dr.
(435) 679-8400

Escalante:
Circle D Motel
475 W. Main
(435) 826-4297

Prospector Inn
380 W. Main
(435) 826-4653

Boulder:
Boulder Mtn. Lodge
20 N. Hwy 12
(435) 335-7460

Torrey:
Days Inn
825 E. Hwy 24
(435) 425-3111

Best Western Capitol Reef Resort
2600 E. Hwy 24
(435) 425-3761

RECOMMENDED DINING:

Panguitch:
Flying M Restaurant
614 N. Main
(435) 676-8008

Cowboy's Smokehouse
95 N. Main
(435) 676-8030

Harold's Place
3066 E Hwy 12
(435) 676-2350

Bryce Canyon:
Cowboy's Buffet & Steak Room
26 S. Main St.
(435) 834-5342

Foster's Steak House
Hwy 12
(435) 834-5227

Tropic:
Clarke's Restaurant
141 N. Main (SR 12)
(435) 679-8383

Escalante:
Cowboy Blues
530 W. Main
(435) 826-4577

Boulder:
Hell's Backbone Grill
20 Hwy 12
(435) 335-7464

Burr Trail Grill
10 Hwy 12
(435) 335-7511

Torrey:
The Rim Rock Restaurant
2523 E. Hwy 24
(435) 425-3388

Broken Spur Inn & Steakhouse
955 Hwy 24
(435) 425-3775

Black Canyon to Bryce
"The Road Less Traveled"

Cabin ruin in Black Canyon

Motorcycle touring is, of course, about the trip itself. Motorcyclists care little for efficiency in travel, in fact they shun it. Finding the interesting route is more important than getting there quickly. If you agree, then this ride is exactly what you're looking for. Here, you'll roll across wide open prairie through tiny backwater towns and pass via an obscure canyon trail to race the length of Johns Valley down to color country and the spectacle of Bryce Canyon National Park.

Wandering through central Utah one day with no destination in mind, I stumbled upon this route. I knew it was there but had never ridden it. Before giving much thought to where I was going, I found myself at Bryce Canyon and realized I had not encountered another vehicle on the road, of any sort, for almost 100 miles. Suddenly the last stanza of Robert Frost's poem came to mind. Was this route symbolic of Frost's poetic metaphor, the road less traveled by?

Of course not, I thought, laughing at myself. Don't be ridiculous! It's just a fun ride. Enjoy!

Black Canyon to Bryce Route Map

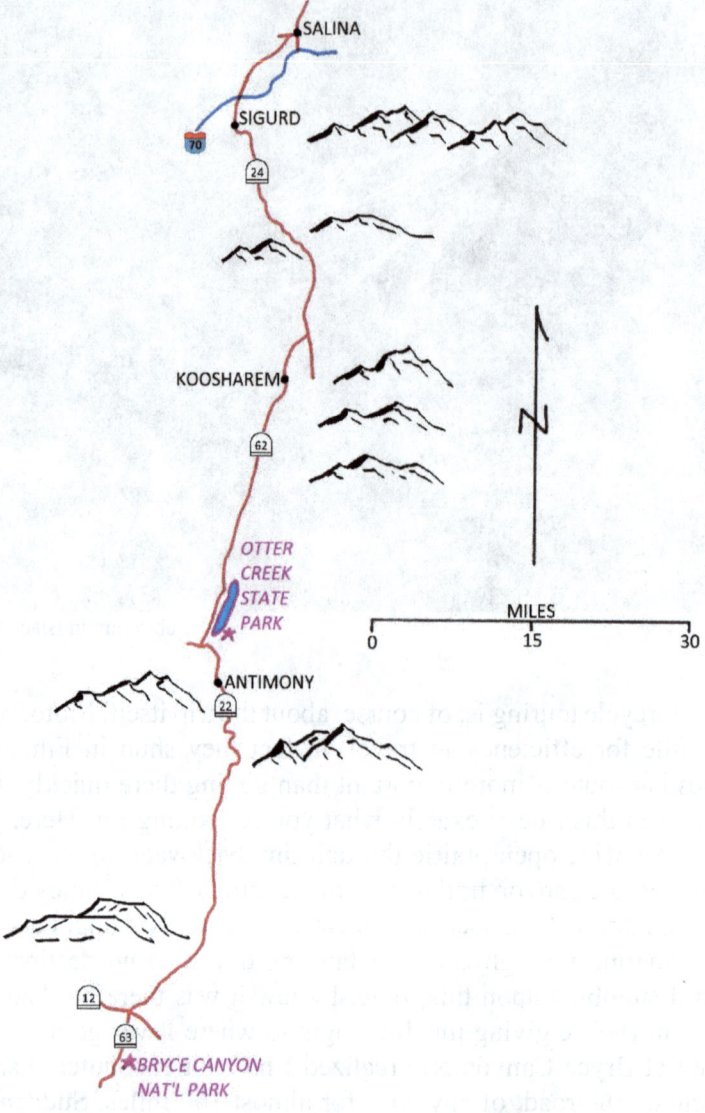

ROUTE: From Salina, take SR 24 southbound to the junction with SR 62. Take SR 62 southbound to the junction with SR 22 at Otter Creek Reservoir. Take SR 22 southbound to the junction with SR 12 and SR 63 – Ruby's Junction. Take SR 63 south to Bryce Canyon National Park.

Section III: Southern Utah

On the road...

What do you look for when you plan a ride? Certainly, many factors influence which route you choose. Sometimes it's the fastest route you're after, which, we all know, is not necessarily the shortest route. Sometimes the most developed route is important, which isn't always the most direct. Sometimes, you just want to go out of the way, which doesn't have to mean literally going out of the way.

This ride illustrates what I'm talking about. Let's take a scoot to Bryce Canyon from up north. Look at a map and you'll see that this route runs the shortest distance and appears to be the most direct. It is also apparent that this is probably the slowest and certainly the least developed route, taking you through the fewest vestiges of civilization. It literally takes you out of the way by going in a straight line. Appealing, isn't it?

We'll start in Salina because its central location makes a good launch point. Take SR 24 south from town, which can be found splitting off from US 50 a few blocks west of the US 50/US 89 junction in the center of town. The first several miles of SR 24 parallel I-70 to the southwest. This stretch is a flat, straight affair that takes you through the rural communities between Salina and Richfield. About halfway to Richfield, SR 24 turns sharply to the south at the junction with SR 118. Turn left (south) at this junction.

Here the road rolls through more rural countryside, passing the communities of Vermillion and Sigurd. South of Sigurd, the route bends abruptly to climb into the Rainbow Hills. Layers of soft pink and gray line the slopes.

Past the Rainbow Hills, the highway presents an agreeably twisting ride as it winds through Kings Meadow Canyon. The pavement is in great shape here and the road is well laid out, making the canyon a stretch to have some fun. Ten miles of gentle *twisties* bring you to where the road drops out of the hills and bends down into Plateau Valley.

Rolling south through the valley you'll find a wide-open landscape of meadow and sage. The highway is broad, straight and flat with seemingly unlimited visibility. This stretch beckons you to open up the throttle, perhaps getting around any traffic you've come upon, to make a speed run past Koosharem Reservoir.

A couple miles south of the reservoir, you'll come to the junction with SR 62. Though well marked, this road junction can sneak up on you. Look for it on the right (west) side of the highway. Turn right onto SR 62 at this T-intersection.

SR 62 makes an unbending level run of over 30 miles down the length of Grass Valley. In June of 1873 Brigham Young sent a party, led by Albert Thurber, to explore Grass Valley for settlement. One of the party's objectives was to establish a peaceful relationship with the indigenous Indians. Traveling with the group was Chief Tabioona in the capacity of interpreter and diplomat. The group camped near Fish Lake on June 22, 1873 and in early July organized a summit with local chiefs. At this meeting, the chiefs made a pledge of peaceful co-existence to the settlers with a handshake. This vow of friendship was never broken.

About seven miles off of SR 24 you'll roll through the tiny community of Koosharem. This interesting name derives from an Indian word for an edible tuber that grows in the valley and once provided a food staple for the Indians. You can find food and refreshment in this small settlement, and even gas, but not high octane. If you started out with a full tank, fuel shouldn't be a worry on this ride.

Moving south from Koosharem, Grass Valley is a sweeping panorama of prairie, bound by the Parker Mountains to the east and the Sevier Plateau to the west. Through the middle runs Otter Creek. Not quite halfway down the valley you'll see signs indicating that you are passing through Greenwich, a community that makes Koosharem look like urban sprawl. Don't look for services here.

Near the bottom of the valley you'll ride past Otter Creek Reservoir. At capacity, this lake is over six miles long. With Otter Creek State Park at the southern end of the reservoir, the area is a popular summer recreation site.

Here, SR 62 comes to a T-intersection where it joins with SR 22. To the right (west), SR 62 continues through Kingston Canyon before coming to an end upon meeting US 89, between Junction and Circleville. To the left (east) SR 22 begins. Turn left onto SR 22 and follow the road as it bends south into Antimony.

Antimony, originally known as Coyote, is a charming community founded in 1873 as an agrarian settlement. In 1880, antimony (stibnite) was discovered in a nearby canyon and the town became a mining camp as well. In 1921, Coyote was renamed Antimony after the metal mined here. In town you can find basic services, such as gas (mid-grade), food and lodging.

Osiris Creamery in Black Canyon

South of Antimony, state maintenance of the highway ends and this rapidly becomes very apparent. Some maps even show this route as unpaved at the point where state responsibility ends and SR 22 becomes a local road. This is unfortunate, for it probably keeps some from riding what is in fact a good motorcycle route. While the road becomes narrow and lane markings disappear, the path is paved and entirely passable. This point actually marks the beginning of one of the ride's most enjoyable segments.

Coming out of town, the road winds into Black Canyon, twisting tightly back and forth through the rocks while it follows the East Fork of the Sevier River. This is a slow ride, the road becoming very narrow in spots with many blind curves. With no lane markings, no shoulder, and several rough spots, it's obvious that this trail doesn't enjoy a large maintenance budget, but its scenic value makes the ride worthwhile. Winding through the tight turns of the canyon, it's easy to imagine exploring this ravine on horseback more than a century ago. It's likely that little has changed in that time, other than the pavement beneath you.

Near the bottom end of Black Canyon you will come upon an interesting derelict structure that appears to be some sort of abandoned mining operation. This is actually an old creamery, and later a grain processing plant. The creamery and other nearby ruins mark what remains of Osiris, now a ghost town. This village was founded in the late 1920s by E.F. Holt, who built the creamery and a large summer house, which still remains, overlooking it.

Only a mile or so past Osiris, Black Canyon opens into Johns Valley, another broad prairie landscape, this one spotted with occasional groves of evergreen. The valley splits the Dixie National Forest and SR 22 splits the valley. To the west lie the bold cliffs of the Sevier Plateau, while the color of the Paunsaugunt Plateau is visible to the south. On the east, the valley is contained by the Black Ridge and the Escalante Mountains beyond. A long, wide-open and nearly unbending stretch of 26 miles lies before you. As you move further south through the valley, anticipation builds. The panoramic views ahead of you begin to hint that you are coming into color country. With growing excitement comes the temptation to grab some throttle and sprint headlong into the wind.

You're in the home stretch of the ride at this point and it's a speed run. The dash down Johns Valley makes up for time spent loitering in Black Canyon. The highway is well maintained here, with only a few bumps and some rough cattle guards, but nothing that stands in the way of a high-speed sprint. Be careful to keep an eye out for stock and wildlife.

At the bottom of Johns Valley, SR 22 meets SR 12 and SR 63 at a four-way intersection known as Ruby's Junction. Continue straight through the intersection and you leave SR 22 behind as you enter SR 63. This is the road into Bryce Canyon National Park, our destination.

Just south of the highway intersection you will find an array of services: plenty of gas, camping or lodging options and a variety of food. This commercial resort community, formerly known as Ruby's Inn, sits at the entrance to Bryce Canyon National Park on the old homestead of Reuben "Ruby" Syrett. In the summer of 2007, the community incorporated as Bryce Canyon City. Beyond, the road takes you into the park where you can spend hours, if you wish, exploring the fascinating geology of Bryce Canyon.

Bryce Canyon is Utah's second National Park, officially designated in 1928. Truly one of the world's greatest natural wonders, this grand amphitheater was scooped from the edge of the Paunsaugunt Plateau by the forces of erosion over millions of years. Wildly carved spires and pinnacles called hoodoos populate the bowl

Bryce Canyon Nat'l Park

like a great tribe of warriors cast in stone. Set against the Pink Cliffs, this colorful display of Nature's sculpture is breathtaking to behold. Gazing across the expanse of the canyon you will find that your imagination begins to define shapes, both fantastic and familiar, from the rock formations below.

The main park road runs for 18 miles along the ridge of the plateau and provides easy access to the park's main attractions. Just past the visitor center, Sunrise Point, Sunset Point, Inspiration Point and Bryce Point overlook Bryce Amphitheater. Farther into the park the road traces the Pink Cliffs to Rainbow Point, where it comes to an end. Along the way, several spectacular overlook sites give the opportunity to examine Bryce's beauty in detail. Riding the park can be a quick joyride or an extended study, depending on your mood at the moment. Either way, it's a must-do ride.

This brings us to the end of the road less traveled. Are there quicker ways to get to the attractions of southern Utah from the cities in the north? Of course there are. Are there any more enjoyable? You decide. The next time you come upon two roads diverging, I bet you take "the one less traveled by". Frost was right – it makes all the difference!

Black Canyon to Bryce – Notes

Pit Stops:

Salina:
Maverik
195 W. Main (US 50)
(435) 529-7990

Don's Sinclair
215 W. Main (US 50)
(435) 529-3531

Antimony:
Antimony Merc
70 N. Hwy 22
(435) 624-3253

Bryce Canyon:
Ruby's General Store
26 S. Main
(435) 834-5341

Accommodations & Camping:

CAMPGROUNDS:
National Park Campgrounds/Bryce Canyon Nat'l Park info: (435) 834-5322 or www.nps.gov/brca

Utah State Parks Campgrounds info: (800) 322-3770 or www.stateparks.utah.gov .
Otter Creek State Park - Antimony

Commercial Campgrounds
Antimony Merc Campground
70 N. Hwy 22
Antimony
(435) 624-3253

Ruby's Inn RV Park/Campground
300 S. Main
Bryce Canyon
(435) 834-5301

HOTELS:
Salina:
Econo Lodge
1225 S. State (US 89)
(435) 529-7455

Rodeway Inn
1400 S. State (US 89)
(435) 529-1300

Antimony:
Rockin' R Ranch
775 Hwy 22
(435) 624-3350

Bryce Canyon:
Best Western Ruby's Inn
26 S. Main St.
(435) 834-5341

RECOMMENDED DINING:
Salina:
Mom's Café
10 E. Main (US 50 & US 89)
(435) 529-3921

Bryce Canyon:
Cowboy's Buffet & Steak Room
26 S. Main St.
(435) 834-5342

Foster's Steak House
Hwy 12
(435) 834-5227

Mileage between Utah's National Parks

				Arches
			Bryce Canyon	270
		Canyonlands	327	66
	Capitol Reef	235	120	145
Zion	204	372	84	328

All Utah National Parks are open year round, 24 hours a day. Visitor centers and other facilities may close periodically and hours of operation vary. See *www.nps.gov* for current hours of operation.

Arches National Park
Visitor Center is open every day except Christmas Day.

Bryce Canyon National Park
Visitor Center is open every day except Thanksgiving Day, Christmas Day and New Year's Day.

Canyonlands National Park
Island in the Sky Visitor Center is open year round "except some winter holidays". Needles Visitor Center is open mid-February through November, except Thanksgiving Day.

Capitol Reef National Park
Visitor Center is open "daily except for some major holidays".

Zion National Park
Zion Canyon Visitor Center is open every day except Christmas Day. Kolob Canyons Visitor Center is open every day except Thanksgiving Day and Christmas Day.

Capitol Reef to Canyonlands

Riding through Capitol Reef Nat'l Park

Touring southern Utah's five great national parks is a motorcycling adventure par excellence. Sometimes I think that if I hadn't run out of gas money, I'd still be there.

This ride takes you through two of these magnificent gems on a scenic route that rivals SR 12 as one of the best roads in the nation. Along the way, Natural Bridges National Monument and Glen Canyon National Recreation Area add to the journey's marvel.

This run is a long one, not only in terms of distance, but also time. Plan on an early start, for a full day of riding thrills and sensory overload is ahead. You'll begin the day by watching the sunrise over the grand megaliths of Capitol Reef, then ride on across a stunning desert reminiscent of a lunar landscape. A dash through color country will bring you to cross the mighty Colorado River between the bold red rock walls of Glen Canyon. You'll then take a front row seat in the amphitheater of infinity as a time lapse of geologic history unfolds before you. Climbing over the Abajo Mountains, you'll ride like The Duke through the set of a John Ford western to chase the setting sun into Canyonlands. The end of the day will find you with an empty gas tank, a full camera, and a single word on your lips – WOW! Enjoy!

Capitol Reef to Canyonlands Route Map

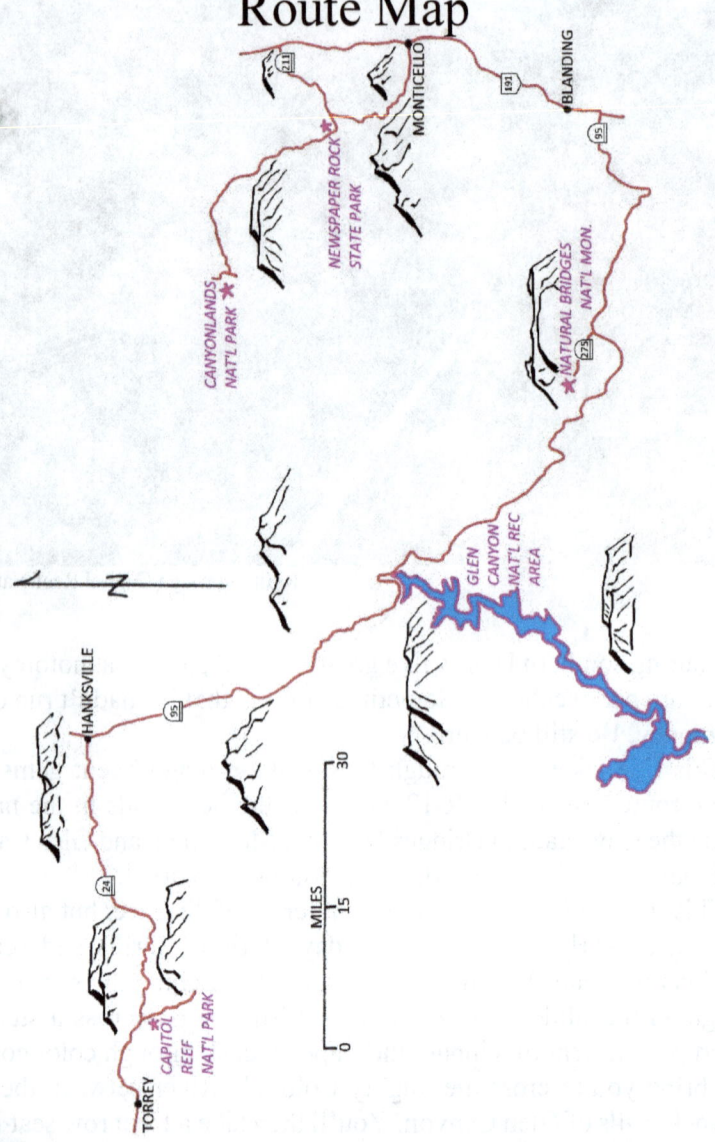

ROUTE: From Torrey, take SR 24 eastbound through Capitol Reef Nat'l Park to the junction with SR 95 in Hanksville. Take SR 95 south through Glen Canyon NRA. At SR 275, turn north to tour Natural Bridges Nat'l Monument. Continue eastbound on SR 95 to the junction with US 191 at Blanding. Take US 191 north to Monticello. At Monticello, take Rt. 2432 west to the junction with SR 211. Take SR 211 west to Canyonlands Nat'l Park.

On the road...

One could spend weeks touring southern Utah without risking boredom. The indescribable scenic beauty captures one's attention as the underlying stories of science and history begin to pry open the imagination and spark a child-like curiosity. Of course, on a motorcycle the urge to examine is tempered by the desire to keep moving.

Riding a bike on the scenic byways that link the region's national parks and monuments allows us to do both in a fashion unimaginable to tourists plodding the roads in their soulless mini-vans. Racing the wind, we get to experience the wonders we pass through, while satisfying the urge to remain in motion.

This is such a ride – an experience that can only be fully savored from the saddle. If you budget a full day, you'll have plenty of time to explore and examine the wonders you encounter and still have that comfortable stiffness in the seat of your pants that comes from a good long ride.

This trip links two of the five crown jewels that are Utah's national parks. We'll begin in Torrey, just west of Capitol Reef and end up in the southern part of Canyonlands, known as The Needles. Plan on an early start to give yourself plenty of flexibility.

Torrey is a neat little resort town on the edge of Capitol Reef National Park. It's a nice place to stay and makes a good base from which to tour the surrounding area. Getting there is fun too. From the north, take SR 24 out of Salina and you'll enjoy a scenic run along the red cliffs of the Fremont River. From the south or west, SR 12 is an unbeatable ride. Once there, you're sure to enjoy Torrey's warm hospitality, fine dining, and comfortable lodging.

Start the day with a full tank of gas and head east out of town on SR 24. As you pass the junction with SR 12 you'll go around a bend to the north and suddenly...POW! A grand panoramic view of brilliant color smacks you in the face. A broad red rock valley lies before you, across which the highway runs to the foot of Cooks Mesa and Meeks Mesa beyond. At the base of Meeks Mesa, the highway bends to the east again and takes you on a run of stunning color along the face of the cliffs.

Roughly five miles from Torrey you'll enter Capitol Reef National Park. This is the only national park in Utah without an entrance station. Rather than pay an entrance fee at the gate, as is common at other

Chimney Rock - Capitol Reef Nat'l Park

parks, you can pay any required fees or show your park pass at the visitor center, another six miles up the road.

Riding into the park you'll be treated to a series of unique rock formations carved from the red sandstone. Twin Rocks, Chimney Rock, and The Castle are each on the north side of the highway before the visitor's center. On the south side of the road you'll see the turnout to Panorama Point and Goose Necks overlook.

Eleven miles from Torrey you'll come to the visitor center on the south side of the highway. Turn right (south) here and you can take a short scenic spur into the park. This road winds through the Fruita Historic Area, an old Mormon pioneer settlement, where you'll find pioneer homes, a blacksmith shop and other period exhibits. Past Fruita, the road turns into a narrow paved trail that runs for about six and a half miles down to Capitol Gorge. At the head of the trail is a self-service fee station: $5 or a NP pass is required. Though narrow, the trail is very well maintained and winds through a spectacular landscape. This short detour treats you to a symphony of color as you ride through a dynamic painted desert to Capitol Gorge.

Back on SR 24, continue east from the visitor center. You'll quickly come to the historic Fruita schoolhouse, a quaint little one

Petroglyphs - Capitol Reef Nat'l Park

room school built in 1897 and used until 1941, after which time the school's students were bussed to Loa and Bicknell. Across the road from the school you'll see a pastoral setting of fruit orchards from which the town took its name. The NPS maintains these orchards today and sells the fruit to wayward bikers and others looking for a refreshing treat. Munching on a fresh apple while relaxing in this peaceful retreat, with the tiny schoolhouse, the orchards and the Fremont River flowing through a cool green oasis in the narrow rock canyon, one cannot help but be struck by what a lovely place Fruita must have been a hundred years ago. The pioneers who settled here sure got it right.

Not far beyond the school, you can find petroglyphs left by the ancient Fremont Indians etched into the rock walls just off the road. There are several marvelous examples of their rock art along a short stretch of the canyon. Some appear to be fading and unfortunately may not be visible for long. Others are in great condition. Examining these petroglyphs, I have often pondered the question: are they art or graffiti? To a large extent, the fact that they are several centuries old tends to make them the former rather than the latter. But was this mural left by ancient artisans in a spiritual expression of communion with Nature, or was it just a couple of mischievous teenagers drawing unflattering caricatures of the local chief? Maybe their parents grounded them when their deed was discovered. Consider the fact that if you did the same thing on the same wall today, you would be facing a hefty fine and possibly jail time, even if you were only expressing yourself spiritually. Of course, in a few hundred years, tourists may gather to admire your inscription and call it art. Don't try this at home, kids. Just check out the petroglyphs. Graffiti or art? You decide.

Continuing east, the road runs through a narrow stone gorge which offers a twisting ride of overwhelming beauty. Shortly, you will come to the turnout to Hickman Bridge and Capitol Dome, from which the park gets its name. Tradition holds that the rock formations in this area reminded early settlers of ocean reefs. The prominent white stone called Capitol Dome resembles just that, hence the name Capitol Reef. Now how is it that we've come to label such fascinating tales as trivia?

As you make your way past Capitol Dome you'll notice the color of the canyon start to change. The rocks gradually fade from bold red to subtler shades of pink and tan. The Fremont River leaves a bright splash of green across the floor of the gorge, adding to the scenic palette. The road continues its tantalizing run through this narrow canyon to the parks eastern boundary, where you'll find an orientation pullout and a restroom.

Leaving the park, you'll see the terrain open up to a stark desert. Vegetation quickly disappears almost entirely as you follow the river across Blue Flats. Bending north, the road traces the Caineville Reef through a landscape that I imagine must look much like the surface of the moon. It's almost eerie how void of life this area appears. Aside from a few hardy roadside weeds, nothing seems to stir in this vast lunar-like desert. Bluish-gray and black escarpments mark the path of the highway. Giant monoliths reminiscent of forbidding Gothic cathedrals stand watch over the valley. The Red Desert, more tan and gray than red, stretches out to the north. This countryside is strikingly beautiful in its desolation.

As the highway splits the Caineville Reef, a small desert oasis appears out of nowhere, a patch of green on the Fremont River that is the town of Caineville. Almost as quickly as it appeared, it is gone and the ride returns to barren desert.

Here the road stretches out before you on a straight speed run between the Caineville mesas across a flat desert valley. Factory Butte stands alone in the distance to the north. Then, dropping off Factory Bench into Blue Valley, the highway finds the green vegetation of the river again as it rolls into Hanksville. The pavement on this stretch

Rider hits the twisties in North Wash

from Caineville to Hanksville is in decent shape, but the road surface is old. There were many tar snakes the last time I rode through, something to bear in mind on a hot day.

Hanksville is a cute little whistle-stop at the junction of state routes 24 and 95. You'll find it a nice place to pull over for a rest, maybe to grab some lunch or top off the tank. Gassing up here is well advised, since fuel will be scarce for the next 125 miles or so. There are a few pit stops at or near the highway junction, but none more amusing than Hollow Mountain Station, a gas station and C-store carved into the face of the rock. Figuratively, as well as literally, this little cave is a cool place to stop and take a break.

At Hanksville, the ride leaves SR 24 and continues on SR 95 to the south. A long straightaway, virtually flat, climbs only subtly for 16 miles as it crosses Dry Valley. To the west you'll see the South Pinto Hills, and farther south, the cliffs of the Henry Mountains. Reaching Poison Springs Bench, the ride becomes quite colorful again as the road climbs and weaves through gentle curves and wide, sweeping bends. Gradually the landscape starts to narrow near the red rock cliffs of Little Egypt off to the west.

Steel bridge spans the Dirty Devil River

Riding past the junction of SR 276, you'll roll into a tight canyon of vivid red sandstone. This ravine is quite narrow and makes for a wonderful ride of twisty, tight turns. Running playfully through a fold in the mountains, the road follows a seasonal river bed called North Wash. Enough water apparently flows through the gorge to leave a stripe of green on the floor of the wash. Rugged red rock walls hug the highway tightly for a thirteen mile romp down to Lake Powell at Glen Canyon.

At the south end of the wash the terrain opens up to the dazzling panorama of Glen Canyon National Recreation Area. Traversing the canyon wall overlooking Lake Powell, the ride here is utterly breathtaking. Spectacular red mesas and bold cliffs present a view somewhat reminiscent of the Grand Canyon.

The highway takes you up around the north tip of Lake Powell, where the confluence of the Dirty Devil and Colorado rivers was before Glen Canyon Dam was built. Today the lake covers the spot where these rivers actually merge, but the lake's low water level from years of drought has made the joining of these rivers more apparent recently. Bending back to the south as it rounds the apex of the lake,

Section III: Southern Utah

the highway crosses the Dirty Devil over a steel bridge that spans a picturesque gorge.

Don't be surprised to find the ride through Glen Canyon to be a slow one. This is not at all due to the road, which is well built and very well maintained, nor is it a result of heavy traffic, which I have never found to be a problem on this ride. The simple fact is that this sensational vista can literally slow you to a crawl.

A couple of miles past the Dirty Devil you'll get to cross the Colorado via a slender bridge that spans Narrow Canyon. This bridge is a flat concrete span that allows you to steal a glimpse into the deep gorge as you cross. On the other side you'll climb away from the lake behind you and find the cutoff to Hite Landing. You may find food and gas at this marina but you must pass through a fee station to get to them.

Dashing over Browns Rim, the road shortly brings you to White Canyon. Here begins a delightful stretch of highway that runs the length of this gorge and in doing so, presents for you a grand mural of geologic history. I always find White Canyon to be a fascinating ride. It makes me wish I had a deeper understanding of the science of geology. The highway doesn't actually run through White Canyon, but rather parallels the gorge for miles through a broader basin. Layers of rock deposits in multiple colors play out a time-lapse presentation of the area's creation through the magic of your imagination. The oldest layer, a base of white sandstone, forms the walls of the gorge and the foundation which underlies the surrounding valley. On top of that, layers of softer red sandstone have eroded into marvelous shapes, taking their place on the stage of millennia to showcase Nature's power to create through the forces of destruction.

The road bed on this segment is very well maintained and mildly twisty, making it a thoroughly pleasant ride. Roughly 15 miles past the boundary of Glen Canyon National Recreation Area you'll come to a bend in the road at Fry Canyon Lodge. Climbing a bench to the north, your ride takes you for a further run along White Canyon. Again, you'll see the white stone of the gorge beneath sculpted red sandstone formations. The most prominent of these is a rock called The Cheesebox. Look for it north of the highway. Now, I don't know what a cheesebox is supposed to look like – I've grown accustomed to storing my cheese in the refrigerator – but this mound looks just like a cookie jar to me, complete with a lid and knob handle on top.

Sipapu Bridge - Natural Bridges Nat'l Monument

Riding here along a finger of the Red House Cliffs to your right, with White Canyon on your left, the scenery is dramatic. Shortly, the road drops down off a bench and leaves the red rock country behind as it brings you onto Cedar Mesa, a gigantic base of tan colored sandstone that covers hundreds of square miles. Here you'll roll past SR 276 again and then come to SR 275 eight miles later.

SR 275 is a short spur that leads to Natural Bridges National Monument. Turning left (north) on this road will take you on a scenic detour that is *sine qua non* the Utah experience. Five miles from the road junction, a visitor center offers park information, as well as water and restroom facilities. From there, a paved nine mile scenic loop takes you to three natural bridges spanning White Canyon.

Natural bridges and arches are, in my opinion, the essence of Utah's scenic wonder. Bridges differ from arches in that the former are formed by the erosive force of moving water, such as a river or stream. The three bridges within this monument are some of the most magnificent examples of this natural architecture extant. Also found within the park are the ruins of Ancestral Puebloan dwellings. A detour into Natural Bridges National Monument is a marvelous diversion that I recommend.

Back on SR 95, you'll climb through a forest of cedar and juniper and, no doubt, will take note of how much the landscape has changed

Section III: Southern Utah

over the course of this ride. Running across the top edge of greater Cedar Mesa, you'll be able to see the canyons of color country to the south, especially at Salvation Knoll. This roadside viewpoint captures a sweeping panorama of the remarkable terrain to the south. Though dust and pollution often limit visibility, I imagine that on a clear day, one could easily see into Valley of the Gods from this vantage point, perhaps even to Monument Valley beyond.

Past Salvation Knoll, the road begins a gradual descent off the mesa towards Comb Wash. This section of highway is part of a loop known as Trail of the Ancients for the abundance of prehistoric ruins found in the area. One of these sites, at Mule Canyon, sits right off the highway about midway between Salvation Knoll and Comb Wash.

Dropping through a forest of cedar, pinion and juniper into the wash, the road appears to be headed for a collision with the solid rock wall of Comb Ridge, when at the bottom of the wash it bends to traverse the wall via a big looping switchback. At the top of the ridge, a gap in the rocks provides passage to the other side, and like passing from one room into another, again you'll notice a subtle change in the landscape.

A few miles up the road you will see a cutoff for another set of prehistoric aboriginal ruins at Butler Wash. This site is several miles off the highway along a dirt road and is probably better left to vehicles other than road bikes. Near this cutoff, by the Cheese and Raisin Hills, the road takes you on a short frolicking ride, rising and falling through a twisty stretch before straightening out to end at an intersection with US 191, called Shirttail Junction.

Turning left (north) at the junction takes you into Blanding, where there are plenty of gas, food and lodging options. Continue north through Blanding on US 191. Outside of town, the highway climbs into a mountain forest setting, twisting a bit past Recapture Lake before settling into a relatively straight and pleasant sprint to Monticello.

In Monticello, look for the road sign marking the turnoff to Canyonlands National Park at 200 South. The sign can be easy to miss, but 200 South is not. Turn left (west) here. Two and a half blocks west you will find Abajo Drive cutting off to the left. Abajo Drive is Route 2432 and will take you out of town. This road runs arrow straight and relatively flat to the foot of the Abajo Mountains, where it begins a climb into the forest. Take note that this road runs open range, from the edge of town to the other side of the mountain. I have encountered

Newspaper Rock

a lot of cattle on this road and the large, ignorant beasts don't seem to think it necessary to yield the right of way. On one trip over this mountain, however, the most striking thing was the number of deer I passed, both on and immediately beside the road. I counted more than two dozen in a stretch of less than ten miles, a number way beyond what I would expect to be the norm. I don't know if this was just a freak anomaly or not but I quickly came to the conclusion that the posted speed limit of 40 mph was probably a good idea.

The ride over the Abajos is an enjoyable one. Route 2432 is off the beaten path and will take you on a winding jaunt through cool dense mountain forests, in bold contrast to the open deserts through which you passed earlier in the day. Cresting the summit you'll come to a roadside viewpoint from which you can see the colorful deserts of Canyonlands laid out to the northwest. From here the road descends rapidly to a T-intersection with SR 211.

At the junction with SR 211, turn left (west). The road quickly drops off a plateau into a little draw. This marks the beginning of yet another distinctive segment of the ride, one of the most scenic. Descending down through the draw you'll quickly find a narrow canyon. Big, bold rock walls hug the road tight, making a slow, yet thoroughly enjoyable ride. Not far into this canyon you'll find Newspaper Rock State Historical Monument.

Newspaper Rock is one of the largest and most popular petroglyph sites in the west. Hundreds of figures have been etched into this slate panel by people from several cultures spanning two thousand years. This is where the discussion of art versus graffiti is really appropriate. Personally, I see a rock that is clearly defaced, yet I find this to be one of the most fascinating historic sites in the western US. Here is a spot where passers-by, from ancient Anasazis to more recent Navajo, Ute, and even Anglo pioneers, have left their mark. This is one of the most easily accessible petroglyph panels in the state and one that can be examined quite closely. Take a moment to check it out.

Beyond Newspaper Rock you will find yourself on a winding canyon road that follows Indian Creek. In the middle of the canyon, a lush grove of cottonwood and undergrowth paints a cool strip of green. Gradually, the canyon opens up to reveal a broad valley of brilliant red. Giant sandstone mesas float like ships in a harbor. This panorama reminds me of the setting for a John Ford western. I almost expect to encounter John Wayne riding up on a big horse to warn me of Apaches on the warpath. Go ahead and indulge yourself in a little swagger when you climb out of the saddle here, but try not to speak in a cheesy John Wayne accent. Trust me, it'll only make your riding companions groan and roll their eyes.

An open run of about 15 miles across this colorful valley brings you to the entrance station at Canyonlands National Park. Canyonlands is divided by the Green and Colorado rivers into three distinct regions; Island in the Sky, The Maze and The Needles. This road takes you into the Needles area.

The Needles region is one of stunning natural sculpture, filled with canyons, grabens, potholes, arches and spires. The most prominent formations are the layered rock pinnacles from which this district draws its name. Just past the entrance station, the park's visitor center is located on the north side of the road. Excellent displays of artifacts, natural history and biology, along with interpretive film presentations and, of course, the ever helpful NPS rangers are here to enhance your visit to the park. Of equal importance, restroom facilities and water are available here as well. Past the visitor center a short paved road will take you roughly five miles into the park, where you can examine an Ancestral Puebloan ruin, Wooden Shoe Arch, Pothole Point and Big Spring Canyon. You'll ride past great mushroom shaped rocks that look like a patch of giant toadstools and see gnarled, multi-layered rock pinnacles scattered about the landscape. While there is much less

The Needles - Canyonlands Nat'l Park

paved road in this region than in Island in the Sky to the north, The Needles is nonetheless a spectacular ride. The scenic attractions in this area feel much closer and more accessible.

By now you are near the end of a long, but exciting day in the saddle. No doubt, you are ready for hot meal, a cold drink and a place to rest your weary bones. If you're into camping, one of the park's campgrounds makes a great place to call it a day. However if, like me, your definition of camping is any night not spent in your own bed, take heart. A juicy steak, a cold draft, and clean sheets are just a short ride away.

When you've finished exploring Canyonlands, head out of the park back to SR 211 and retrace your path back to Newspaper Rock. This ride is just as fun the second time. Past Newspaper Rock, rather than turning back onto Route 2432, continue straight on SR 211, a quicker path back to US 191. Going this way is probably safer late in the day, with all the deer on the Abajo road, and a change of scenery is always welcome. The road here runs a straight course across an open valley. Peters Point Ridge walls off the landscape to the right, with an open desert plateau to the left. Passing through Photograph Gap, the highway descends gently down a long straightaway to the junction with US 191. Here you'll spot three peculiar rock formations; Sugar Loaf Rock to the north of SR 211, George Rock to the south and

Church Rock directly to the west of US 191. Turn south on US 191 to find gas, food and lodging in Monticello, 14 miles away. To the north, a scenic ride of about 39 miles takes you to Moab.

The run from Capitol Reef to Canyonlands packs an awful lot into a single day, but this is what makes it such a grand riding adventure. Even though you'll be on the road from sunrise nearly to sunset, the great natural attractions along the way break up the time spent in the saddle with opportunities to get off the bike and explore. Fantastic roads, breathtaking scenery and striking variety make this one of the truly great rides in the western United States.

Capitol Reef to Canyonlands – Notes

Pit Stops:

Torrey:
Phillips 66
Jct. Hwy 12 & Hwy 24
(435) 425-3302

Sinclair
875 Hwy 24
(435) 425-3956

Hanksville:
Hollow Mtn. (Phillips 66)
60 Hwy 95
(435) 542-3298

Stan's Chevron
150 Hwy 95
(435) 542-2017

Blanding:
Shell
861 S. Main
(435) 678-2770

Canyon Country Chevron
12 W. Center
(435) 678-3900

Monticello:
Shell
17 N. Main (US 191)
(435) 587-2555

Maverik
265 E. Center (US 491)

Accommodations & Camping:

CAMPGROUNDS:
National Forest Campgrounds info: (877) 444-6777 or www.reserveusa.com.
Dalton Springs – Rt. 2432
Buckboard – Rt. 2432

National Park Campgrounds
Capitol Reef Nat'l Park info: (435) 425-3791 or www.nps.gov/care
Canyonlands Nat'l Park info: (435) 259-7164 or www.nps.gov/cany
Glen Canyon NRA info: (435) 684-2278 or www.nps.gov/glca

BLM Campgrounds info:
BLM Monticello Field Office
365 N. Main
Monticello, UT 84535
(435) 587-1500
Newspaper Rock – SR 211
Hamburger Rock – SR 211

Commercial Campgrounds
Needles Outpost
SR 211 at Canyonlands Nat'l Park
(435) 979-4007

HOTELS:
Torrey:
Days Inn
825 E. Hwy 24
(435) 425-3111

Best Western Capitol Reef Resort
2600 E. Hwy 24
(435) 425-3761

Blanding:
Gateway Inn
88 E. Center
(435) 678-2278

Quality Inn of Blanding
711 S. Main
(435) 678-3271

Monticello:
Inn at the Canyons
533 N. Main (US 191)
(435) 587-2458

Wayside Inn
197 E. Center (US 491)
(435) 587-2261

RECOMMENDED DINING:
Torrey:
The Rim Rock Restaurant
2523 E. Hwy 24
(435) 425-3388

Broken Spur Inn & Steakhouse
955 Hwy 24
(435) 425-3775

Hanksville:
Stan's Burger Shak
100 Hwy 95
(435) 542-3330

Blondie's Eatery
30 Hwy 95
(435) 542-3255

Blanding:
Old Tymer Restaurant
733 S. Main
(435) 678-2122

Homestead Steak House
121 E. Center
(435) 678-3456

Monticello:
Wagon Wheel Pizza
156 S. Main
(435) 587-2766

MD Ranch Cookhouse
380 S. Main
(435) 587-3299

Moab Area Rides

(Photo by Kyle Magdiel)   Rider in Arches Nat'l Park

Situated at the northeast corner of Utah's colorful Canyonlands country, Moab has become an outdoor recreation mecca and international tourist destination. Off-road vehicle enthusiasts test their skills on the area's many rugged jeep trails. Mountain bikers take their sport to the extreme on the slickrock megaliths that abound. Hikers and campers find a wealth of primitive backcountry to explore in the nearby state and national parks. International tourists seek out the unique beauty of Arches and Canyonlands National Parks. With ample scenic byways and spectacular vistas, the Moab area also draws bikers from all over the western US.

Too awesome to be covered in just one ride, Moab is best exploited in a series of day rides. Set up a base camp in town and devote two or three days to fully experience an area you will come to appreciate as one of the finest motorcycle touring experiences in Utah. Enjoy!

Moab Area Rides Route Map

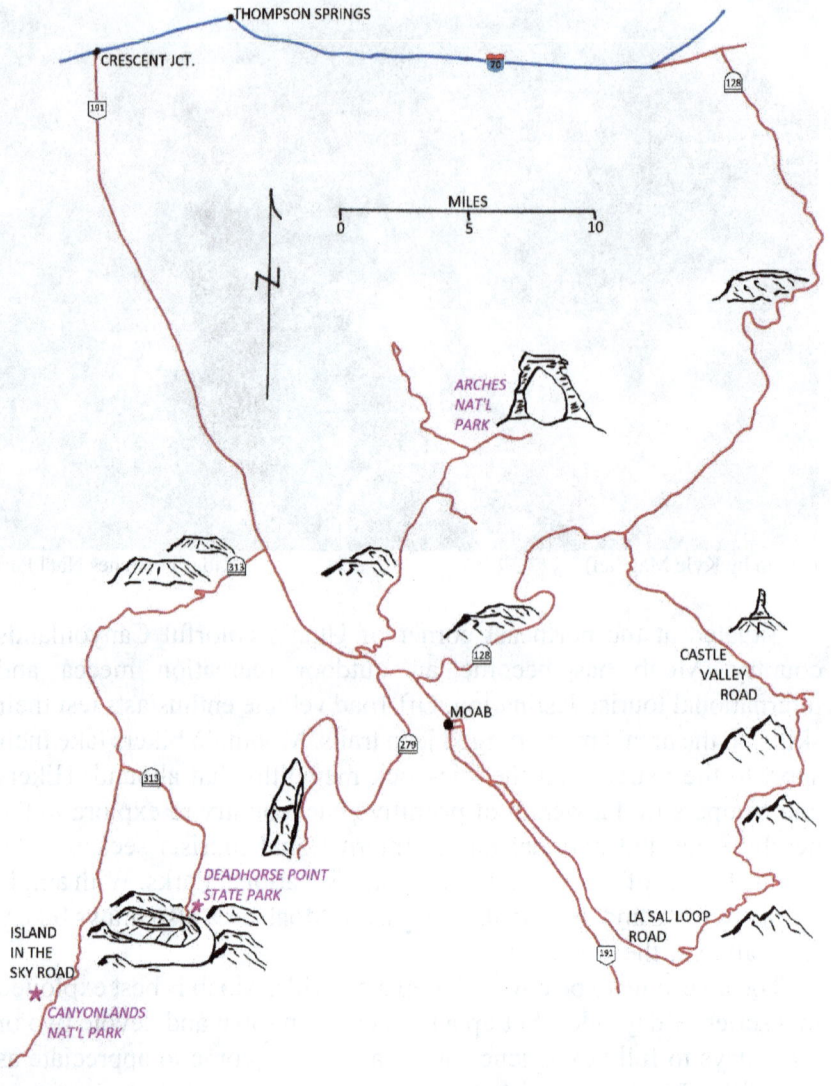

ROUTES: See text, saddle up, and ride 'em all!

Colorado River Loop

This loop will take you up one of the greatest stretches of canyon road in Utah. At the risk of being accused of hyperbole, I must say that there are no words to adequately describe riding SR 128. While not a particularly long loop, you could stretch this ride to 3 hours or more. I promise it will leave you awestruck.

From Moab, head north on US 191 (Main Street). At the north end of town, just before you cross the Colorado River, turn right (east) on SR 128. Immediately, you enter the mouth of a canyon cut through the red rock by the Colorado River. Although your ride has just begun don't be surprised if you feel the urge to pull over and soak in the awesome spectacle before you. Believe it or not, it gets better. Keep your camera handy!

SR 128 traces the muddy waters of the Colorado on a winding northeasterly path through a brilliant red rock canyon. This is a relatively slow stretch of road, more due to its scenic qualities than anything else. Settle in and enjoy the ride. To your left is the powerful, silt-laden river. You can almost see it carving the canyon deeper and imagine what it must be sculpting. To your right the road hugs the canyon wall, so closely in places that you can almost reach out and touch it.

There are several campground and picnic area turnouts on the river side of the highway, each of which offers an excellent place to absorb the vistas and take some pictures. Look for a series of campgrounds in rapid succession as you come to the Big Bend area roughly five miles into the canyon. Another good photo stop is the Takeout Beach picnic area, just past Big Bend, about the ten miles into the canyon.

Roughly eleven miles up the highway, the canyon opens up into Professor Valley, a small green oasis in the red desert populated by a handful of ranches. Here the road steps away from the river a bit and straightens out for a dash across the valley. Ten miles later, the road and river rejoin for another delightful canyon run.

This second canyon segment hugs the river, just as before, as it twists through more spectacular red rock country. About six miles past Professor Valley (roughly thirty miles into the ride), you will cross the river at Dewey. Note the old suspension bridge as you ride past. With the river now on your right, the terrain begins to open up and, less than five miles from the bridge, the road and the river part ways as SR 128 climbs up to Windy Mesa.

Riders on the Colorado River

I've run this canyon many times, and each time feels like the first. This stretch of SR 128 will overwhelm your senses and bring you to an emotional crescendo. Roads like this are why we ride motorcycles.

Climbing out onto the mesa, SR 128 makes a brief dash north to I-70. Just before reaching the freeway the road comes to a T-intersection. Follow the freeway signs to the left (west) to get on I-70 westbound at mile 204.

I-70 takes you on a short and usually windy dash across Sagers Flat. Seven miles down the freeway, at exit 187, you'll find Thompson Springs with a gas station and C-store. Five miles beyond, at exit 182, lies Crescent Junction. Take exit 182 and jump on US 191 southbound.

US 191 is a straight thirty mile run south into Moab. This road is the northern gateway to the color country of Canyonlands. Although lacking any twists or turns, the approach to Moab is a scenic delight.

Before calling this ride complete, let's explore a short spur off of US 191. Coming into Moab, just over a mile past the gate to Arches National Park, you will find SR 279 off the right (southwest) side of US 191. This road traces the Colorado River downstream from our earlier run up SR 128. Here too, the river cuts a path through a red rock canyon, yet it is one that is much wider. SR 279 only covers about sixteen miles before it runs out of pavement but it is well worth riding to the end and back. For much of the way, the highway runs flush against towering vertical rock walls. These rock faces are a favorite of climbers and often, you will be treated to the spectacle of spider-like adrenaline junkies scaling the cliffs. Also along this short stretch of road, look for prehistoric petroglyphs and an interesting rock formation called Jug Handle Arch.

After running to the end of SR 279 and back, turn right (south) on US 191 for the short run back into Moab. By now you should have a camera full of memories and a powerful thirst from the desert heat, a perfect excuse to head into town and relax at one of Moab's superb watering holes.

Dead Horse Point/Canyonlands

This ride, while covering relatively little distance, can fill as much of your day as you wish. You'll visit some of the most famous picture postcard vistas in the state on this run, so be sure to keep your camera within easy reach.

You might consider launching this run at, or even before, dawn. While the ride is no less enjoyable at any time of the day, sunrise over Dead Horse Point is absolutely breathtaking and embarking early allows you to beat several hours of oppressive desert heat.

Go north out of Moab on US 191. About ten miles out of town, on the left (west) side of the highway, you will come to SR 313. The road is clearly marked with signs pointing to Dead Horse Point State Park, and Canyonlands National Park. Turn left (west) and you're on Seven-mile Canyon Road (SR 313), another stretch of highway that will validate your decision to ride a motorcycle.

A few miles down SR 313 you'll see Monitor Butte and Merrimac Butte off to the north of the highway. These two massive monoliths dominate the surrounding landscape, facing each other down like their Civil War ironclad namesakes. Two view areas just beyond the double hairpin curves in the road offer excellent vantage points from which to observe the timeless battle between these two giants.

About fifteen miles from the junction, the road bends to the south and then forks. SR 313 veers off to the east at nearly a right angle and takes you to Dead Horse Point State Park. The road that continues south becomes Island in the Sky Road and leads to Canyonlands National Park. Turn left with SR 313 and check out what many consider to be Utah's most scenic state park.

Dead Horse Point State Park has a campground, picnic area and visitor center but the centerpiece attraction, of course, is the overlook. Perched on the rim of the canyon, Dead Horse Point overlook presents one of the most famous vistas in Utah. Next to Delicate Arch, this view has probably graced more postcards, travel brochures, and landscape murals than any other natural wonder in the state. Hundreds of feet below, the Colorado River winds through a deep and colorful gorge of sandstone and mud sediment. Formed through millions of years of sediment deposition and subsequent erosion, the gorge and river take a dramatic bend around the Goose Neck Ridge. Dead Horse Point, at the tip of this promontory, gets its name from the nineteenth century Mustang round-ups that occurred here. The promontory forms a natural corral, its only access through a thirty yard neck of land

Section III: Southern Utah

Sunrise at Dead Horse Point

controlled with a gate. After driving a herd of Mustangs onto the point, wranglers would cull less desirable specimens from the herd and leave them to make their own way off the ridge through the open gate. Legend tells of a group of culls that would not leave, despite the open gate, and died of thirst within view of the cool waters of the Colorado River just two hundred feet below.

After leaving the state park, turn left onto Island in the Sky Road for an excursion into the north end of Canyonlands National Park. This area of the park lies on a large mesa known to the aboriginal natives as the Island in the Sky. Access to the mesa is via a narrow strip of land called The Neck, which sits just beyond the visitor center. Before crossing The Neck, check out Shafer Canyon viewpoint, one of many stunning view areas in the park.

Crossing The Neck places you on Grand Viewpoint Road. The road shortly comes to a fork, the right leading to Upheaval Dome while overlooking the Green River on a ride past majestic rock towers. The left fork leads ultimately to Grand Viewpoint overlook and offers spectacular views of the massive desert canyons on both sides of the mesa. At Grand Viewpoint, you will find the beauty of Monument Basin and see the confluence of Colorado and Green rivers in the distance. Both of these roads are worthy of exploration, every viewpoint along each is a scenic delight.

When finished in the park, retrace your path back to SR 313 and US 191. It's time to head back into Moab for some good food and a cold draft, both of which you'll find in abundance.

Delicate Arch - Arches Nat'l Park

Arches National Park

Arches National Park is a geologic wonderland boasting the greatest density of natural arches in the world. There are more than two thousand cataloged arches in the park, most of which you'll have to hike to in order to find. If so inclined, throw on a set of hiking boots and make a day out of walking the back trails. On the other hand, if you prefer to stay in the saddle, fret not! There is more than enough natural wonder to see from your bike. This ride is a must while in Moab.

Again, take US 191 north out of Moab. Just a few miles beyond the north edge of town you will find the entrance to the park clearly marked on the right (east) side of the highway.

The road into Arches, like Canyonlands, is a simple in-and-out affair, with three branches. To do the park justice, I would encourage taking a few hours and exploring each fork of paved road. With its close proximity to town however, the park offers some great afternoon quickies and can be enjoyed by breaking it up into two or three segments over as many days. This may be an option to consider after completing one of the other Moab area rides, when it's too early to call it a day, but too late to embark on another long ride.

Some of the high points I recommend hitting include Park Avenue, Courthouse Towers Viewpoint, Balanced Rock, Double Arch and The

Windows, Skyline Arch, Devil's Garden and of course, Delicate Arch. Park Avenue is a fascinating formation illustrative of the sandstone fins from which arches are formed. At Courthouse Towers, one can easily imagine an arch, gone many thousands of years now, which once stood in the remnant formations near Sheep rock. More recently, Wall Arch, on the Devil's Garden trail, suffered the same fate when it collapsed on August 4, 2008. The road to Double Arch and The Windows leads you past the intriguing rock formations of the Garden of Eden. Delicate Arch is arguably one of the most recognized landscapes in the world, a geologic wonder that has become synonymous with Utah itself, appearing on countless postcards, travel posters and brochures, as well as the Utah license plate.

Arches National Park is small, relative to others in the National Parks system but there is much to see and enjoy. Its small area and proximity to Moab make it easy to exploit and you'll definitely want to add it to your riding menu while in the Moab area.

La Sal Loop

The La Sal loop offers a "beat the heat" diversion from the slickrock desert rides described so far. This ride will take you into the cool green woods of the Manti-La Sal National Forest to traverse the face of the La Sal Mountains and overlook scenic Castle Valley below. The La Sal range is Utah's second highest, with Mt. Pearle rising to an elevation of 12,721 feet. This fun little loop can be completed in a couple of hours.

This time, we'll head south out of Moab, just to change things up a bit. About eight miles south of the center of town, look for a sign pointing to the La Sal Mountain Loop Road. Turn left (east) on this local road. In about a half mile, this road comes to a T-intersection with Spanish Valley Drive. Turn right on Spanish Valley Drive. This road becomes La Sal Mountain Loop Road and will take you into the mountains.

La Sal Mountain Loop Road (also shown on some maps as Geyser Pass Road) begins a twisty assent into the Manti-La Sal National forest almost immediately. You'll enjoy a refreshing temperature drop as the road makes the climb into evergreen forest. This path is rough and poorly maintained in places, almost new in others. It climbs aggressively in spots, with tight, narrow curves. Watch for occasional patches of gravel. Though its condition varies over the length of the route, the road is paved and passable through the entire loop and the views are great.

You might consider bringing along a picnic lunch and stopping to enjoy a break from the hot desert below. Traversing across the face of the La Sal range, you'll be treated to majestic views of the desert canyons and slickrock country below. Near the northwest corner of the loop an overlook presents a striking vista of scenic Castle Valley and (on a clear day) Arches National Park beyond.

Shortly after the overlook, the road begins it's descent into Castle Valley. At the edge of the valley the road comes to a T-intersection. Turn left (northwest) on Castle Valley Road (shown on some maps as county road 96). The run through Castle Valley may look familiar to you, even on your first ride through. This area has been a popular setting for TV and movie production. The road will take you past colorful Adobe Mesa, as well as the Castle Rock and Priest & Nuns formations.

At the mouth of Castle Valley, the road meets SR 128. Turn left (west) for another spectacular run along the banks of the mighty

Riders in Castle Valley

Colorado River, this time downstream into Moab. At the intersection with US 191, a left turn takes you back into town.

Moab

After a day in the saddle, the city of Moab is a welcome oasis. With many fine eateries and a veritable cornucopia of cool watering holes, you'll undoubtedly want to plan your day to end up in town. Relaxing poolside at the hotel or cooling off in the comfort of a local cantina are perfect settings to reflect on the day's ride and plan tomorrow's fun.

Moab is truly a Utah treasure, an excellent centerpiece for a fabulous riding vacation.

Moab Area Rides – Notes

Pit Stops:

Moab:
Maverik
435 N. Main
(435) 259-8718

Shell
220 N. Main
(435) 259-3557

Walker's
299 S. Main
(435) 259-6030

Chevron
817 S. Main
(435) 259-0500

Thompson Springs:
Out West Food & Fuel (Shell)
I-70 exit 187
(435) 285-2230

Accommodations & Camping:

CAMPGROUNDS:
National Park Campgrounds
Arches Nat'l Park info: (435) 719-2299 or www.nps.gov/arch
Canyonlands Nat'l Park info: (435) 259-7164 or www.nps.gov/cany

Utah State Parks Campgrounds info: (800) 322-3770 or
www.stateparks.utah.gov.
Dead Horse Point State Park – SR 313

BLM Campgrounds info:
BLM Moab Field Office
82 E. Dogwood
Moab, UT 84532
(435) 259-2100
Goose Island Campground – SR 128
Negro Bill Camping Area – SR 128
Drinks Canyon Camping Area – SR 128
Hal Canyon Campground – SR 128

Section III: Southern Utah

Oak Grove Campground – SR 128
Big Bend Campground – SR 128
Upper Big Bend Camping Area – SR 128
Hittle Bottom Campground – SR 128
Dewey Bridge Campground – SR 128
Jay Cee Park Campground – SR 279
Williams Bottom – SR 279
Goldbar Camping Area – SR 279
Kings Bottom Camping Area – Kane Creek Rd.
Moonflower Camping Area – Kane Creek Rd.
Ken's Lake Campground – US 191
Sand Flats Recreation Area – Sand Flats Rd.

Commercial Campgrounds

Archview Campground
US 191 @ SR 313
(435) 259-7854

Canyonlands Campground
555 S. Main
(435) 259-6848

Edge of the Desert
1251 S. Millcreek
(435) 259-3337

Kane Springs Campground
1705 Kane Creek Rd.
(435) 259-8844

Sand Flats Recreation Area
Sand Flats Rd.
(435) 259-2444

Moab KOA
3225 S. Hwy 191
(435) 259-6682

Moab Rim Campark
1900 S. Hwy 191
(435) 259-5002

Moab Valley RV Resort
1773 N. Hwy 191
(435) 259-4469

OK RV Park
3310 Spanish Valley Dr.
(435) 259-1400

Pack Creek Campground
1520 Murphy Lane
(435) 259-2982

Riverside Oasis
1871 N. Hwy 191
(435) 259-3424

Slickrock Campground
1301 ½ N. Hwy 191
(435) 259-7660

Spanish Trail RV Park
2980 S. Hwy 191
(435) 259-2411

HOTELS:
Moab:
Aarchway Inn
1551 N. Hwy 191
(435) 259-2599

Apache Motel
166 S. 400 E.
(435) 259-5757

Best Western Greenwell
105 S. Main St.
(435) 259-6151

Bowen Motel
169 N. Main St.
(800) 847-5439

Gonzo Inn
100 W. 200 S.
(435) 259-2515

Holiday Inn Express
1515 N. Hwy 191
(435) 259-1150

JR's Desert Inn
1075 S. Hwy 191
(435) 259-8352

Lazy Lizard Hostel
1213 S. Hwy 191
(435) 259-6057

Up the Creek
210 E. 300 S.
(435) 260-1888

Adventure Inn
512 N. Main St.
(435) 259-6122

Best Western Canyonlands
16 S. Main St.
(435) 259-2300

Big Horn Lodge
550 S. Main St.
(435) 259-6171

Days Inn
426 N. Main St
(435) 259-4468

Hampton Inn
488 N. Main St.
(435) 259-3030

Inca Inn Motel
570 N. Main St.
(435) 259-7261

La Quinta Inn
815 S. Main St.
(435) 259-8700

Moab Valley Inn
711 S. Main St
(435) 259-4419

Section III: Southern Utah

Motel 6
1089 N. Main St.
(435) 259-6686

Ramada Inn
182 S. Main St.
(435) 259-7141

Red Rock Lodge
51 N. 100 W.
(435) 259-5431

River Canyon Lodge
71 W. 200 N.
(435) 259-8838

Rustic Inn Motel
120 E. 100 S.
(435) 259-6177

Sleep Inn
1051 S. Main St.
(435) 259-4655

Super 8
889 N. Main St.
(435) 259-8868

Quality Suites
800 S. Main
(435) 259-5252

Red Cliffs Lodge
14 Hwy 128
(435) 259-2002

Red Stone Inn
535 S. Main St.
(435) 259-3500

Rodeway Inn - Landmark
168 N. Main St.
(435) 259-6147

Silver Sage Inn
840 S. Main St.
(435) 259-4420

Sorrel River Ranch
Hwy 128 Mile 17
(435) 259-4642

Virginian Motel
70 E. 200 S.
(435) 259-5951

RECOMMENDED DINING:
Moab:

Broken Oar
53 W. 400 N.
(435) 259-3127

Buck's Grill House
1393 N. Hwy 191
(435) 259-5201

Eddie McStiff's
57 S. Main St.
(435) 259-2337

Jeffrey's Steak House
218 N. 100 W.
(435) 259-3588

La Hacienda
574 N. Main
(435) 259-6319

Moab Brewery
686 N. Main St.
(435) 259-6333

Moab Diner
189 S. Main St.
(435) 259-4006

River Grill Restaurant
Hwy 128 Mile 17
(435) 259-4642

Sunset Grill
900 N. Hwy 191
(435) 259-7146

Twisted Sistas' Café
11 E. 100 N.
(435) 355-0088

Zax Restaurant
96 S. Main
(435) 259-6555

Four Corners Loop

Riders at Four Corners Monument

Here's a fun day ride that will take you through the heart of "Indian Country" on a two-wheeled field trip of discovery. You'll roll through four states as well as the Mountain Ute and Navajo Nations while enjoying the splendor of magnificent desert southwest landscapes. Along the way you can indulge in some archeology, sample the hospitality of modern Native American culture and examine the colorful geology of the Colorado Plateau.

This is the kind of ride that I find particularly enjoyable – one that combines an engaging day in the saddle with opportunities to satisfy innate curiosity by visiting points of interest. Three separate tourist attractions lie along this loop, breaking up the ride with opportunities to stop and explore. First, we'll visit the pre-Columbian ruins of an Ancestral Puebloan village at Hovenweep Nat'l Monument. We'll then ride on to find the only spot in the US common to four states. After that, we'll cruise through the awesome red buttes of Monument Valley to call it a day and wash away a dusty desert thirst with a cold drink and a hot meal. The next time you see one of these famous places on TV or in the movies, you'll smile and say, "I've been there." Enjoy!

Four Corners Loop
Route Map

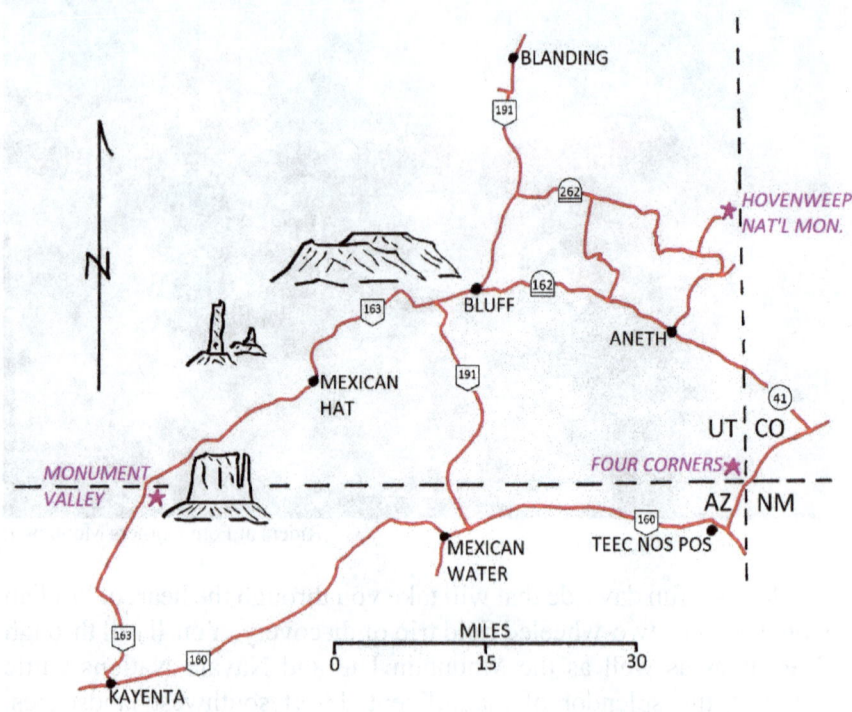

ROUTE: From Blanding, take US 191 south to SR 262. Take SR 262 east to Hatch Trading Post Rd. (Indian Route 5099). Continue east on IR 5099 to Hatch Trading Post. Turn south on Mesa Rd. (County Road 401), follow signs to Hovenweep Nat'l Monument. From Hovenweep, take CR 401 east/south to Ismay Trading Post Rd. (IR 5066). Take IR 5066 west/south to Aneth. At Aneth, turn east on SR 162. Take SR 162 / CO 41 to US 160. Take US 160 west to Four Corners Monument. Continue westbound on US 160 to US 163 at Kayenta. Take US 163 northbound to Monument Valley, continue to Bluff. Take US 191 north back to Blanding.

Section III: Southern Utah

On the road...

Utah is full of interesting attractions that draw tourists from all over the world. Hopefully, this book has demonstrated that Utah is also full of great roads for the motorcyclist. Riders are the most fortunate of Utah tourists, for we can exploit both of these characteristics simultaneously, and in doing so take the experience to the level of adventure.

This ride, like many others in southern Utah, is such an adventure, a delightful day in the saddle riding through some of the most dazzling desert landscapes imaginable, that will take you to attractions ranging from obscure to world famous.

We'll begin this ride at Blanding, a city that makes an excellent base from which to explore the southeast corner of the state. (The town of Bluff roughly twenty-five miles to the south is another good choice.) Head south out of Blanding on US 191 for about fourteen miles, where you will come to the junction with SR 262. The highway junction is clearly marked with road signs indicating the way to Hovenweep and Four Corners. Turn left (east) onto SR 262.

Right away, SR 262 is a rough road – a real kidney-jarring ride. The road travels into the Navajo Nation across a desert plateau known as McCracken Mesa, with rather unremarkable scenic quality. About eight miles east of the highway junction, the route forks, with SR 262 bending south to the right and the cutoff to Hovenweep continuing straight on the left. Follow the road signs to Hovenweep and stay to the left.

The road you are now on is designated on various maps as Hovenweep Road, Hatch Trading Post Road, Route 2416, County Road 414 or Indian Route 5099. I tend to favor the Indian Route references because these seem to be the only markers you will actually encounter on the roads in this area. Regardless of what you call it, it's not as confusing as it sounds. The trail to Hovenweep National Monument is clearly marked by road signs the entire way and there just aren't enough paved roads in this patch of desert to get lost.

This local road too, is a rough one. Ride too fast and you may feel your back teeth coming loose. You'll be crossing through open range and may encounter a horse or two near the road. A short way past the cutoff, this trail brings you to Hatch Trading Post, a splash of green in an otherwise colorless desert.

At Hatch Trading Post, the pavement bends abruptly to the right. Another Hovenweep road marker indicates this is the way to go. Some maps show a paved road continuing to the east from Hatch Trading Post that leads directly to Hovenweep through Black Steer Canyon. This is misleading, for while the road is there, it is definitely not paved. The emblem on the front fender of my bike reads "Road King", not "Off-Road King", so I opted to follow the recommendation of the sign and stay on the pavement. If you're on a heavy road bike as well, I suggest turning right (south) here with the asphalt.

This turn to the south puts you on County Road 401, in case you're keeping track, and almost immediately past the turn you may see the pavement end. Now, after the preceding discussion about staying with the pavement, you're probably thinking 'What the hell, Dave?' Don't be dismayed, my friends. If it hasn't been covered by the time you make this ride, this patch of hard-pack dirt only lasts about 30 feet. Another stretch of roughly 300 feet lies a short way to the south but after that it's asphalt all the way, I promise. Just past these rough spots the road bends to the east and climbs a small mesa, where coincidently it is called Mesa Road. A quick four miles east from here you'll find the turn into Hovenweep National Monument, again clearly marked. Turn left (north) on this road to get to the park's visitor center.

Hovenweep National Monument is comprised of five separate prehistoric villages spread out in a line of roughly sixteen miles. Each site lies at the head of a different canyon along the Utah-Colorado border. Today's ride has brought you to the monument's primary facility and visitor center at the Square Tower Unit. This site is the only one accessible by paved roads. A stop at the visitor center will acquaint you with the history and archeology of the site. From there you can take a short walk of about two miles around the rim of Little Ruin Canyon, where you may examine the ruins up close. The Rim Trail Loop is an easy, enjoyable and fascinating little hike along the canyon – a diversion I highly recommend.

The dwellings of the Square Tower Unit are remarkably well preserved and offer a captivating glimpse into the technology and culture of the pre-Columbian inhabitants of this region. Archeologists believe these buildings were constructed between 1235 and 1240 and were inhabited for no more than 70 years. By ca. 1300, the people of this region abandoned these villages and migrated south into Arizona and New Mexico.

Hovenweep Castle - Hovenweep Nat'l Monument

After visiting the monument, return to Mesa Road (County Road 401) along Hovenweep Road. From here, you'll be following the road signs to Aneth. At Mesa Road, turn left (east). This road loops around to the south and meets the Ismay Trading Post Road, which is County Road 402, or as I prefer, Indian Route 5066. Again following the signs to Aneth, turn right (west). This road also bends south and joins SR 162 at Aneth.

At Aneth, you'll want to turn left (east) on SR 162, following the road signs to Four Corners. Gas and refreshment are available at Aneth before you follow the highway southeast towards Colorado. A run of about ten miles through the arid desert brings you to the border, where the highway becomes CO 41. This stretch of road runs arrow-straight for another ten miles or so to meet US 160.

At the junction with US 160, turn right (west) towards Four Corners Monument. A short stretch of no more than five miles brings you across the San Juan River into New Mexico. A short distance past the border, you'll find the cutoff to Four Corners Monument on the right side of the highway.

Four Corners Monument is a Navajo Tribal Park administered by the Navajo Nation. This unique geographic location is the only spot in

Four Corners Monument

the United States where the borders of four separate states meet at a single point. Aside from the political significance, this desolate patch of desert is rather unremarkable, yet it is this very significance that tugs at one's curiosity and draws thousands of visitors annually. When you get there, take a moment to enjoy the silly antics of your fellow visitors. You're likely to see someone bent over the marker with a hand or foot in each state, mimicking a geographic version of the game Twister. No doubt you'll witness a tourist or two circling the datum point and mumbling to themselves, "now I'm in Colorado, now I'm in New Mexico…" as they cross each state line. If you linger long enough, you're sure to overhear someone else muse about running from the law and evading capture by simply jumping from state to state (never mind the fact that legal jurisdiction on every side of the marker rests with the Navajo and Mountain Ute Nations and they probably aren't that concerned with state lines). When you've drawn enough amusement from the behavior of your fellow travelers, try to resist indulging in a little silliness of your own. I bet you can't do it. That's all right, though. Go ahead and enjoy yourself. Someone else is probably getting a smile from watching you.

While at the park, you're sure to experience the warmth and hospitality of the Navajo people. Guests are welcomed with a genuine kindness and friendship that makes the visit more fun. The site hosts a visitor center with area information and several vendor kiosks displaying native art. Food and refreshment are also found within the park.

When leaving Four Corners, turn right (west) on US 160. Just past the monument, the highway crosses the Arizona border and runs south for a few miles to the junction with US 64 at Teec Nos Pos. Here you will find gasoline, something to drink and the favorite attraction of Indian reservations across the country, tax-free cigarettes. At the highway junction, turn right to continue westbound on US 160.

US 160 runs west across the northern Arizona desert for seventy-two miles to Kayenta. This stretch of highway is a relatively straight and flat speed run. The first half of this leg is also fairly colorless, not much scenery and a whole lot of desert. Thirty-one miles past Teec Nos Pos, you'll come to another trading post at Mexican Water where again you can find gas, refreshment and more tax free tobacco. Continuing west, the landscape begins to change. About half-way to Kayenta, flashes of red begin to appear, hinting of the bold color that lies ahead. Roughly 30 miles out of Kayenta, the distant red mesas surrounding Monument Valley come into view. Dramatic hoodoo formations stand next to the highway near Dinnehotso while the scenery builds to a crescendo of red and you roll into the colorful desert at Kayenta.

Kayenta sits at the junction of US 160 and US 163. Each time I travel through here, I'm struck by the hot, dry wind that seems to blow constantly and I wonder if it ever stops. Carried on the breeze are tiny grains of sand, continuing the timeless work of carving the surrounding mesas and stinging the face and eyes of riders passing through. In spite of the constant sandblasting, Kayenta is a pleasant crossroads, where you will find anything you might need after a run across the desert, including gas, food and lodging.

At the highway junction, turn right (north) onto US 163. This road runs through the town of Kayenta and climbs into the colorful country beyond. As you roll through town and into the hills to the north, note the petrified sand dunes by the roadside and in the nearby cliffs. You can still see ripples in the sand that were frozen into stone when these great dunes solidified.

Ride Utah!

Monument Valley

US 163 is in good shape, a very well maintained road. The highway usually sees a lot of traffic in the summertime, but this is not a big problem. The twenty-four mile stretch from Kayenta to the Utah border is a speed run. As you near the border (about ten miles out), the mesas of Monument Valley come into view, an awe inspiring site that gets better as you draw closer.

Monument Valley straddles the Utah-Arizona border on the northern edge of the Navajo Nation. This area is one of the most recognizable landscapes in the world, having been the setting for countless movies, television programs and commercials. Perhaps no one has done more to popularize the region than John Ford, who used Monument Valley as a location for several classic western films including, *Stagecoach* (1939), *My Darling Clementine* (1946), *She Wore a Yellow Ribbon* (1949), *Rio Grande* (1950), *The Searchers* (1956), *How the West Was Won* (1962) and *Cheyenne Autumn* (1964). Recognizing the dramatic impact of this bold landscape, many film and television artists have followed Ford's lead in using Monument Valley as a backdrop for their projects, including Dennis Hopper, who filmed a portion of his 1969 motorcycle cult-classic *Easy Rider* here. So many movies, television programs and commercials have been

Section III: Southern Utah

made here that, even upon visiting the valley for the first time, you are likely to find the area very familiar, as though you have been here many times before.

Like Four Corners, Monument Valley is a Navajo Tribal Park. Just over the Utah border, you will find the road to the park's visitor center on the right (east) side of the highway. The visitor center complex contains a campground, restaurant, gift shop and restroom facilities, as well as park information. Visitors can board a tour bus for a guided drive through the valley or take a self-guided trip with their own vehicle. The trail through the valley is unpaved and I wouldn't recommend attempting it on a heavy road bike. The observation deck at the visitor's center offers spectacular views of the surrounding mesas. If you want a closer look, I suggest the guided tour option.

Continuing north on US 163 from the visitor center, you'll be treated to more fascinating views of the castle-like rock formations of Monument Valley. As you approach, these grand sculpted mesas will grab and hold your attention. Then as you move past them, a change in perspective brings a change in shape. There are several turnouts on this stretch of road from which you may view these massive sculptures and capture the memory with your camera.

The highway climbs to Monument Pass and as you ride through on the other side, check out the valley in your rearview mirror for another interesting perspective. A couple of miles ahead, you will find Redlands viewpoint which offers a final magnificent look at the valley from a distance.

Making a straight run across the desert plateau, you'll see the red cliffs of Douglas Mesa in the distance to your left. Ahead of you lay the red rock gorges of the San Juan River and a striking view of Raplee Ridge. This spellbinding pink and gray striped mountain will captivate your attention as you approach. Perhaps millions of years in the making, this marvelous mountain ridge still only represents a mere fraction of the earth's four-and-a-half-billion year span. Such a realization can at once inspire excitement and awe while making you feel somewhat small and insignificant.

As you draw nearer to the San Juan River, the highway drops off the plateau into a brilliant red valley and twists pleasantly to the river gorge. Here sits the town of Mexican Hat, nestled along the cliffs of the gorge. This cool little burg has gas, food and lodging.

On the far side of Mexican Hat, the road bends to the north and just outside of town you'll come to the rock for which it is named. Mexican

Mexican Hat Rock

Hat Rock is an interesting balanced rock formation, and yes, it really does look like a Mexican hat. You can't miss it on the right (east) side of the highway.

As you move north and east from the San Juan River gorge, you may get the sensation that you are climbing a series of steps. Though the actual elevation change can be very subtle, each bench or ridge you cross marks a far less subtle change in the geology of the landscape. If you pay close attention, it is almost like climbing a staircase of time.

A couple of miles north of Mexican Hat Rock, the highway skirts the edge of Valley of the Gods, a kind of mini Monument Valley. Unfortunately, the roads into this valley are unpaved. It's too bad that US 163 doesn't bend through the valley, but the view from the highway is good nonetheless. You can also find some good vistas by taking a short detour up SR 261. Note how the rock formations here look much older and more eroded.

Just past Valley of the Gods, your ride climbs up another step, and like stepping into another geologic era, the landscape changes. Less red and more tan, pink, and hints of orange in the buff sandstone color the terrain as you make a flat run parallel to Lime Ridge. Ahead is a rugged ridge of red sandstone, looking like the teeth of a giant saw. The highway runs straight at this menacing landscape, as if playing chicken with the ridge. Approaching, you can't help but wonder how the road will pick its way through this forbidding obstacle. Then, almost last minute, the highway veers right and drops into Comb Wash before sneaking up through a hole in Comb Ridge.

Once again, you seem to have moved up another step and once again, the landscape changes as the road drops off the ridge into a little river valley surrounding the San Juan. Shortly after passing the junction with US 191, you'll roll into Bluff, another cool desert oasis.

Bluff was founded by Mormon pioneers in 1880, and the ruins of their first settlement, historic Fort Bluff, are still to be found within the town limits today. The livelihood of this community has ridden the changing tides of Indian relations, agriculture, mining, oil exploration, and more recently, the arts and tourism over its 130-plus year history. Gas, good food, and nice lodging are available here, in this lovely little escape from the harsh desert, and you may wish to make Bluff the end of your ride.

If you choose to continue back to our start point in Blanding, you'll find that US 163 ends on the east side of Bluff, where the highway becomes northbound US 191. Just out of town, you'll climb through a delightfully narrow canyon at the base of Bluff Bench, and in doing so, climb through another layer of time back to the high desert where we started. A relatively straight run of about twenty-five miles through this somewhat featureless desert will bring you back to Blanding and its complete array of services. If your itinerary calls for visiting points north, Monticello, twenty-one miles north of Blanding, or Moab, fifty-three miles beyond Monticello, make good places to end the day.

This delightful ride has taken you on a fun tour of both human and natural history. Because it lies so far south, you can almost run the loop year round. With the versatility to be a simple half-day ride or one that you can stretch into a full day, the Four Corners loop is a ride that fits easily into a southern Utah touring itinerary. Better still, it's just plain fun!

Four Corners Loop – Notes

Pit Stops:

Blanding:
Shell
861 S. Main
(435) 678-2770

Canyon Country Chevron
12 W. Center
(435) 678-3900

Teec Nos Pos, AZ:
Teec Nos Pos Trading Post
Jct. Hwy 160 & 64
(928) 656-3224

Kayenta, AZ:
Kayenta Chevron
120 US 160
(928) 697-3425

Giant Conoco / C-store
Jct. Hwy 160 & 163
(928) 697-3525

Monument Valley:
Goulding's Trading Post
1000 Main Street (off US 163)
(435) 727-3231

Mexican Hat:
Out West Feed & Fuel
2256 Hwy 163
(435) 683-2214

Bluff:
K&C Trading Post
161 Hwy 191
(435) 672-2221

Accommodations & Camping:

CAMPGROUNDS:
National Park Campgrounds
Hovenweep National Monument info: (970) 562-4282 or www.nps.gov/hove

Monument Valley Navajo Tribal Park info:
P.O. Box 360289
Monument Valley, UT 84536
(435) 727-5870

Commercial Campgrounds
Cadillac Ranch RV Park
Hwy 191, Bluff, UT
(435) 672-2262

HOTELS:
Blanding:
Gateway Inn
88 E. Center
(435) 678-2278

Quality Inn of Blanding
711 S. Main
(435) 678-3271

Kayenta, AZ:
Hampton Inn
Hwy 163
(928) 697-3170

Monument Valley Inn
Jct. Hwy 160 & 163
(928) 697-3211

Wetherill Inn
1000 Main St.
(928) 697-3231

Mexican Hat:
Hat Rock Inn
120 Hwy 163
(435) 683-2221

Canyonlands Motel
Hwy 163
(435) 683-2230

Mexican Hat Lodge
2265 Hwy 163
(435) 683-2222

San Juan Inn
Hwy 163
(435) 683-2220

Bluff:
Desert Rose Inn & Cabins
701 Main St. (US 191)
(435) 672-2303

Kokopelli Inn
161 E. Main (US 191)
(435) 672-2322

Recapture Lodge
220 E. Main (US 191)
(435) 672-2281

RECOMMENDED DINING:
Blanding:
Old Tymer Restaurant
733 S. Main
(435) 678-2122

Homestead Steak House
121 E. Center
(435) 678-3456

Bluff:
Cottonwood Steak House
409 W. Main (US 191)
(435) 672-2282

Section IV

Riding Through

Utah is blessed with a well-developed freeway infrastructure that facilitates travel within and through the state. I-15, the major north-south corridor, connects all the state's urban concentrations. Two substantial east-west corridors, I-70 and I-80 traverse the state as well, while I-84 connects northern Utah to the Pacific Northwest. The interstate freeway system has made Utah and the country much smaller. For speed and efficiency, it can't be beat.

Often, though, when traveling by motorcycle, speed and efficiency are far from being the primary objectives. While some stretches of Utah's freeways offer enjoyable rides (segments of I-70, I-80 and I-84 come to mind), motorcycle travel is much more about the journey itself than simply getting to where you're going. Fortunately, there are plenty of secondary highways on which bikers can travel through and within the state while avoiding the freeways entirely. We'll examine a few of these alternative corridors in this section.

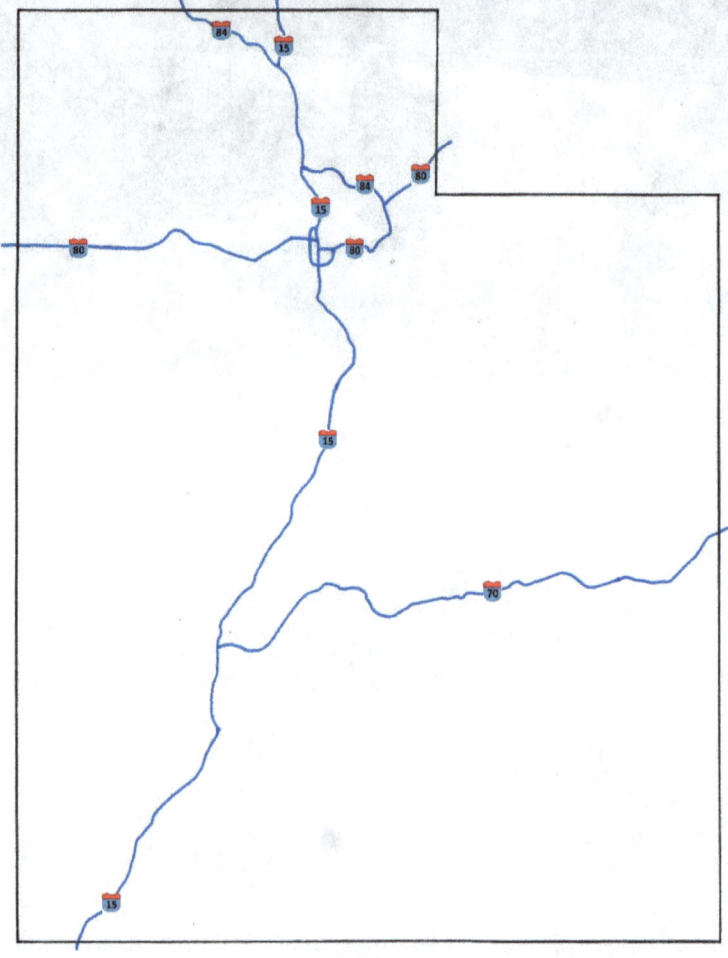

I-15 Alternatives

(Photo by Carl Benson)   Riders on the super-slab near Salt Lake City

Via I-15, one could travel from the Arizona border to Idaho in less than a day. Veterans Memorial Highway, as it is sometimes called, is an excellent stretch of interstate freeway, well designed and well maintained, that strings together Utah's major population centers. It's a great way to go when you want to get there quickly.

On a motorcycle, though, one of the first questions to ask yourself when picking a route is, "What's the hurry?" Many riders view freeways as a necessary evil at best, and at the worst, something to be avoided, whatever it takes. If you lean towards the latter way of thinking, take heart. Traveling through Utah need not be done in a hurry and need not involve the I-15 corridor. Pull over and get out your map while we examine some creative ways around the "super-slabs".

US 89 – "Heritage Highway"

US 89 runs parallel to, and just to the east of I-15 from Arizona to the Idaho border, making it the most obvious alternative route to the north-south freeway corridor. At their point of greatest separation on the Arizona border, these highways are some 85 miles apart, while between Utah Valley and Salt Lake Valley, US 89 actually piggybacks on I-15. For traveling longitudinally through the state, particularly outside the Wasatch Front, US 89 is the front running substitute for the slabs of I-15.

US 89 crosses the Arizona border just north of Page and runs west across the southern edge of the Grand Staircase–Escalante National Monument to Kanab where it joins US 89A. US 89A splits off of US 89 some 25 miles south of Page, AZ and shoots west across the picturesque northern Arizona desert to cross the border north of Fredonia, AZ and rejoins US 89 at Kanab. However you enter the state, you'll have a wonderful ride up 89 all the way to the urban centers of the Wasatch Front.

North of Kanab, the Heritage Highway (US 89) runs through a delightful red canyon along Kanab Creek, then crosses the Sand Hills to find the East Fork of the Virgin River near Mt. Carmel Junction. Here, the road enters the bottom end of Long Valley and makes a magnificent scenic run through this valley up to Panguitch. Cool green forests and meadows between granite mountains and colored cliffs set the backdrop for this segment of your ride.

Running north from Panguitch will find you on a straight and fairly flat dash through a broad valley of farms and ranches. The highway has chosen the Sevier River as its guide for this stretch of the journey, and moving in close to hug the river in the hills south of Circleville, it offers you an amusing canyon frolic before settling down again as it rolls through town. This slice of the trip has brought you into the country where one Robert Leroy Parker, a.k.a. Butch Cassidy was born and raised. Here, on the ranches near Circleville, Butch learned the cattle trade and the business of rustling.

North of Circleville, the highway settles in for another short, straight stretch, descending gently through a valley between Junction and Marysvale. Just north of Junction, Piute Reservoir and Piute State Park lie to the east of the road.

Past Marysvale, the road gets spunky again and treats you to a splendid, yet all too short romp through Sevier Canyon. For most of this stretch, the road clings tightly to the river, making the ride

Big Rock Candy Mountain

wonderfully twisty. Mountain forests and a rock canyon provide a sublime scenic quality. Near the south end of the canyon sits Big Rock Candy Mountain, an odd colored hill where you can find gas and food stops on both sides of the highway – a great place to stop and take a break.

Way too soon, the frivolity ends where the road meets I-70, and it's back to business for a while. Technically, US 89 piggybacks on I-70 up to Elsinore, which is only nine miles northeast of the junction. However, a frontage road, also labeled 89, runs closely parallel to the freeway through Joseph and up to Elsinore. This little sidecar allows the obsessed purist to stay off the slabs, but since the going is substantially slower, especially through Richfield and the surrounding farmland, and the secondary road offers no advantage in either scenery or ride character, most riders take the pragmatic choice of running I-70 up to Salina.

To the north of Salina, US 89 runs flat and straight through the farmlands of the Sevier Valley. This stretch of road may seem longer than it actually is, particularly on a hot day. Speed limits drop through the communities of Centerfield and Gunnison and sometimes rural traffic slows the pace of the ride. At least you're off the freeway, however, and the run up the valley is still quite enjoyable.

At Gunnison, Heritage Highway veers to the east to run up the Sanpete Valley. Strung along the highway in rapid succession are the little towns of Manti, Ephraim, Mount Pleasant and Fairview. North of Fairview, the road climbs into the hills to find Thistle Creek and twists its way up to a junction with US 6. Highways 6 and 89 then run in tandem a short way down Spanish Fork Canyon to the edge of the city of Spanish Fork, where they again separate.

From the mouth of Spanish Fork Canyon, US 89 runs north through Springville and along the west face of the Wasatch Mountains to Provo, closely paralleling I-15. Upon reaching Provo, the highway melts into the urban sprawl of the Utah Valley all the way up through American Fork and into Lehi, where it meets I-15. You've really got to hate freeway riding in a bad way to ride this stretch of the highway through the city. Again the pragmatic approach is to hop on I-15 somewhere between Spanish Fork and Provo.

From Lehi over Point-of-the-Mountain, US 89 shares the road with I-15 before splitting off again on the south edge of Sandy. Here the highway runs the length of the Salt Lake Valley as State Street and as is the case through Utah Valley, the heavy urban terrain makes the freeway a better choice. This remains true all the way up to Farmington.

Just north of Farmington, US 89 splits off I-15, after piggybacking on the freeway once again from Bountiful. This section of the highway offers a pleasant suburban ride along the face of the mountains up through the Fruit Heights and Kaysville areas to South Ogden. At Ogden, the highway becomes Washington Blvd. through town, and like State Street through Salt Lake City, it's a stop and go urban crawl. Rather than riding through downtown Ogden, you might consider jumping on I-84 westbound at the mouth of Weber Canyon. I-84 merges with I-15 in Riverdale and the two run in tandem to the north past Ogden.

On the north side of Ogden, US 89 again becomes a viable and welcome freeway alternative. In town, the highway forks off of Washington Blvd. to the left at 2nd Street. If riding the freeway, just about any exit past exit 349 will allow you to escape the slabs and regain the Heritage Highway to the east.

Between Ogden and Brigham City the highway takes you through Utah's famous Fruit Way. Here, orchards and farmer's markets line

Section IV: Riding Through

Steel horses taking a break at Bear Lake Summit on US 89

the road. I love this stretch of the highway for all the reasons that bikers look for alternatives to freeways. Traffic is much lighter here and the ride more relaxing. Roadside fruit stands offer multiple opportunities to stop for a break and a fresh treat. Furthermore, I've found that on a hot summer day, the ambient temperature seems substantially lower here than on the freeway, just a short distance away.

At Brigham City, US 89 begins what is perhaps its most delightful segment, as it climbs into the mountains for its run to the Idaho border. Here the highway merges with US 91 at the mouth of what is popularly referred to as Sardine Canyon. (This is something of a misnomer, for the real Sardine Canyon runs northeast from Sardine Summit towards Hyrum, away from the road. Why argue with tradition, though?) Together these highways wind up to Sardine Summit and dip through a high valley before dropping through Wellsville Canyon into the Cache Valley. This segment of highway is favored with a broad, four-lane road bed, making it a wonderful and scenic speed run through the mountains.

At Logan, US 89 and US 91 separate. US 91 runs due north through Cache Valley to the border, itself a worthy alternative to I-15 some 16 miles to the west. US 89 veers abruptly east into the mountains for a splendid run up the Logan Canyon Scenic Byway.

Logan Canyon is a wonderful stretch of twisty mountain road that traces the Logan River up to Bear Lake Summit. (See Bear Lake Loop, for a detailed discussion of this ride.) This stretch of road is not only one of Utah's most scenic gems, it is one of the best motorcycle roads in the state.

After cresting the mountains at Bear Lake Summit, US 89 makes a winding descent down to Garden City on the shores of Bear Lake, then bends north and hugs the lakeshore on its way into Idaho.

When traveling the length of Utah, the outstanding scenery and character of US 89 can't be beat. If staying off the freeway is your goal, the Heritage Highway should be your number one alternative to the I-15 corridor.

The Western Corridor

Running through western Utah are a string of often overlooked secondary highways that mirror I-15 and offer riders a route from Cedar City to Tooele without setting a tire on the freeway. While this route lacks some of the scenic appeal and road character of US 89, it is not without merit and in fact rivals I-15 for speed of travel.

Riding north out of Cedar City on Main Street, you'll find yourself on SR 130. This highway crosses I-15 at exit 62 and leaves the city behind as it dashes north across the high desert. SR 130 is also known as the Minersville Highway, and after a short straight run up the Cedar Valley, it climbs through the Black Mountains and winds pleasantly down Parowan Canyon to its namesake, the town of Minersville. Here it meets SR 21 and continues north under that designation.

Running fairly flat and straight north of Minersville, SR 21 makes a speed run across Milford Flat on the northern edge of the Escalante Desert into the small town of Milford. Here the highway forks, with SR 21 veering west to find US 50 in Nevada, while SR 257 takes over the journey northbound. Continue north on SR 257.

SR 257 north of Milford presents a virtually flat desert straightaway on which to open up the throttle. Rolling across the broad expanse of Beaver Bottoms, the Mineral Mountains lie to the east while the San Francisco Mountains and Cricket Mountains conceal the dry bed of Sevier Lake to the west. Sharing the ride along a close, parallel path, the Union Pacific / Amtrak rail line follows the highway north to Delta.

In the town of Delta, SR 257 comes to an end where it meets US 6. Turning right (east) at the highway junction will take you through

Delta to continue the ride north on US 6. Just out of town, the road takes you along the white sand dunes of the Little Sahara National Recreation Area. Climbing subtly, the highway carries you north with few bends up to Tintic Valley where it meets SR 36 just west of Eureka.

At Tintic Junction, turn left to ride SR 36 northbound and leave US 6 behind as it bends east to Eureka. SR 36 gently rises and falls, with mild turns as it carries you northwest through the Vernon Hills. Turning sharply north at Vernon, the highway makes a straight dash up Rush Valley towards Stockton. Hopping over the hills north of Stockton, the road gently descends into the Tooele Valley.

Running north through the city of Tooele, SR 36 continues past the communities of Erda and Stansbury Park for another twelve miles before meeting I-80 at Lake Point. From here, I-80 offers a westbound route to Nevada or a short eastbound run to Salt Lake City and the heart of the Wasatch Front.

Because this route is well maintained and sees little more than local traffic, you'll find the Western Corridor rivals I-15 for speed. Incredibly straight for a secondary route, with little in the way of *twisties*, this ride offers the opportunity to open the throttle and blow out your pipes on desolate desert straightaways. With a unique scenic appeal as a bonus, this route is a worthy alternative to the slabs of I-15.

The Central Corridor

Lying in the center of the state, SR's 24 and 28 form the backbone of a secondary north-south corridor that allows riders to escape the heat and traffic of the freeway. SR's 22, 62 and segments of US 89 extend this corridor well into southern Utah.

From the southwest, riding US 89 to the junction with SR 62 accesses this central route. SR 62 takes a short yet enjoyable run east through Kingston Canyon before turning north for a sprint across Grass Valley to join SR24.

To the east, SR 22 offers a scenic dash up Johns Valley from Bryce Canyon City (SR 12), before picking its way slowly through Black Canyon and the town of Antimony to join SR 62 at the bottom of Grass Valley. While portions of SR's 22 and 62 are narrow and poorly maintained, this route is nonetheless worth seeking out.

SR 62 merges into SR 24 where the latter skirts the Praetor Slopes just south of Koosharem Reservoir (about fourteen miles northwest of

Loa). A short dash up the Plateau Valley brings SR 24 to the mouth of Kings Meadow Canyon for a pleasantly winding romp north through the Rainbow Hills to the little towns of Sigurd and Vermillion.

At Vermillion, SR 24 merges with US 89 and the two share the roadbed north into Salina where SR 24 comes to an end. Riding north on US 89 out of Salina takes you to the town of Gunnison, where SR 28 can be found forking to the left off of US 89.

Riding SR 28 north out of Gunnison takes the ride around the west side of the San Pitch Mountains for a run north through the farm country of the Juab Valley. The farms along this route, particularly north of Levan, seem to absorb the oppressive heat of summer. This natural cooling effect is dramatic and easily discernible. I have often found air temperatures to be several degrees cooler along SR 28 than on I-15 just a few miles to the west.

SR 28 comes to an end where it intersects I-15 on the south edge of Nephi. While one truly committed to shunning the freeway could cobble together a route of secondary roads to continue a journey northward, this is effectively the limit of the Central Corridor. Though it doesn't transit the entire length of the state, it certainly offers riders a viable, fast alternative to the freeway. More to the point, it allows riders to escape the heat and doldrums of what is arguably the least enjoyable segment of I-15.

The Eastern Corridor – US 191

US 191 runs the length of the state from Arizona to the Wyoming border along the eastern edge. As with US 89, travelers can completely transit the state without leaving the highway, and like its more popular cousin, US 191 possesses, on the whole, that special combination of scenic quality and ride character that make it more than just an alternative route.

Crossing into Utah just north of Mexican Water, AZ, US 191 runs through the sand dunes on northern edge of the Navajo Nation to join US 163 near Bluff. Sharing the road through Bluff, these routes separate on the west end of town and US 191 continues its journey north through the color country of southeast Utah.

Running north from Bluff to Blanding, the highway is designated a scenic route on the official Utah Highway Map published by the state Dept. of Transportation. Colorful canyons and high desert plateaus give the ride the distinct flavor of the desert southwest so common to southern Utah.

The scenic buffet continues north of Blanding as the road passes through the forests surrounding Recapture Lake and lopes lazily up and down across open desert into Monticello. Beyond Monticello, riders are treated to pockets of *twisties* and ever increasing color as the road approaches the slickrock country around Moab.

Rolling through Moab, riders of US 191 see the world turn brilliant red. A landscape of sculpted sandstone surrounds the little resort oasis, while the snow-capped La Sal Mountains stand watch to the east.

North of Moab the highway is a straight shot through the red desert to Crescent Junction where it meets I-70. Here, it hitches a ride on the freeway for twenty-four miles to the west.

At exit 157, US 191 leaves the freeway and continues its trip north, this time sharing the road with US 6. For roughly fifty miles the road makes a speed run, flat and straight through a broad desert valley, curving almost imperceptibly to the west to conform to the shape of the bold Book Cliffs off to the east. On the top end of this desert dash, the road finds the cities of Wellington and Price nestled in a valley with the fortress-like walls of the Book Cliffs wrapping around them to the north.

Moving past Price, our highway finds the town of Helper perched on the edge of the mountains at the mouth of Price Canyon. A couple of miles into this scenic canyon, US 191 parts company with US 6, forking to the right to trace Willow Creek into the hills.

The next forty-four miles of the highway are again designated a scenic route by UDOT. Somehow though, simply marking this road with dots on a map seems akin to damning with faint praise, for this is one of the finest motorcycle highway segments in the state. Looping around PacifiCorp's Carbon Plant, the road is soon embraced tightly by rocky canyon walls and begins a delightful ascent up a sinuous forested gorge.

Ten miles or so up the road, the landscape opens up and you will find an interesting monument just off the highway near the intersection of Emma Park Road. This is the Bamberger Monument, a marker erected by state prisoners in 1918 to honor Simon Bamberger, governor of Utah from 1917- 1920. At face value, this monument seems to have little significance other than to serve as evidence that the vanity of Utah politicians is nothing new.

Again the landscape closes in as the road makes a steep climb through a beautiful forested canyon. The ascent is wonderfully twisty making for a fantastic ride.

Bamberger Monument

The highway summits at over 9,300 feet at a gap between Reservation Ridge and the Badland Cliffs near the border of the Ashley National Forest. Beginning an equally amusing descent down Indian Canyon, the road runs through a thick forest of aspen and pine that becomes a particular delight to ride in the fall as autumn colors begin to burst.

About fifteen miles south of Duchesne the highway leaves the Ashley National Forest and the trees give way to sandstone cliffs. Gently twisting along the west side of the canyon, the road traces the edge of a broad swath of green down the middle of the gorge, dotted with pastures and ranches. Here and there cabins pop up, some of which appear quite old, as if they may be nineteenth century derelicts.

At the mouth of Indian Canyon lies the town of Duchesne, where US 191 meets US 40. These highways share the road for a fifty-eight mile run east to the city of Vernal. On the way, the ride will take you through some lovely desert landscapes, reminiscent of the color country to the south.

In Vernal, US 191 says goodbye to US 40 and runs due north into the hills. Again, the road earns scenic route designation from UDOT, and again, this doesn't begin to describe the amusing qualities of this stretch of highway. Not far out of Vernal a scenic desert, full of fossils and other geologic intrigue, forms the setting for the ride. Then, climbing a staircase of ten hairpin switchbacks, the road comes to the mountain forests on the south slope of the Uinta Range. Slipping through the Uintas, the highway crosses the top of Flaming Gorge Dam and picks its way around the reservoir for a dash across Antelope Flat into Wyoming.

US 191 is an excellent road throughout – well designed and well maintained. Top notch road characteristics and scenic quality make this highway a route highly suited to motorcycle enthusiasts. Location and north-south orientation give this road the added bonus of being an outstanding alternative to I-15.

East – West Routes

A derelict service station offers a shady rest stop on US 6

No description of alternative routes is complete without examining a couple of the significant east-west throughways. Crossing Utah from west to east or vice versa is easy and convenient via I-70, I-80, and I-84. Unlike I-15, which sees much more traffic and lacks much in the way of scenic quality, segments of these lateral freeways are actually quite enjoyable to ride. These virtuous segments are sporadic however, and (in the case of I-80) often disappear beyond the state border. So, for the purist intent on steering clear of the super-slabs, here's a look at some alternate east-west routes.

US 40

US Highway 40 finds its western terminus in northern Utah where it meets I-80 at Silver Creek Junction, just east of Salt Lake City. Beginning on the shores of the Atlantic Ocean in New Jersey, this grand American byway once ran from coast to coast and was known popularly as "The National Road". Since 1975, all segments west of Silver Creek Junction have been decommissioned in favor of I-80, yet it is still possible to ride the Golden Highway (another popular nickname for US 40) from Park City to Atlantic City.

The segment of US 40 that we'll examine here, from I-80 to the Colorado border, is a thoroughly enjoyable ride, but more important, what lies beyond the border makes this road an outstanding alternative to I-80 for extended eastbound travel. When traveling by motorcycle from the Wasatch Front to the urban corridor ranging from Denver, CO to Cheyenne WY, US 40 is certainly the superior ride.

At its origin just off I-80, US 40 is a four lane divided highway of freeway style construction. The road makes a comfortable high speed run to the south along the eastern edge of Park City down to Heber City. Gently climbing and descending through the mountains along the way, the ride is both scenic and fun.

Becoming Main Street in Heber City, the highway takes you south through town where it bends to the southeast and dashes into the hills. After a short, flat straightaway running away from the Heber Valley, the road climbs into Daniels Canyon for a marvelous run through the mountains. Daniels Canyon is a top rate ride, with both twisty road character and wonderful scenic quality. In autumn, this lovely canyon explodes in color as the aspen groves turn a bright, almost neon shade of yellow.

Cresting the mountain at 7,980 feet, the highway finds its way through Daniels Pass. At the road summit, a resort lodge with gas, a convenience store and restaurant makes an enjoyable rest stop. Beyond the pass, the highway begins its descent down the eastern slope towards Strawberry Reservoir. Wide and well maintained, this stretch of road is also a joy to ride. Mild *twisties* alternate with broad straightaways to carry the ride out of the mountains, offering a grand view of Strawberry Reservoir along the way.

A short romp through Deep Creek Canyon brings the road to the high country farms and rangelands of Duchesne County. A dash across the plateau finds Starvation Reservoir, where a bridge spanning a finger of the lake carries the ride over the water, offering a scenic view in the process.

Just beyond Starvation Reservoir, the town of Duchesne sits at the edge of the Uinta Basin. Here, US 191 hops on US 40 and hitches a ride. East of Duchesne, these tandem highways roll through farmlands past the town of Roosevelt to cross a delightfully scenic desert and find their way into the city of Vernal, where US 191 jumps off and makes its way north.

Carrying the ride through the heart of Vernal and the neighboring town of Naples, US 40 then makes a fairly flat and straight speed run to the Colorado border. In doing so, our highway once again crosses a marvelously scenic desert along the edge of Dinosaur National Monument before continuing its journey east into the beauty of Colorado.

Riding US 40 from Park City to Colorado will take less than three hours, but three delightful hours they will surely be. Continuing eastbound into Colorado, the ride is equally enjoyable. When traveling to northeastern Colorado or southwest Wyoming, you'll find this route far superior, in terms of road character and scenic quality, to crossing the desert plains of southern Wyoming via I-80.

US 50

Like US 40, US 50 once ran from sea to sea, until being truncated in California in 1973. This highway still retains most of its grandeur as a transcontinental route, however, running from Ocean City, MD to West Sacramento, CA.

Known as the "Loneliest Road in America" as it crosses Nevada, this epithet is certainly apropos in western Utah as well. Crossing the Nevada border near Great Basin National Park, this desolate highway makes a straight, flat dash across the desert to cross the Confusion Range via Kings Canyon. Dropping down across the Tule Valley, the road then hops over the House Range at Skull Rock Pass, skirting along the north shore of dry Sevier Lake as it crosses the Sevier desert to the town of Delta.

Running east out of Delta, US 50 then continues its desert dash to the southeast, passing through the sand dunes of the Pahvant Valley before veering north to parallel I-15 near the little town of Holden. Jumping on I-15 at exit 178, US 50 hitches a ride on the freeway for ten miles north to the town of Scipio, where leaving I-15 it resumes its course southeast through Round Valley to the town of Salina.

At Salina, US 50 meets I-70 and rides this freeway east over the Colorado border to Grand Junction. Though more than half of US 50's journey through Utah shares the road with I-70, this highway still makes the cut as a worthy alternate route, particularly for riders coming from the west who are faced with crossing Nevada via I-80, which is a truly dismal ride. I-70, on the other hand, is not bad for a freeway. Even though it's a super slab, this route has a degree of character and enough scenic appeal to qualify it as a decent motorcycle ride. Those with a fanatical aversion to the slabs (as I occasionally tend to be) can take heart in the assurance that they are riding US 50 rather than I-70 and thus enjoy the trip with a clean conscience.

Rand McNally designates US 50 as a scenic route for its entire run across the state, from Nevada to Colorado. While I've found the venerable map maker to be somewhat liberal with scenic route designation in the past, I applaud their bold statement with US 50 in Utah, particularly in recognizing the unique beauty of the desolate west desert. When coming to Utah from points west, traveling the Great Basin via America's Loneliest Road beats the tedium of I-80 every time.

US 6

Once the longest transcontinental highway in America, US 6 ran from the waters of Cape Cod at Provincetown, MA to the shores of the Pacific at Long Beach, CA. In 1964, the highway was truncated to Bishop, CA, putting it in second place behind US 20 as the country's longest road. Still, with over 3200 miles of pavement under its markers, this ribbon of highway is a substantial route. Known as "The Grand-Army-of-the-Republic Highway", it is indeed a grand memorial to the Civil War army to which it pays tribute.

US 6 shares the road with US 50 for much of its Utah crossing. Entering from Nevada at the Great Basin, the routes run in tandem to Delta, where US 6 separates on a large loop to the north, rejoining US 50 on the back of I-70 near Green River. It is this loop through north-central Utah that makes US 6 an amusing, albeit more time consuming alternative, to a mid-state crossing on US 50.

Running northeast out of Delta, US 6 crosses the sand dunes of Little Sahara National Recreation Area and climbs gently into the Tintic Valley. Just west of Eureka, the road bends east, passing through this small mining town as it crosses the East Tintic Mountains and drops into Goshen Valley on the other side.

US 6 through the Goshen Valley

Sprinting across the valley to Santaquin, the highway intersects I-15 and bends north to roughly parallel the freeway on the east side, sharing the road with SR 198. Looping through the cities of Payson and Salem, this highway tandem makes its way to Spanish Fork where it bends abruptly east and merges with US 89.

Here US 6 and US 89 share a short ride up Spanish Fork Canyon before separating at Thistle Junction. US 6 continues east, tracing Soldier Creek up a marvelous mountain draw where the road is wide, smooth and very well maintained. This section of highway offers what motorcycle author Marty Berke calls the "Triple R", a ride configuration where road, river and railroad run in parallel. Crisp mountain air and scenic terrain indulge the senses while a road of magnificent character, tight *twisties* and sweeping high speed curves provide the rider with an injection of pure adrenaline. Yes, this stretch of road is a true joy to ride. But before you let loose with too much exuberance, take note of the road sign near the mouth of Spanish Fork Canyon that warns of increased traffic enforcement between Spanish Fork and Price. The warning is no bluff. This stretch of highway has a history of fatal traffic accidents and the Utah Highway Patrol has responded with aggressive traffic enforcement. Their program should be applauded as a tremendous success, for the ride to Price is once again a safe and enjoyable trip for responsible motorists and riders. Give 'em a wave of thanks as you ride through.

The highway peaks at Soldier Summit, cresting nearly 7,500 feet, then descends with equal excitement through Price Canyon into the city of Price. Just above the town of Helper, near the mouth of the canyon, US 191 merges from the east to tag along on the ride down to Green River.

South of Price, US 6/191 makes a long straight dash through a high desert valley along the face of the Book Cliffs. A stunning view of this marvelous range accompanies the highway for its entire run south to Gunnison Valley, where it joins I-70 west of Green River.

At the freeway junction, US 6 joins US 50 on its piggyback ride along I-70 to the Colorado border. As I've indicated above, this stretch of freeway is not bad as far as super-slabs go. Running across Crescent Flat, Sagers Flat, Windy Mesa and through Grand Valley into Colorado, with mountains to the north and east, this triple highway holds plenty of scenic merit.

Crossing the state on an east-west axis, US 6 and US 50 are really just two sides of the same coin. One route is somewhat more direct, holding to a southern track, while the other offers the diversion of swinging north to cross the lower Wasatch. Both are wonderful alternate routes which should receive primary consideration for riders crossing the state with the track of the sun.

Ride Utah!

Keeping the road safe - Utah Highway Patrol

Appendix A
Motorcycle Dealers
(Alphabetically by make; North-South, West-East)

BMW:

BMW Motorcycles of Utah
339 W. 9000 S.
Sandy, UT 84070
(801) 618-2700
www.bmwmotorcyclesofutah.com

CAN-AM:

Renegade Sports
1903 S. 800 W.
Logan, UT 84321
(435) 755-7111
www.renegadesports.us

Renegade Sports
240 N. Frontage Rd.
Centerville, UT 84014
(435) 292-1492
www.renegadesports.us

Weller Recreation
2972 N. 900 E.
Kamas, UT 84036
(435) 783-4718
www.wellerrec.com

Moto Zoo
1295 E. Red Hills Pkwy
St. George, UT 84770
(435) 652-2640
www.mzpowersports.com

ADS Motorsports
284 W. 12th St.
Ogden, UT 84404
(801) 393-4561
www.adsmotorsports.com

High Adventure Power Sports
1846 S. 5070 W.
Salt Lake City, UT 84104
(801) 924-9244
www.highadventureps.com

Utah Valley Powersports
135 N. 2000 W.
Springville, UT 84663
(801) 491-4242
www.utahvalleypowersports.com

DUCATI:

Salt Lake Motorsports
916 S. Main St.
Salt Lake City, UT 84111
(801) 478-4000
www.saltlakelemotorsports.com

HARLEY-DAVIDSON:

Saddleback Harley-Davidson
2359 N. Main St.
Logan, UT 84341
(435) 787-8700
www.goldenspikeharley.com

Harley-Davidson of SLC
2928 S. State St.
Salt Lake City, UT 84115
(801) 487-4647
www.utahharley.com

South Valley Harley-Davidson
8886 S. Sandy Parkway Dr.
Sandy, UT 84070
(801) 563-1110
www.utahharley.com

Timpanogos Harley-Davidson
555 S. Geneva Rd
Lindon, UT 84042
(801) 434-4647
www.timpharley.com

Golden Spike Harley-Davidson
892 Riverdale Rd.
Ogden, UT 84405
(801) 394-4664
www.goldenspikeharley.com

Park City Harley-Davidson
324 Main St.
Park City, UT 84060
(435) 214-5099
www.utahharley.com

Beers Harley-Davidson
2029 W. Hwy 40
Vernal, UT 84078
(435) 789-5196
www.beersharley.com

Zion Harley-Davidson
2345 N. Coral Canyon Blvd.
Washington, UT 84780
(435) 572-4322
www.zionhd.com

HONDA:

Cache Honda Yamaha
3765 N. Hwy 91
Hyde Park, UT 84318
(435) 563-6291
www.cachehy.com

Newgate Motorsports
3745 S. 250 W.
Ogden, UT 84405
(801) 394-3403
www.newgatemotorsports.com

Appendices

Honda / Suzuki of Salt Lake
2354 S. State St.
Salt Lake City, UT 84115
(801) 486-5401
www.hondasuzuki.com

Steadman's
916 N. Main St.
Tooele, UT 84074
(435) 882-3344
www.steadmans.net

Summit Honda
6407 Business Park Loop Rd.
Park City, UT 84098
(435) 649-7433

Vernal Sports Center
2029 W. Hwy 40
Vernal, UT 84078
(435) 789-5196
www.beersharley.com

Rocky Mountain ATV
4510 N. Hwy 6
Helper, UT 84526
(435) 472-8862
www.rockymountainatvmcdealership.com

Ron's Sporting Goods
138 S. Main St.
Cedar City, UT 84720
(435) 586-9901
www.ronssportinggoods.com

Moto Zoo
1295 E. Red Hills Pkwy
St. George, UT 84770
(435) 652-2640
www.mzpowersports.com

Plaza Cycle
1379 W. 3300 S.
Salt Lake City, UT 84119
(801) 972-8725
www.plazacycle.com

Honda World
10764 S 300 W
So. Jordan, UT 84095
(801) 572-9800
www.hondaworldslc.com

Monarch Honda
398 W. 800 N.
Orem, UT 84057
(801) 224-4070
www.monarchhonda.com

Garrett Honda Motorsports
563 N. Main St.
Nephi, UT 84648
(435) 623-0823
www.garretthondamotorsports.com

Jorgensen's
980 S. Cove View Rd.
Richfield, UT 84701
(435) 896-6408
www.jhsport.com

Hondaland
935 E. Hwy 491
Monticello, UT 84535
(435) 587-2818

Ride Utah!

INDIAN:
(No dealers yet in Utah)
www.indianmotorcycle.com

KAWASAKI:

Renegade Sports
1903 S. 800 W.
Logan, UT 84321
(435) 755-7111
www.renegadesports.us

Big Boys Toys
2529 N. Hwy 89
Ogden, UT 84404
(801) 782-6125
www.bigboyspolaris.com

Renegade Sports
240 N. Frontage Rd.
Centerville, UT 84014
(435) 292-1492
www.renegadesports.us

South Valley Motorsports
11553 S. State St.
Draper, UT 84020
(801) 576-1899
www.southvalleymotorsports.com

White Knuckle Motorsports
889 N. 2000 W.
Springville, UT 84663
(801) 489-0393
www.whiteknucklekawasaki.com

Tony Basso ATV
1152 S. Carbon Ave.
Price, UT 84501
(435) 637-4224
www.tonybassoatv.com

Vescos Motorsports
816 N. Main St.
Brigham City, UT
(435) 734-9424
www.vescosmotorsports.com

Newgate Motorsports
3745 S. 250 W.
Ogden, UT 84405
(801) 394-3403
www.newgatemotorsports.com

Plaza Cycle
1379 W. 3300 S.
Salt Lake City, UT 84119
(801) 972-8725
www.plazacycle.com

Duff Shelley Kawasaki
260 E. Main St.
American Fork, UT 84003
(801) 756-3613
www.duffshelley.com

Rocky Mountain ATV
4510 N. Hwy 6
Helper, UT 84526
(435) 472-8862
www.rockymountainatvmcdealership.com

Delta Sports Center
299 N. Hwy 6
Delta, UT 84624
(435) 864-6432
www.deltasports.com

Appendices

Jorgensen's
980 S. Cove View Rd.
Richfield, UT 84701
(435) 896-6408
www.jhsport.com

Rocky Mountain ATV
204 Playa Della Rosita
Washington, UT 84780
(435) 673-2444
www.rockymountainatvmcdealership.com

SUZUKI:

Renegade Sports
1903 S. 800 W.
Logan, UT 84321
(435) 755-7111
www.renegadesports.us

Big Boys Toys
2529 N. Hwy 89
Ogden, UT 84404
(801) 782-6125
www.bigboyspolaris.com

Layton Cycle & Sports
60 N. Main St.
Layton, UT 84041
(801) 544-2241
www.laytoncycle.com

Honda / Suzuki of Salt Lake
2354 S. State St.
Salt Lake City, UT 84115
(801) 486-5401
www.hondasuzuki.com

The Edge Powersports
14301 Minuteman Dr.
Draper, UT 84020
(801) 495-3278
www.get2theedge.com

Vernal Sports Center
2029 W. Hwy 40
Vernal UT 84078
(435) 789-5196
www.vernalsuzuki.com

Escape Motorsports
1480 N. State Street
Provo UT 84604
(801) 374-0602
www.escapemotorsports.com

White Knuckle Motorsports
889 N. 2000 W.
Springville, UT 84663
(801) 489-0393
www.whiteknucklekawasaki.com

Rocky Mountain ATV
4510 N. Hwy 6
Helper, UT 84526
(435) 472-8862
www.rockymountainatvmcdealership.com

Jorgensen's
980 S. Cove View Rd.
Richfield, UT 84701
(435) 896-6408
www.jhsport.com

Ride Utah!

D&P Performance
110 E. Center St.
Cedar City UT 84720
(435) 586-5172
www.dandpperformance.net

Moto Zoo
1295 E. Red Hills Pkwy
St. George, UT 84770
(435) 652-2640
www.mzpowersports.com

TRIUMPH:

Triumph Motorcycles of Utah
339 W. 9000 S.
Sandy, UT 84070
(801) 618-2700
www.triumphofutah.com

VICTORY:

Renegade Sports
1903 S. 800 W.
Logan, UT 84321
(435) 755-7111
www.renegadesports.us

Big Boys Toys
2529 N. Hwy 89
Ogden, UT 84404
(801) 782-6125
www.bigboyspolaris.com

Tri-City Performance
461 S. 800 W.
Centerville, UT 84014
(801) 298-8081
www.tricityperformance.com

Tri-City Performance Inc.
1350 S. 2000 W.
Springville, UT 84663
(801) 794-3005
www.tricityperformance.com

YAMAHA:

Cache Honda Yamaha
3765 N. Hwy 91
Hyde Park, UT 84318
(435) 563-6291
www.cachehy.com

Careys Cycle Center
4450 S. 700 W.
Riverdale, UT
(801) 394-3469
www.careyscycle.com

Layton Cycle & Sports
60 N. Main St.
Layton, UT 84041
(801) 544-2241
www.laytoncycle.com

Plaza Cycle
1379 W. 3300 S.
West Valley City, UT 84119
(801) 972-8725
www.plazacycle.com

Weller Recreation
2972 N. 900 E.
Kamas, UT 84036
(435) 783-4718
www.wellerrec.com

Plaza Cycle
1379 W. 3300 S.
Salt Lake City, UT 84119
(801) 972-8725
www.plazacycle.com

Plaza Powersports
345 N. Main St.
Heber City, UT 84032
(435) 654-7073
www.plazapowersports.com

Escape Motorsports
1480 N. State St.
Provo, UT 84604
(801) 374-0602
www.escapemotorsports.com

Rocky Mountain ATV
4510 N. Hwy 6
Helper, UT 84526
(435) 472-8862
www.rockymountainatvmcdealership.com

Jorgensen's
980 S. Cove View Rd.
Richfield, UT 84701
(435) 896-6408
www.jhsport.com

Steadman's
916 N. Main St.
Tooele, UT 84074
(435) 882-3344
www.steadmans.net

South Valley Motorsports
11553 S. State St.
Draper, UT 84020
(801) 576-1899
www.southvalleymotorsports.com

York Motorsports
591 S. 1500 W.
Vernal, UT 84078
(435) 789-7463

Big Pine Sports
340 N. Milburn Rd.
Fairview, UT 84629
(435) 427-3338
www.bigpinesports.com

Delta Sports Center
299 N. Hwy 6
Delta, UT 84624
(435) 864-6432
www.deltasports.com

Moto Zoo
1295 E. Red Hills Pkwy
St. George, UT 84770
(435) 652-2640
www.mzpowersports.com

Appendix B
Clubs and Organizations

BMW:

BMW Motorcycle Owners of America – factory sponsored BMW club
www.bmwmoa.org

Internet BMW Riders – online BMW club and mailing list
www.ibmwr.org

Beehive Beemers MC of Utah – Utah chapter of BMW MOA
www.beehive-beemers.org

CAN-AM:

Spyder Owners and Ryders –
www.facebook.com/pages/Spyder-Owners-and-Ryders/301653903224220

DUCATI:

Desmo Owners Club – factory sponsored Ducati club
www.ducatiusa.com/club/index.do

Desmo Owners Club – online community
www.ducati.net

Ducati Monster – online forum for Ducati Monster owners
www.ducatimonster.org

Bevelheads – online forum for vintage Ducati enthusiasts
www.bevelheaven.com

Ducati Meccanica – online forum for classic Ducati enthusiasts
www.ducatimeccanica.com

Appendices

HARLEY-DAVIDSON:

Harley Owners Group (HOG) – factory sponsored H-D club
www.harley-davidson.com
www.members.hog.com
1-800-CLUB HOG

Saddleback Chapter / HOG – Logan area chapter of Harley Owners Group
www.facebook.com/HOGSaddlebackChapter2169

Northern Utah Chapter / HOG – Ogden area chapter of Harley Owners Group
www.goldenspikeharley.com; www.facebook.com/nuhog.hog

Great Salt Lake Chapter / HOG – SLC area chapter of Harley Owners Group
www.gslhog.org

Central Utah Chapter / HOG – Provo / Orem area chapter of Harley Owners Group
www.cuhog.org

High Uintas Chapter / HOG – Vernal / Uinta Basin area chapter of Harley Owners Group
www.facebook.com/HighUintasHogChapter5213

Southern Utah Chapter / HOG – Saint George area chapter of Harley Owners Group
www.suhog.com

HONDA:

Honda Riders Club of America – factory sponsored Honda club
hrca.honda.com

HRCA chapters – contact local Honda Dealer for information on HRCA chapters in your area

Gold Wing Road Riders Association – national club for Gold Wing and Valkyrie riders
www.gwrra.org

GWRRA Utah District – Utah district of Gold Wing Road Riders Association
    Chapter H: Northern Utah Area chapter
    Chapter M: Salt Lake City Area chapter
    Chapter R: Orem/Provo Area chapter
http://home.comcast.net/~gwrrautah/

The Sabre Group – online forum for owners of the Honda Shadow Sabre
www.thesabregroup.com

Valkyrie Owners Association - club for owners of the Honda Valkyrie
www.valkyrie-owners.com

KAWASAKI:

Riders of Kawasaki – factory sponsored Kawasaki club
www.kawasaki.com/ROK/
1-877-ROK-CLUB

American Voyager Association – Voyager riders club
www.amervoyassoc.org

Concours Owners Group – sport touring club for Concours owners
www.cog-online.org

SUZUKI:

Suzuki Owners Club of North America – Suzuki brand motorcycle owners club
www.suzukiownersclub.net

Marauder Intruder Group – online forum for Marauder, Intruder and Boulevard owners
www.migcruisers.com

TRIUMPH:

Triumph International Owners Club
www.tioc.org
(508) 946-1939

VICTORY:

Victory Riders Association – factory sponsored Victory club
www.victorymotorcycles.com/en-us/community/vra/membership-benefits.aspx

Victory Motorcycle Club – Victory motorcycle owners club
www.thevmc.com

Wasatch Victory Riders – Northern Utah Chapter of the Victory Motorcycle Club
www.wasatchvictoryriders.com

YAMAHA:

STAR Touring and Riding Association– factory sponsored STAR motorcycle club
www.startouring.org

STAR Salt Lake City chapter 152
www.star152.org

STAR Provo chapter 431
www.star431.org

STAR St. George chapter 513
www.starrouring.org/chapterlist.aspx

International STAR Riders Association – STAR riders club
www.international-star-riders.com

MISCELLANEOUS:

Bikers Against Child Abuse
www.bacaworld.org

Blue Knights – Law enforcement motorcycle club
www.blueknights.org
www.blueknightsutah4.blogspot.com

Canyonchasers – online forum for sport touring enthusiasts
www.canyonchasers.net

Iron Butt Association – long distance riders association
www.ironbutt.com

Motormaids – club for women riders
www.motormaids.org

Salt Lake Motorcycle Club – SLC area riders club, all makes welcome
www.slmc1.com

Wind and Fire – Firefighters motorcycle club
www.anglefire.com/ca2/windandfiremc/

Appendix C
Motorcycling on the Web

EDUCATION / INFORMATION / SAFETY:

American Motorcyclist Association – www.americanmotorcyclist.com
Discover Today's Motorcycling – www.motorcycles.org
Motorcycle Industry Council – www.mic.org
Motorcycle Safety Foundation – www.msf-usa.org
Utah Rider Education – www.utahridered.com

MOTORCYCLIST RIGHTS / LEGISLATIVE:

ABATE – www.utahabate.org
Helmet Law Defense League – http://usff.com/hldlhome.html
International Riders Rights Directory – http://ridersrights.org
Motorcycle Riders Foundation – www.mrf.org
Bikers Rights Online – www.bikersrights.com

MAJOR MANUFACTURERS:

BMW – www.bmwmotorcycles.com
Can-Am – www.can-am.brp.com
Ducati – www.ducatiusa.com
Harley-Davidson – www.harley-davidson.com
Honda – http://powersports.honda.com
Indian – www.indianmotorcycle.com
Kawasaki – www.kawasaki.com
Suzuki – www.suzukicycles.com
Triumph – www.triumphmotorcycles.com
Victory – www.victorymotorcycles.com
Yamaha – www.yamaha-motor.com

GENERAL INTEREST:

Biker Net – www.bikernet.com
Cycle Matters – www.cyclematters.com
Cycle News – www.cyclenews.com

Motorcycle.com – www.motorcycle.com
Motorcycle Cruiser Links – http://cruiserlinks.com
Motorcycle Guide – www.motorcycleguide.net
Motorcycling Online – www.motorcyclingonline.com
Motorcycle USA – www.motorcycle-usa.com
Moto Guide – www.motoguide.com
Ultimate Motorcycling – www.ultimatemotorcycling.com
Vintage Motorcycles Online – www.vintagemotorcyclesonline.com

Appendices

Appendix D
Travel Information Resources

TRAVEL & TOURISM INFO:

Utah Office of Tourism
300 N. State St.
Salt Lake City, UT 84114
(800) 200-1160
www.visitutah.com

Ogden/Weber CVB
2438 Washington Blvd.
Ogden, UT 84401
866-867-8824
www.visitogden.com

Davis Area CVB
1572 N. Woodland Park Dr., Ste 510
Layton, UT 84041
888-777-9771
www.visitdavisareautah.com

Box Elder County Tourism
1 S. Main St.
Brigham City, UT 84302
(877) 390-2326
www.boxeldercounty.org

Morgan County Visitors Bureau
87 N. Commercial St
Morgan, UT 84050
(801) 829-6390

Cache Valley Tourist Council
160 N. Main St.
Logan, UT 84321
800-882-4433
www.tourcachevalley.com

Bear Lake CVB
P.O. Box 55
Garden City, UT 84028
800-448-2327
www.bearlake.org

Visit Salt Lake
90 S. West Temple
Salt Lake City, UT 84101
800-541-4955
www.visitsaltlake.com

Tooele County Tourism
154 S. Main St.
Tooele, UT 84074
800-378-0690
http://tooelechamber.com

Mountainland Travel Region
586 E. 800 N.
Orem, UT 84097
(801) 229-3800
www.mountainland.org

Park City CVB
1910 Prospector Ave.
Park City, UT 84060
(435) 649-6100
www.visitparkcity.com

Utah Valley CVB
111 S. University Ave.
Provo, UT 84601
800-222-8824
www.utahvalley.com

Dinosaurland Travel Board
55 E. Main St.
Vernal, UT 84078
800-477-5558
www.dinoland.com

Piute County Tourism
550 N. Main
Junction, UT 84740
(435) 577-2949
www.piute.org

Millard County Tourism
71 S. 200 W.
Delta, UT 84624
888-463-8627
www.millardcounty.com

Sevier County Tourism
250 N. Main St.
Richfield, UT 84701
800-662-8898
www.sevierutah.net

Kane County Travel Council
78 S. 100 E.
Kanab, UT 84741
800-733-5263
www.visitsouthernutah.com

St. George CVB
1835 Convention Center Dr.
St. George, UT 84770
800-869-6635
www.utahsdixie.com

Beaver County Travel Council
40 S. Main St.
Beaver, UT 84713
866-891-6655
www.beavercountytravel.com

Juab County Tourism
4 S. Main St., P.O. Box 71
Nephi, UT 84648
800-748-4361
www.juabtravel.com

Capitol Reef Country
Junction Hwy 12 & 24
Torrey, UT 84773
800-858-7951
www.capitolreef.org

Sanpete County
345 W. 100 N.
Ephraim, UT 84647
800-281-4346
www.sanpete.com

Castle Country Travel Region
90 N. 100 East #2
Price, UT 84501
800-842-0789
www.castlecountry.com

Garfield County Travel Council
55 S. Main
Panguitch, UT 84759
800-444-6689
www.brycecanyoncountry.com

Cedar City & Brian Head Tourism
581 N. Main St.
Cedar City, UT 84720
800-354-4849
www.scenicsouthernutah.com

Moab Area Travel Council
40 N. 100 E.
Moab, UT 84532
800-635-6622
www.discovermoab.com

San Juan County Visitor Services
117 S. Main St.
Monticello, UT 84535
800-574-4386
www.utahscanyoncountry.com

Emery County Travel Bureau
PO Box 1035
Castle Dale, UT 84513
888-564-3600
www.emerycounty.com/travel

OTHER TOURISM WEBSITES:

Outdoor Utah: www.outdoorutah.com
Utah Office of Tourism: www.travel.utah.gov
Utah Travel Center: www.utahtravelcenter.com
Visit Utah: www.visitutah.org

NATIONAL PARKS & MONUMENTS:

Arches National Park
Moab, UT
(435) 719-2299
www.nps.gov/arch

Bryce Canyon National Park
Bryce Canyon, UT
(435) 834-5322
www.nps.gov/brca

Canyonlands National Park
Moab, UT
(435) 719-2313
www.nps.gov/cany

Capitol Reef National Park
Torrey, UT
(435) 425-3791
www.nps.gov/care

Cedar Breaks Nat'l Monument
Cedar City, UT
(435) 586-9451
www.nps.gov/cebr

Glen Canyon NRA
Page, AZ
(928) 608-6200
www.nps.gov/glca

Golden Spike NHS
Brigham City, UT
(435) 471-2209
www.nps.gov/gosp

Natural Bridges Nat'l Mon.
Lake Powell, UT
(435) 692-1234
www.nps.gov/nabr

Rainbow Bridge Nat'l Mon.
Page, AZ
(520) 608-6404
www.nps.gov/rabr

Timpanogos Cave Nat'l Mon.
American Fork, UT
(801) 756-5238
www.nps.gov/tica

Zion National Park
Springdale, UT
(435) 772-3256
www.nps.gov/zion

Dinosaur Nat'l Monument
Jensen, UT
(435) 781-7700
www.nps.gov/dino

STATE PARKS:

Utah State Parks & Recreation
1594 W. North Temple, Ste. 116
Salt Lake City, UT 84114
(801) 538-7220
www.stateparks.utah.gov

FEDERAL CAMPGROUNDS:

National Recreation Reservation Service
877-444-6777
www.reserveusa.com

UTAH TRAVELER INFORMATION:

Road conditions, construction, and weather links:
www.udot.utah.gov

Traffic: udottraffic.udot.gov

WEATHER:

The Weather Channel: www.weather.com
Weather Underground: www.wunderground.com
NOAA Nat'l Weather Service: weather.gov

Index

A

Abajo Mountains, 233, 243, 244
Ajax, William, 76
Alpine Loop, 64, 68
Alpine Summit, 69
Ambrose, Stephen, 21
American Fork, 93, 288
   Canyon, 70
   Creek, 70
American West Heritage Center, 6
Anasazi State Park & Museum, 217
Anasazis, 245, *See also* Ancestral Puebloan
Ancestral Puebloan, 199, 242, 245, 269
Aneth, 270, 273
Antelope Flat, 136, 295
Antelope Valley, 158
Antimony, 226, 227, 291
Arches National Park, 232, 251, 254, 259, 260, 261
Arizona, 166, 192, 204, 272, 275, 276, 285, 286, 292
Ashley National Forest, 88, 124, 131, 294
ATK/Thiokol, 19, 27

B

Badland Cliffs, 294
Baker Archeological Site, 155, 156
Baker, NV, 152, 155, 156, 157
Balanced Rock, 259
Bald Mountain, 31, 35, 37, 38, 93
Bald Mountain Pass, 31, 37, 38
Bamberger Monument, 293
Bamberger, Simon, 293
Barn Hills, 155
Barrick Gold Corp, 74
Bear Canyon, 91
Bear Lake, 4, 9, 15, 54
   Overlook, 8
   Summit, 9, 290
Bear Lake Raspberry Days, 9
Bear River, 28
Beaver Bottoms, 161, 290
Beaver Creek, 34
Beaver Dam Creek, 94

Beaver Dam Mountains, 192
Berke, Marty, 300
Beryl Junction, 180, 182
Bicknell, 237
Big Bend, 253
Big Flat, 215
Big Spring Canyon, 245
Black Canyon, 223, 224, 227, 228, 291
Black Hawk War, 100
Black Mountains, 290
Black Ridge, 228
Black Steer Canyon, 272
Blacktail Ridge, 47
Blanding, 234, 243, 270, 271, 279, 292, 293
Blue Flats, 238
Blue Spring Hills, 27
Blue Valley, 238
Blues, The, 214
Bluff, 271, 292
Bluffdale, 77
Book Cliffs, 88, 293, 301
Bothwell, 27
Boulder, 216, 217
Boulder Mountain, 209, 217, 218
Bountiful, 288
Box Elder County, 19, 22
Box Elder LDS Tabernacle, 22
Boynton Lookout, 216
Boynton, John F., 216
Braffit Ridge, 171
Brian Head, 171
Bridal Veil Falls, 67
Bridgerland, 3, 9
Brigham City, 5, 13, 19, 20, 21, 22, 28, 54, 288, 289
Brigham Young University, 94, 156
Brown, John, 60
Browns Rim, 241
Bryce Canyon City, 228, 291
Bryce Canyon National Park, 169, 171, 204, 212, 214, 220, 223, 224, 225, 228, 230, 232
Burbank Hills, 158
Burnout Canyon, 145, 146
Burr Trail, 217
Butler Wash, 243
Butterfield Canyon, 78

321

C

Cache Valley, 289
Caineville, 238, 239
Caineville Reef, 238
Calf Creek, 216
California Road, 184, *See also* California Trail
California Trail, 60
Camp Floyd, 75
Camp Williams, 77
Cannonville, 213
Canyonlands National Park, 232, 233, 234, 235, 243, 244, 245, 246, 247, 248, 251, 254, 256, 257, 259, 264
Canyons of the Escalante, 216
Capitol Dome, 238
Capitol Gorge, 236
Capitol Reef National Park, 110, 217, 218, 232, 233, 234, 235, 238, 247, 248
Cart Creek Bridge, 134
Cassidy, Butch, 129, 286
Castle Country, 88
Castle Valley, 148, 261
Castle, The, 236
Cedar Breaks, 167, 168, 169, 170, 171, 173, 175, 177, 181
Cedar Canyon, 172
Cedar City, 54, 153, 160, 168, 169, 172, 179, 180, 181, 182, 184, 186, 290
Cedar Fort, 75
Cedar Hills, 146
Cedar Mesa, 242, 243
Cedar Valley, 290
Centerfield, 287
Central Pacific, 21, 25, 26
Checkerboard Mesa, 204
Cheese and Raisin Hills, 243
Chessman Ridge, 170
Chimney Rock, 236
Chocolate Cliffs, 215
Church Rock, 247
Circleville, 226, 286
Clark, Frank, 7
Claron Formation, 170
Clear Creek, 144
Cleveland Reservoir, 147
Coal Creek, 172
Cockscomb, The, 215

Colorado, 88, 166, 272, 273, 274, 297, 298, 299, 301
  Plateau, vii, 146, 151, 160, 166, 269
  River, 35, 129, 131, 216, 217, 233, 240, 241, 245, 253, 254, 256, 257, 262
Colton, 142, 143
Comb Ridge, 243, 279
Comb Wash, 243, 279
Confusion Range, 155, 298
Cooks Mesa, 235
Copperton, 78
Corinne, 20, 23, 24, 25
Courthouse Towers, 259
Coyote, 226
Crescent Flat, 301
Crescent Junction, 254, 293
Cricket Mountains, 160, 161, 290
Croydon, 62
Crystal Hot Springs Resort, 28

D

Daggett County, 133
Daimler, Gottlieb, 143
Dammeron Valley, 185
Daniels Canyon, 45, 297
Daniels Pass, 45, 297
Daniels Summit, 45
Dead Horse Point, 256, 264
Deep Creek, 46
  Canyon, 46, 297
Deer Creek Dam, 68
Deer Creek Reservoir, 67
Delicate Arch, 256, 260
Delta, 152, 153, 154, 160, 161, 290, 298, 299
Deseret
  State of, 24
  town, 161
Deseret Chemical Weapons Depot, 73
Devil's Garden, 260
Devil's Kitchen, 92
Devil's Slide, 33, 62
Dewey, 253
Deweyville, 28
Diamond Valley, 185
Dinnehotso, 275
Dinosaur National Monument, 88, 298
Dirty Devil River, 240, 241
Dixie Hollow, 56, 62

Index

Dixie National Forest, 218, 228
Donner-Reed Party, 57, 60
Double Arch, 259
Douglas Mesa, 277
Dry Fork Canyon, 137
Dry Valley, 239
Duchesne, 43, 44, 46, 47, 48, 54, 294, 295, 298
   County, 297
   River, 35, 48, 49, 121, 122
   Tunnel, 35
Duck Creek, 174
Dutch John, 130, 133, 136
Dutton, Charles E., 197

E

East Canyon, 56, 60, 61, 62
   Creek, 60, 61
   Reservoir, 60, 61, 62
   Resort, 60
East Tintic Mountains, 76, 299
Eccles Canyon, 141, 144
Echo Junction, 33
Elberta, 76, 77
Electric Lake, 146, 147
Emerald Pools, 202
Emery County, 143
Emigration Canyon, 57, 59
Enterprise, 61, 183
Ephraim, 97, 98, 100, 101, 288
Erda, 291
Escalante, 54, 210, 214, 215, 216
   Desert, 290
   Mountains, 228
   River, 214, 216
   State Park, 215
   Valley, 182, 183
Escalante, Silvestre Velez de, 214
Eureka, 76, 79, 291, 299

F

Factory Bench, 238
Fairview, 146, 288
   Canyon, 141, 146
   Lake, 147
Fancher, Alexander, 183
Farmington, 21, 288
Festival of the American West, 6
Fifty Mile Mountains, 216

Fish Lake, 107, 108, 111, 226
   Hightop Plateau, 107
   National Forest, 88, 107, 109
Flaming Gorge, 88, 129, 130, 131, 133, 134, 135, 136, 137
   Dam, 129, 130, 131, 133, 135, 136, 295
   Reservoir, 129, 134
Ford, John, 233, 245, 276
Forsyth Reservoir, 110
Fort Deseret, 161
Fountain Green, 98, 99
Four Corners, 269, 270, 271, 273, 275, 277, 279
Four Corners Junction. *See* Saratoga Crossroads
Fox Bench, 110
Fox, Jesse W., 22
Francis, 44, 51, 118, 119, 120, 121
Fredonia, AZ, 286
Fremont Indians, 137, 156, 237
Fremont Junction, 108, 109, 148
Fremont River, 110, 209, 235, 237, 238
Fremont, J.C., 28
Frisco, 159
Frisco Summit, 159, 160
Frost, Robert, 223
Fruit Heights, 21, 288
Fruita Historic Area, 236
Fry Canyon Lodge, 241

G

Garden City, 4, 5, 9, 290
Garden of Eden, 260
Garfield County, 211, 216
Garrison, 157, 158
Glen Canyon, 199, 233, 234, 240, 241, 248
   Dam, 240
Golden Spike, 19, 20, 21, 23, 24, 25
Gooding Jr., Cuba, 136
Goshen Valley, 299
Goto Monument, 50
Goto, Masashi, 50, 120, 121
Grand Junction, CO, 299
Grand Staircase, 166, 170, 197, 204, 215
Grand Staircase-Escalante National Monument, 209, 214, 215, 286

323

Grand Valley, 301
Grass Valley, 226, 291
Gray Cliffs, 215
Great Arch, 202
Great Basin, 35, 146, 151, 152, 153, 154, 157, 158, 160, 298, 299
    National Park, 151, 152, 155, 156, 157, 298
Great Salt Lake, 2
Green River
    river, 129, 131, 135, 245, 257
    town, 299, 301
Green River, WY, 136, 137
Greenwich, 226
Grotto Trail, 202
Gunlock, 190, 192
    Reservoir, 189, 192, 193, 196
Gunnison, 98, 102, 103, 287, 288, 292
Gunnison Valley, 301

Hite, 241
Hogan Pass, 109
Hogback, 209, 216
Hogle Zoo, 57
Holden, 298
Hollow Mountain Station, 239
Hopper, Dennis, 276
Horn Silver Mine, 159
House Range, 154, 155, 298
Hovenweep National Monument, 269, 270, 271, 272, 280
Huntington Canyon, 141, 142, 146, 147, 148
Huntington Creek, 145, 147
Huntington Reservoir, 147
Huntsville, 4, 10, 11, 12, 13, 82
Hurricane, 171, 172, 197, 199
Hurricane Cliffs, 171, 172, 197, 200
Hyrum, 289

H

Halfway Hills, 158
Halfway Summit, 158
Hamblin, Jacob, 191
Hampton's Ford, 20, 28
Hanks, Ebenezer, 182
Hanksville, 234, 238, 239
Hanna, 48, 49, 118, 119, 121, 122
Hatch, 175, 211
Hatch Trading Post, 271, 272
Hayden Pass, 38
Hayden Peak, 37, 38
Haymaker Bench, 216
Head-of-Rocks Overlook, 215, 216, 218
Heber City, 32, 34, 43, 44, 45, 51, 66, 67, 297
Heber Creeper, 67
Heber Valley Railroad. *See* Heber Creeper
Helper, 293, 301
Henefer, 33, 60, 62
Henrieville, 214
Henry Mountains, 239
Heritage Highway, 100, 101, 102, 175, 286, 288, 290
Herriman, 78
Hickman Bridge, 238
Hidden Valley, 47, 48
Hinckley, 154

I

Idaho, 2, 285, 286, 289, 290
Indian Canyon, 294, 295
Indian Creek, 245
Iron City, 182
Iron Mission, 182
Iron Mountain, 181, 182
Island in the Sky, 232, 245, 246, 256, 257

J

Johns Valley, 223, 228, 291
Jordanelle Reservoir, 51
Juab Valley, 91, 103, 292
Jug Handle Arch, 255
Junction, 226, 286

K

Kaiparowits Plateau, 215
Kamas, 32, 33, 34, 51, 118, 119
Kanab, 204, 286
Kayenta, 270, 275, 276
Kaysville, 21, 288
Kennecott, 73, 78
Kimball Junction, 33, 65, 66
Kings Canyon, 155, 298
Kings Meadow Canyon, 112, 225, 292
Kings Peak, 37, 116

Index

Kingston Canyon, 226, 291
Kodachrome Basin, 213
Kodachrome Basin State Park, 213, 220
Kolob Terrace, 173
Koosharem, 112, 225, 226
Koosharem Reservoir, 112, 225, 291

L

La Sal Mountains, 261, 293
La Verkin, 199, 200
Lake Bonneville, 19, 25
Lake Mountains, 77
Lake Point, 59, 73, 291
Lake Powell, 240
Laketown, 9
Lampo Junction, 25, 27
Last Chance Creek, 109
Leavitt, Dixie, 181
Leavitt, Mike, 181
Legacy Loop Highway, 179, 180, 186, 187
Lehi, 288
Lehman Caves, 157
Levan, 98, 103, 292
Little Dell Reservoir, 57
Little Denmark, 100
Little Dutch Hollow, 60
Little Egypt, 239
Little Mountain, 24
Little Pinto, 182
Little Ruin Canyon, 272
Little Sahara, 291, 299
Littleton, 61
Loa, 109, 237, 292
Logan, 4, 5, 6, 7, 13, 54, 289
   Canyon, 3, 4, 6, 7, 15, 289, 290
   LDS Temple, 6
   River, 8, 290
   Tabernacle, 6
Long Valley, 174, 175, 197, 204, 286
Long Valley Junction, 168, 174
Lost Creek Reservoir & State Park, 62
Lucerne Valley, 137
Lyman, WY, 137

M

Magna, 73, 78
Main Canyon, 62

Manila, 130, 137
Manti, 97, 98, 101, 288
   LDS Temple, 101
Manti-La Sal National Forest, 88, 148, 261
Markagunt Plateau, 167, 170, 173
Marysvale, 286
Maze, The, 245
McCracken Mesa, 271
Meeks Mesa, 235
Mercur, 74, 75
Merrimac Butte, 256
Mexican Hat, 277, 278
Mexican Water, AZ, 292
Milford, 152, 153, 160, 290
Mill Meadow Reservoir, 110
Milton, 61
Mineral Mountains, 160, 161, 290
Minersville, 290
Mirror Lake, 32, 38
   Scenic Byway, 34
Moab, 54, 251, 252, 263, 293
Monitor Butte, 256
Monte Cristo, 3, 10, 15
Monticello, 234, 243, 293
Monument Pass, 277
Monument Valley, 269, 270, 275, 276, 277, 281
Moon Lake, 117, 118, 124, 125
Morgan, 61, 62
   Valley, 33, 61
Mormon, 6, 10, 19, 23, 56, 57, 60, 65, 88, 97, 99, 100, 101, 116, 146, 161, 184, 191, 199, 236, 279
   Pioneer Trail, 56, 62
Mormon Miracle Pageant, 101
Moroni, 97, 98, 99
Mount Nebo, 89, 93
Mount Pleasant, 146, 288
Mount Timpanogos Wilderness Area, 68
Mountain Green, 62, 63, 81
Mountain Home, 118, 123, 124
Mountain Home Range, 158
Mountain Meadows, 181, 184, 185
   Massacre, 183
Mt. Carmel Junction, 198, 204, 286
Mt. Pearle, 261
Mule Canyon, 243
Mytoge Mountains, 107

N

Naples, 298
Narrow Canyon, 241
Narrows, The, 202
Natural Bridges National Monument, 233, 242
Navajo, 174, 245, 269, 271, 273, 274, 275, 276, 277, 292
Navajo Lake, 174
Needles, The, 158, 232, 235, 245, 246
Nephi, 54, 90, 91, 97, 98, 99, 102, 103, 292
Nevada, 88, 152, 154, 155, 158, 166, 290, 291, 298, 299
New Mexico, 272, 273, 274
Newcastle, 182
Newspaper Rock, 244, 245, 246
Nobletts Creek, 119
Nobletts Trailhead, 51
North Wash, 240

O

Ogden, 2, 4, 5, 13, 21, 54, 63, 288
  Canyon, 3, 4, 12, 13, 82, 83
  River, 82
Old Ephraim, 7
Old Iron Town State Park, 181
Ophir, 74
Oquirrh, 78
Oquirrh Mountains, 59, 78
Orem, 32, 34, 67
Osiris, 228
Otter Creek, 226
Otter Creek Reservoir, 224, 226
Otter Creek State Park, 226, 230
Overland Stage, 60, 65

P

Page, AZ, 286
Pahvant Valley, 298
Palisade State Park, 102, 104
Panguitch, 54, 168, 169, 204, 210, 211, 286
  Creek, 169
  Lake, 169, 170
Paradise Valley, 109
  Lake, 109
Park Avenue, 259
Park City, 33, 43, 45, 51, 54, 65, 66, 297, 298
Parker, Robert Leroy, 286
Parley's Canyon, 33, 57, 65
Parley's Summit, 65
Parowan, 168, 169, 172, 216
Parowan Canyon, 171, 290
Parowan Valley, 171
Paunsaugunt Plateau, 209, 211, 228
Payson, 90, 95, 300
  Canyon, 95
  Lakes, 94, 95
Peach Days, 22
Penney's Junction, 73, 74, 76
Peteetneet Creek, 95
Peters Point Ridge, 246
Peterson, 61
petroglyphs, 131, 137, 237, 238, 245, 255
Phipps, Washington, 216
Phipps-Death Hollow, 216
Photograph Gap, 246
Pine Valley, 158, 185, 187
Pineview Reservoir, 11, 82
Pink Cliffs, 167, 173, 212, 215, 229
Pioche, NV, 159
Piute Indians, 184, 199
Piute Reservoir, 286
Plateau Valley, 292
Point-of-the-Mountain, 94, 288
Pony Express, 60, 76
Porterville, 61
Post Hollow, 109
Pothole Point, 245
Powell Point, 214
Powell, John Wesley, 129, 214
Pratt, Orson, 60
Price, 54, 148, 293, 300, 301
Price Canyon, 293, 301
Professor Valley, 253
Promontory, 19, 21, 25
  Mountains, 25
Provo, 2, 50, 54, 65, 67, 93, 94, 288
  Canyon, 34, 64, 67
  Falls, 36
  River, 31, 34, 35, 36, 50, 67, 119
Pruess Lake, 158

R

Rainbow Hills, 112, 225, 292

Index

Randolph, 10
Raplee Ridge, 277
Recapture Lake, 293
Red Canyon, 130, 136, 209, 211, 212
Red Cliffs Desert Reserve, 185
Red Desert, 238
Red Fleet State Park, 131
Red House Cliffs, 242
Red Mountains, 191, 193
Red Rock Ranch, 10
Redford, Robert, 68
Rendezvous Beach, 9, 15
Reservation Ridge, 294
Richfield, 109, 225, 287
Richville, 61
Ricks Springs, 7, 8
Riverton, 77
Rock Creek, 117, 118, 123, 124, 125
Rock Springs, WY, 136
Rockville, 200
Ruby's Junction, 212, 224, 228
Rush Lake, 73
Rush Valley, 73, 76, 77, 291

S

Sage Creek Junction, 4, 9, 10
Sagers Flat, 254, 301
Salem, 300
Salina, 109, 113, 224, 225, 235, 287, 292, 298, 299
Salt Creek, 19, 24, 91, 92, 99
   Canyon, 99
   Peak, 99
Salt Creek Waterfowl Management Area, 19, 24
Salt Lake City, 2, 33, 39, 56, 57, 63, 65, 73, 77, 80, 116, 120, 183, 288, 291, 297
Salt Lake Motorcycle Club, 72
Salt Lake Valley, 57, 59, 60, 65, 94, 286, 288
Salvation Knoll, 243
San Francisco Mountains, 158, 159, 161, 290
San Juan River, 273, 277, 278
San Pitch Mountains, 97, 98, 99, 102, 103, 146, 292
San Rafael Swell, 88
Sand Hills, 204
Sandy, 288

Sanpete County, 100, 101, 145
Sanpete Valley, 97, 99, 100, 146, 147, 288
Santa Clara, 185, 190, 191, 192
   River, 192
Santaquin, 77, 93, 94, 300
   Canyon, 93, 94
Saratoga Crossroads, 75
Saratoga Springs, 77
Sardine Canyon, 3, 5, 13, 289
Sardine Summit, 5, 289
Scandinavian Festival, 101
Scofield, 142, 143, 144
   Reservoir, 143
Sevier Canyon, 286
Sevier Lake, 154, 290, 298
Sevier Plateau, 226, 228
Sevier River, 112, 154, 175, 227, 286
Sevier Valley, 108, 112, 287
Sheep Creek Bay, 130, 137
Sheep Creek Geological Loop, 137
Shirts, Peter, 182
Shivwits Indian Reservation, 192
Sierra Nevada, 153
Sigurd, 112, 225, 292
Silver Creek Junction, 33, 66, 297
Skull Rock Pass, 155, 298
Skyline Arch, 260
Skyline Drive, 88, 141, 142, 146, 147
Skyline Mines, 144
Slate Gorge, 36
Snow Canyon, 186, 189, 190, 193, 194
   State Park, 194
Snow, Erastus, 194
Snow, Lorenzo, 194
Soldier Summit, 142, 143, 301
South Canyon, 169
South Fork Canyon, 50
South Snake Range, 157
Spanish Fork, 288, 300
   Canyon, 288, 300
Springdale, 200, 201
Springville, 288
St. George, 54, 153, 160, 179, 180, 181, 186, 189, 190, 191, 195, 197, 199
St. John's Episcopal Church, 6
Stansbury Park, 291
Starvation Reservoir, 47, 297, 298
Steinaker Reservoir, 131
Stillwater Dam, 123
Stinky Springs, 24

Stockmore Guard Station, 49, 122
Stockton, 73, 291
Straight Cliffs, 215
Strawberry Reservoir, 46, 297
Stuart Guard Station, 147
Sugar Loaf Rock, 246
Sundance, 68, 69
Swett Ranch, 133, 134
Swett, Oscar, 133
Syrett, Reuben "Ruby", 228

Upper Valley Creek, 214
Utah
  County, 75
  Lake, 2, 77, 93, 94
  Valley, 93, 94, 286, 288
Utah Rebellion, 75
Utah State University, 7
Utah's Fruit Way, 5, 22, 288
Utahn, 48
Ute, 116, 245, 269, 274

T

Tabby Mountain, 47
Tabiona, 48, 118, 122
Tabioona, Chief, 226
Takeout Beach, 253
Teec Nos Pos, 275
Temple Fork, 7
Temple of Sinawava, 202
This Is The Place Heritage Park, 57
Thistle Creek, 288
Thistle Junction, 300
Thompson Springs, 254
Thurber, Albert, 226
Timpanogos Cave National
    Monument, 69, 70
Tintic Junction, 291
Tony Grove Lake, 8, 15
Tooele, 54, 73, 290, 291
  Army Depot, 73
Torrey, 210, 218, 234, 235, 236
Trail of the Ancients, 243
Transcontinental Railroad, 19
Trappers Loop, 13, 80
Trappist Monastery, 11
Tropic, 212, 213, 216
Tropic Valley, 212
Tule Valley, 155, 298
Tunnel Spring Mountains, 158
Twin Rocks, 236

U

Uinta National Forest, 91, 121
Uinta Range, 31, 37, 295
Ulrich, Skeet, 136
Union Pacific, 21, 22, 23, 25, 26, 161, 290
Upheaval Dome, 257
Upper Valley, 214

V

Valley of the Gods, 243, 278
Vermilion Cliffs, 215
Vermillion, 112, 292
Vernal, 54, 129, 130, 131, 133, 137, 295, 298
Vernon, 76, 291
Veterans Memorial Highway, 285
Veyo, 185, 190, 192
  Volcano, 185, 193
Virgin, 197, 199, 200
Virgin River, 197, 199, 200, 286
Vivian Park, 67

W

Wah Wah Mountains, 158
Wah Wah Valley, 158
Wall Lake, 37
Wasatch
  Front, 2, 3, 5, 20, 21, 32, 33, 34, 43, 45, 55, 64, 67, 80, 82, 116, 151, 153, 161, 286, 291, 297
  Mountains, 2, 45, 288
  Plateau, 88, 141, 146, 147
  Range, vii, 2, 56, 70, 97, 99, 153
Watanabe, Takeo, 120
Waterpocket Fold, 217
Wayne, John, 245
Weber
  Canyon, 13, 21, 33, 63, 81, 288
  County, 22
  River, 61, 81
Weeping Rock, 202
Wellsville Canyon, 289
Wheeler Peak, 157
  Scenic Drive, 157
White Canyon, 241, 242
White Cliffs, 197, 204, 215

Index

Wide Hollow Reservoir, 215
Willard, 5, 22
Willard Bay State Park, 29
Windows, The, 260
Windy Mesa, 253, 301
Winter Quarters, 144
Winter Quarters Canyon, 143
Wolf Creek, 121
Wolf Creek Pass, 50
Wolf Creek Summit, 118, 119, 121
Wooden Shoe Arch, 245
Woodland, 51, 119, 121
Woodruff, 4, 10
Woodruff, Wilford, 10
Wyoming, 34, 38, 39, 88, 129, 136, 137, 292, 295, 298

Y

Young, Brigham, 22, 60, 94, 183, 226
Yuba State Park, 103, 104

Z

Zion Canyon, 197, 199, 200, 201, 202, 204, 232
Zion National Park, 116, 169, 171, 173, 181, 197, 198, 199, 200, 206, 232
Zion/Mt. Carmel tunnel, 203

About the Author

Dave Magdiel has been riding road bikes for more than 30 years. His journeys have taken him from Canada to Mexico and have covered most of the continental US and Hawaii. For over ten years he has written about his travels.

Dave is a graduate of Boise State University with a degree in economics. A veteran of the US Army, he served with the 2nd Armor Division (FWD) in the 1991 Persian Gulf War. After the military, he made a career in logistics management until leaving to pursue his dream to ride and write.

Always the avid biker, explorer and writer, Dave lives in Stansbury Park, Utah but his true home is in the saddle.

www.ingramcontent.com/pod-product-compliance
Lightning Source LLC
Chambersburg PA
CBHW071652160426
43195CB00012B/1434